Edward Lucie-Smith
was born in 1933 in Kingston, Jamaica,
and in 1946 came to England. He was educated at King's
School, Canterbury, and Merton College, Oxford, where he
read History. Well known as a poet, novelist, biographer,
broadcaster and critic, he is the author of numerous books –
among them *Symbolist Art* (also in the World of Art series),
The Body and, most recently, *The Thames and Hudson
Dictionary of Art Terms*. He has also published
several anthologies and four volumes of
his own verse.

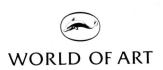

WORLD OF ART

This famous series
provides the widest available
range of illustrated books on art in all its aspects.
If you would like to receive a complete list
of titles in print please write to:

THAMES AND HUDSON
30 Bloomsbury Street, London WC1B 3QP
In the United States please write to:
THAMES AND HUDSON INC.
500 Fifth Avenue, New York, New York 10110

Edward Lucie-Smith

Movements in art
since 1945

New revised edition

249 illustrations, 65 in color

Thames and Hudson

FOR AGATHA SADLER

This new revised edition first published in the USA in 1985 by
Thames and Hudson Inc., 500 Fifth Avenue,
New York, New York 10110

Library of Congress Catalog Card Number 83-51503

Previous editions of this book
were published in the USA under the title
Late Modern: The Visual Arts Since 1945

Printed and bound in Spain by Artes Graficas Toledo S.A.
D.L. TO-575-1984

Contents

CHAPTER ONE

'Late modern'

In 1945, a world war ended. Such dates form convenient dividing lines for the historians of art. In this case, the line is more than merely 'convenient', as it coincides with a genuine crisis in the development of twentieth-century painting and sculpture. It was at about this time that the visual arts embarked on a new course, whose direction might have been difficult to predict in 1939. In part, the changes were due to the war itself. Where so much had altered, art could not expect to survive untouched by events. Europe was battered and exhausted. In the countries invaded by the Germans, modern artists had had great difficulty in surviving. The energies of the Ecole de Paris had been drained by a massive emigration. Meanwhile, the United States had been established (together with Russia, where Stalinism and socialist realism still reigned) as one of the two world powers, and the richer and more powerful of the two. From the early 1930s onwards, the artistic life of America, and especially of New York, had been enriched by wave upon wave of *émigrés*, in flight from the Nazi terror. These new arrivals were absorbed more easily than they would have been elsewhere, because the population of the United States was itself an amalgam from all the European homelands.

It would be too much to claim, however, that post-war art represented something wholly new and unprecedented. Its roots lay deep in the rich soil of modernism, which had got its start as the century dawned. Indeed, the art we now see being created by our contemporaries seems to me 'late modern' almost in the sense that Giovanni Battista Tiepolo is 'late baroque'. If one accepts that modernism can be regarded as a stylistic category – like mannerism, the baroque, or neo-classicism – then it has certainly had a remarkably long run.

Tentative efforts to classify the art of the 1980s as 'post modern' rather than 'modern' have been unconvincing because even art which rebels against established modernist standards still implicitly acknowledges the continuing modernist tradition. Innovation only takes place within an established framework. The art of our times has been more notable for taking existing ideas to extremes than for new invention. This process of exaggeration and ossification has produced a number of striking inconsistencies in late twentieth-century attitudes towards both art and artists.

On the one hand, there has been a continued emphasis on the sacredness of the artist's own individuality. In many cases, this individuality, or sense of uniqueness, has become the subject of the work of art. On the other hand, the artist has wanted to abandon this position, and sink himself in technology; to imitate the procedures of science, and conduct experiments rather than make works of art. While modern art has flourished perhaps most conspicuously in the most capitalist society in the world, that of the United States, the process of democratization has made artists increasingly unhappy with the idea that they

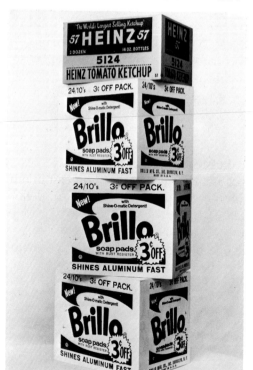

1 ANDY WARHOL
Brillo boxes 1964

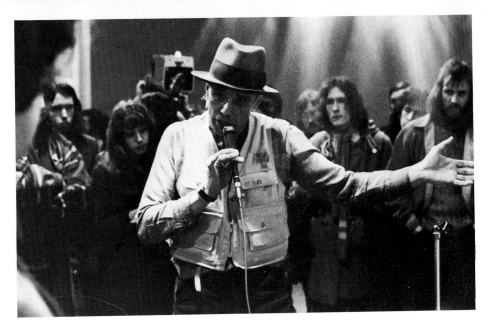

2 JOSEPH BEUYS *Action in 7 Exhibitions* 1972

are producers of goods for a luxury market – goods whose rarity is reflected by the high price which is asked for them. And yet, again, as the emphasis shifted from the artist's product to his personality, many painters and sculptors have been unable to resist the temptation to turn the human being as well as the work into a marketable commodity. The purchaser of certain kinds of pop art – Andy Warhol's Brillo boxes, for example – *Ill. 1* bought not so much an object as a franchise in a certain mode of existence, while Joseph Beuys is clearly even more in demand as a personality than he is as a man who produces items for sale. Art-dealers now market the strictly intangible.

The position of the artist as a kind of favoured outcast in our society creates many difficulties for us in our attempt to define his role. Perhaps the most logical way of dealing with it is to adopt the existentialist position and see the man who makes art as one who offers a challenge to the rest of society and at the same time accepts a kind of bet with existence. In his famous lecture 'Existentialism is a Humanism', delivered in 1946, Jean-Paul Sartre avowed that a basic tenet of his philosophy was that '*existence* comes before essence – or, if you will, that we must begin from the subjective'. For Sartre, the individual should strive to be 'man to the very limit, to the absurd, to the night of unknowingness'. Though existentialism was the most popular of philosophies in the immediate post-war period, it cannot be said that the artists themselves have succeeded in fulfilling its programmes. What existentialism did do, however, was to promote a general feeling that man was alone in the world, was now detached from all systems of belief, and that the creator must find his salvation in art alone, reinventing it from the very beginning. Hence the somewhat tendentious emphasis on the idea of 'originality' – the artist was willing to have descendants, but not ancestors, and was, to that extent at least, as subjective as Sartre could have wished.

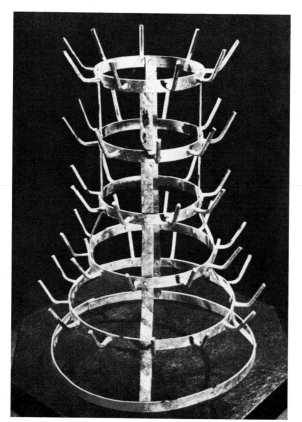

3 MARCEL DUCHAMP
Bottle rack 1914

And yet, ironically, the history of the visual arts during the past forty years has been the story of a series of other, narrower -isms and movements, which have succeeded one another in ever more rapid tempo. Abstract expressionism was succeeded by assemblage, pop art, colour painting, op art, kinetic art, minimal art, conceptual art, super realism and neo-expressionism. The violence and the rapidity of the changes have tended to conceal the fact that all these movements represent a resifting and re-evaluation of ideas which were already known before the war. Abstract expressionism is rooted in surrealism; assemblage and pop art reached back beyond surrealism to dada; op art and kinetic art are founded upon experiments made at the Bauhaus; minimal art interestingly combines both dada and Bauhaus influences; the origins of neo-expressionism are obvious from the name itself. Though art swung from the extremely and almost desperately personal to the coolly impersonal, the terms of the conflict were pre-set. But most of these stylistic 'revivals' differ from the pre-war originals in that they develop and exaggerate the borrowed form, while playing down or entirely jettisoning the content.

Perhaps the most conspicuous example is the relationship of pop art to dada. One of the original dadaists, Raoul Hausmann, remarked gnomically that 'Dada fell like a raindrop from Heaven. The Neo-Dadaists have learnt to imitate the fall, but not the raindrop.' The late Marcel Duchamp was more outspoken, and said in a letter addressed to Hans Richter in 1962:

> This Neo-Dada, which they call New Realism, Pop Art, Assemblage, etc., is an easy way out, and lives on what Dada did. When I discovered ready-mades I thought to discourage aesthetics. In Neo-Dada they have taken my ready-mades and found aesthetic beauty in them. I threw the bottle-rack *Ill. 3* and the urinal into their faces as a challenge and now they admire them for their aesthetic beauty.[1]

These criticisms are just, but perhaps beside the point. Where dada challenged the existing aesthetic and social order, post-war art has built that challenge *into* an order. One symptom of what I have called the 'ossification' of modernism has been the shift from the concept of the *avant-garde* to that of the 'underground'. The underground artist differs from his predecessors of the *avant-garde* in believing himself to be so permanently alienated that little can be done about it. The only solution he can offer is a utopian one, that of setting up an alternative society altogether. Meanwhile, he retreats into a fortress of art about art. Or so he would like to think, for the members of the underground can seldom resist the limelight.

A frontal attack on this attitude was delivered by the leading critic Clement Greenberg, in the course of a discussion of minimal art – that is, art which tried to shed everything extraneous to the aesthetic process, and perhaps most of that process itself. Greenberg said:

> In the Sixties it has been as though art – at least the kind that gets itself most attention – has set itself as a problem the task of extricating the far-out 'in itself' from the merely odd, the incongruous, the socially shocking. Assemblage, Pop, Environment, Op, Kinetic, Erotic and all the other varieties of Novelty art look like so many moments in the working out of this problem, whose solution now seems to have arrived in the form of what is called Primary Structures,

4 CARL ANDRÉ *144 pieces of aluminium* 1967

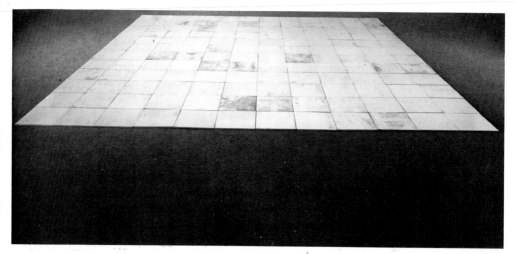

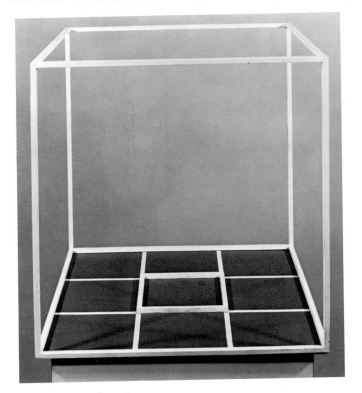

5 SOL LEWITT *A7* 1967

A BC, or Minimal art. The Minimalists appear to have realized, finally, that the far-out in itself has to be the far-out *Ills 4, 5* as an end in itself, and that this means the furthest out and nothing short of that. They appear also to have realized that the most original and furthest-out art in the past hundred years always arrived looking as though it had parted company with everything previously known as art. In other words, the furthest out usually lay on the borderline between art and non-art. The Minimalists have not really discovered anything new through this realization, but they have drawn conclusions from it with a new consistency which owes some of its newness to the shrinking of the area in which things can safely be non-art. Given that the initial look of non-art was no longer available in painting, since even an unpainted canvas now stated itself as a picture, the borderline between art and non-art now had to be sought in the three-dimensional, where sculpture was and where everything material that was not art also was.[2]

Like the more rarefied of the sixteenth-century mannerists, modern artists have been trying to find out what art can do when only art is in question. The answer often seems to be 'very little'. The only point at which I would disagree with Greenberg's analysis is with his feeling that minimal art, then the 'latest' style, somehow came about through an effort of the will.

Yet, despite this, there is more popular interest in modern art than ever before, and willy-nilly, the artist continues to play a role in society. It is worth pausing here, before giving detailed consideration to the various movements I have mentioned, to consider a number of typical patterns in the world of post-war art. It does not seem too naïve, for instance, to bring up the question of the way in which contemporary works of art are exhibited and sold.

Most artists depend for their success on what has been called the 'dealer-critic system'. The means whereby a reputation is made in its early stages still lies for the most part in the one-man show in a private gallery, accompanied by favourable notices in the newspapers and specialized art-magazines. A consistent, coherent show obviously has an advantage. It is easier to promote, from the dealer's point of view, and much easier to discuss, from the critic's. In America, especially, a successful artist during the post-war years has tended to become a 'product', packaged and promoted as such. Pop art gave an open blessing to already established procedures, and neo-expressionism re-confirmed them in the 1980s. Once an artist has become established in the hierarchy, a large number of museums, and a certain number of big collectors, feel com-

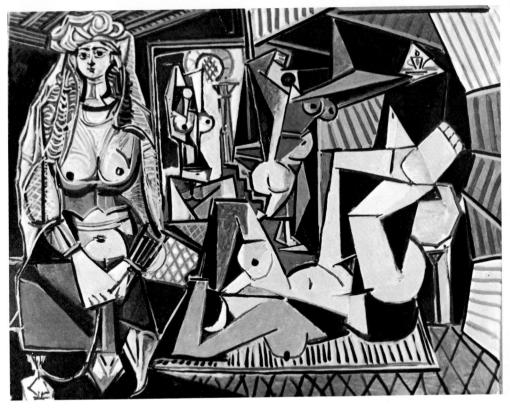

6 PABLO PICASSO *The Women of Algiers* 1955

pelled to buy an example of his work. Once this need is filled,
however, they may well wait to make another purchase until
the artist concerned changes his style.

Inevitably, this has had a certain practical effect. Picasso, with
his various styles or periods, each marked by a break in style and
a new beginning, had already canonized the idea that the artist
should take a single theme or idea, press it to a conclusion, then
choose a new path. In the post-war period, his variations on set
themes (*Las Meninas*, *Women of Algiers*) formed a very large *Ill. 6*
part of his production, and have exercised an important
influence. Picasso's example, allied to purely commercial considerations, has encouraged the contemporary artist to standard-

ize his product, and to move forward, when he needs to, only by dramatic leaps. More often than not, an artist who is holding an exhibition now presents a group of interrelated works which serve to interpret one another; then, after a decent interval, a new and different group will be shown.

To speak only of the artist's relationship with his dealer, the critics, and his immediate patrons is, nevertheless, to mis-represent the role of contemporary art. Any account of the evolution of the visual arts since the war must now take into account the fact that work of an extremely 'advanced' and hermetic nature now reaches the mass public through the medium of ambitious exhibitions, usually staged in museums, and for the most part under government or other official sponsorship.

Immediately after the war, the great figures of modern art were honoured by a spate of shows, all over the world. In one sense, this seemed a reparation for the hostility of the Nazis; in another, it was a way of marking the fact that culture was getting off to a fresh start. The public was ready for these exhibitions; they became, to however minor an extent, an accepted part of mass entertainment. As the years went by, it was no longer simply the established masters who were honoured by these shows. Contemporary art was 'news'; it became part of the common currency of journalism. There was a spate of books about modern art; these in turn helped to educate the public, and thus created an appetite for more exhibitions. Museum directors were for ever on the scent of novelty. A new tendency was no sooner discovered than a show was arranged to consecrate it.

The acceptance of modern art in the post-war world created an anomalous situation which has yet to be resolved. Not only was art in a newly self-regarding phase, but the basic myth of modernism, inherited from before the war, was a myth of revolt against what was established and accepted. And yet, gradually and inevitably, modern art has become involved with the machinery of the State. The State became one of its principal patrons; and the great international art-fairs, such as the Venice Biennale, the Biénale des Jeunes in Paris, the São Paulo Biennale, and the 'Documenta' exhibitions in Kassel, were soon a matter of national prestige. Art aligned itself with sport as one of the means of peaceful warfare among nations. At the same time, modernism, in its new guise, became one of the things which the underdeveloped nations envied and tried to copy from the developed ones.

In places such as India and Japan, traditional culture between the wars was already in a state of decay; it was natural therefore that artists in those countries should try and rebuild upon the European and American model. This worked better in some places than in others. Japan, by then endowed with a technological, urban culture which closely resembled those to be found in the United States and in Europe, produced after the war a crop of artists who rivalled their Occidental equivalents. Even so, though artists like the informal abstractionist Jiro Yoshihara are undoubtedly distinguished, with a flavour of their own which comes from the Japanese calligraphic tradition, they do not strike us as the key artists of their time; they are important on a national, not an international scale. The same is true of the pop and neo-dada artists who represent the younger generation in Japan.

Similarly, national exhibitions, brought to Europe from various South American countries, have done nothing to suggest a new idiom, significantly different from that used by artists in Europe itself, or in the United States. There has been no recurrence of the phenomenon of Mexican populist art, the murals painted by Diego Rivera and his school which aroused great interest in the United States, although the populist tradition has continued in attenuated form in Mexico itself.

What has occupied the scene, internationally, has been the struggle for primacy between Paris and New York, to which has most recently been added a bid for prominence by the late twentieth-century German school. Any visitor to one of the great international art-fairs is familiar with the pattern.

An especially important event in the struggle for primacy between Paris and New York was the triumph of abstract expressionism in Europe during the late 1940s: the first American raid on the European stronghold. The economics of modern art were profoundly affected by it. The United States had long been a good market for European art. American collectors had been early, though not the earliest, purchasers of paintings by the impressionists. The eccentric Dr Albert Barnes once bought the entire contents of Soutine's studio. But there is much testimony to show how difficult it was, in the early years of modernism, to sell contemporary American art to American patrons. Abstract expressionism changed this by triumphing in Europe. It changed it at a moment when, more than ever, the United States had become the world's dominant economic power. In the art boom of the 1950s, American artists were the greatest beneficiaries of a surge of interest in collecting contemporary art. The economic aspect reinforced the stylistic one. Europeans were impressed with American vitality, then with American purchasing power, and thirdly with the importance of American opinion. The lesser art centres of Europe – Milan, Brussels, Zurich, and most of all London – were, perhaps, in the long run, more profoundly affected than Paris.

In fact, England presents an especially interesting case. In the years between the wars, the small and struggling group of English *avant-garde* artists looked almost exclusively to Paris. Clive Bell, one of the most important critics of the period, once expressed the opinion that a first-rate English painter would never rank higher than a second-rate French one. He was thinking of the distance between Sickert and Degas. It would never have occurred to him to make a comparison with an American artist. Then, for a long period, from the late 1950s onward, the English art world became a mere appendage of America, and a trip to New York became as important to young English artists as a trip to Rome was for European painters of the seventeenth century – something which added an essential polish to their work.

But if modern art has had nationalism foisted upon it, there are certain social effects which it has generated on its own account. The example which immediately springs to mind is that of pop art. The painting and sculpture of the immediate post-war years seemed, in their various manifestations, to offer a refuge against the pressures of the urban environment, and a protest against its mechanization and inhumanity. Pop art put forward the view that this environment offered experiences which could be structured. The point went home, notwithstanding the fact that pop art itself contained a strange dichotomy, being as much concerned with the syntax of representation as with what was being represented. A whole new territory became available to artists. For the most part, it was the very territory they lived in: the things which surrounded them.

There grew up, chiefly as a result of this, a sympathy between contemporary art and what has been called 'pop culture' which went deeper than the superficialities of most pop painting. The visual arts began to broaden their popular base still further. It was no longer merely a matter of crowds flocking to the museums, to enjoy the art that the bureaucracy provided. The visitors took note of what they saw, and post-war art, despite its frequent thinness and exaggeration, began to generate new modes. Indeed, these very deficiencies made it in some ways more easily assimilable. The modes it generated did, however, spawn something solid: a new range of social attitudes.

Modernism, and in particular modern art, had begun to create its own social groupings almost from the beginning. Those who gathered in Picasso's studio in 1908, for the purpose of honouring (or mocking) the great self-taught painter Henri Rousseau, formed a society at least as cohesive as that of the young romantics who turned out for the first night of Victor Hugo's *Hernani*. Throughout all the successive phases of modernism, artists have continued to band together with like-minded friends. Sometimes these groups have assumed, or have been given, a title; sometimes they have existed without benefit of baptism. But there was more to it than this. The years between 1918 and 1939 show a slow but ever-increasing acceptance of modernism on the part of at least one segment of the educated public. The surrealists did not lack for rich patrons and fashionable admirers. But acceptance did not extend very far down the social scale. With rare exceptions, *avant-garde* art remained an upper-class, or at least an upper-middle-class, concern.

The post-war years were to change this situation. Modern art was far more widely publicized; it had attracted official support; more and more people came in contact with it. These factors outweighed its hermeticism. While it would be untrue to say that it made conversions *en masse* among the older generation, there began to be an unspoken agreement, even among those who did not like or understand it, that here, for better or worse, was the representative art of the day, and that nothing could be done to put the clock back. There were also more positive effects. Modern art made a particular appeal to the young, and not necessarily only the middle-class young, because it was something by tradition rebellious. In the affluent society, the struggle between the classes was transforming itself into the struggle between the generations. Meanwhile, young people everywhere had more leisure and more education than ever before. They began to create a way of life which was their own. It was to this way of life and this youthful public that modern artists began to address themselves.

The effects of the meeting were explosive. The dynamism of contemporary art, its quick turnover of styles, matched the pace of a culture which based itself on obsolescence. There was also the fact that the nature of fashion was itself changing: more and more, a fashion was not merely the arrival, triumph, and decline of a preference or style, but what might be described as style about style, just as painting and sculpture were art about art. The narcissism of contemporary fashion has often been commented upon.

Gradually, a new phenomenon began to make itself felt: the alliance of the ends against the middle. Art was still slow in disseminating itself when it moved away from its principal centres. But in those centres, it was no longer a matter of an idea slowly filtering out, finding its way from the elect circles by successive stages. Rather, new ideas leapt straight from the leading artists into the world of popular culture, creating a world where the bizarre was accepted as a matter of course, and by-passing the middle aged and the middle class on the way.

Britain supplied a striking example of this kind of development. Here, the post-war period saw a great expansion in the number of art schools, to the point where these began to offer a liberal education which rivalled that to be got from the universities, while being quite different from it in principle (in America, where universities and art schools are often linked, the division is less sharp). In Britain, an art-school education tended to be freer than its university equivalent; it demanded less formal study, but a greater degree of intellectual flexibility. Because it centred upon visual phenomena, it was international rather than national in its emphasis: there was no question of teaching English art as universities taught English literature or English history.

While it is difficult to prove that the various experiments in art education which have been made in Britain over the past forty years have produced better artists, the impact upon popular culture has been undeniable. To take one specialized but important example, the Beatles had close connections with Liverpool College of Art, and practically every major pop-group in Britain between the rise of the Beatles and the triumph of punk has had some kind of link with an art school. Many of the musicians began to play when they were art students. Popular music took over the modern art life-style; and where the musicians led, the fans followed.

The connection between developments in modern art and those in popular music can be seen at its closest in the light-shows staged in the 1960s and 1970s by many groups. The ancestry of the light-show can of course be traced back to the 1920s, and the Bauhaus, where light environments and light theatres were planned, but never executed. The rise of the light-show coincided with the widespread use of hallucinogenic drugs, and these shows were popularly supposed to provide the spectator, or participant, with the same range of sensations.

The light-show is an extreme example of the tendency to redefine the nature of art itself – a theme which runs throughout this book. Art, it seems to me, has been making steady progress in one direction at least: it tends to concern itself less and less with the tangible object, and is merely the agent which sets in motion a series of physiological and psychological changes within the spectator. It is at this point that the romantic doctrine of *le déréglement de tous les sens*, and the worship of technology, finally contrive to link hands with one another.

An art of the kind I have just described is naturally hostile to the dealer-critic system. For this system, which grew up amid the capitalism of the late nineteenth century, is based on the assumption that the work of art *is* in fact tangible, that it is a physical object which must be sold to a customer, this customer being an individual or an institution with the desire to possess the object in question and the money to pay for it. Big-time commercial art-dealing is a classic example of a free market economy, now hard to discover elsewhere in so pure a form. The surprising thing is how successfully it has survived into our own time. In the mid-1960s it seemed that art was rapidly democratizing, as well as dematerializing itself. The French critic Pierre Restany expressed approval:

> Abandoning the old concept of the unique object, the 'luxury product' for individual use, the artist is in the process of inventing a new language of communication between men. Renouncing his ambiguous role, that of the marginal adventurer and independent producer, the artist will be prepared for his overriding role in the society of the future: the organization of leisure.[3]

The technological revolution with its long-term effect of creating mass unemployment clearly makes the 'organization

22

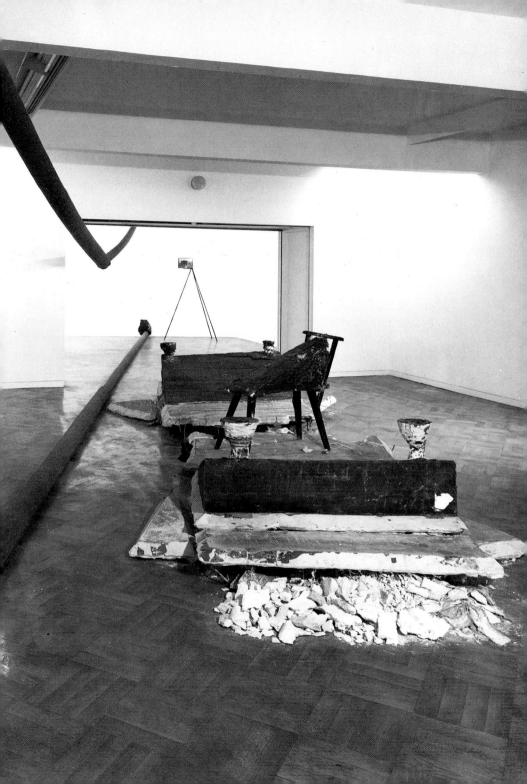

of leisure' crucial. But insofar as they are involved in this situation at all, modern artists play only a very minor role. Instead, they increasingly stress the special, rather than the universal nature of their experience. Beuys' environmental piece *Dernier espace avec introspecteur* has as its kernel the wing-mirror of a car in which the artist suffered a near-fatal car crash. But Beuys does not generalize about the experience, or suggest a comparison with car crashes suffered by victims other than himself. Instead, he incorporates the event into his own magic system, and the cracked mirror becomes a kind of sacred relic.

Beuys' works, whatever the form they take, are items of evidence about a particular range of activities, rather than things which lead an independent existence of their own. They are interesting psychically and psychologically but not formally. They support Beuys' claim to be a conductor for natural forces alien to the society in which he finds himself. He claims to be co-equal with society, rather than being part of it. Yet, paradoxically, that society has proved to be a very favourable arena for his own activities and those of artists resembling him. This is one of the paradoxes, like the survival of the old dealer-critic system, which any history of modern art in the post-war years must seek to accommodate.

CHAPTER TWO

Abstract expressionism

Abstract expressionism, the first of the great post-war art movements, had its roots in surrealism, the most important movement of the period immediately before the war. Surrealism had routed dada in Paris in the early 1920s. It is perhaps most satisfactorily defined by its leading figure, André Breton, in the First Surrealist Manifesto of 1924.

> SURREALISM, n. Pure psychic automatism, by which an attempt is made to express, either verbally or in writing, or in any other manner, the true functioning of thought. . . . Surrealism rests on the belief in the higher reality of certain neglected forms of association, in the omnipotence of dream, in the disinterested play of thought. It tends to destroy the other psychic mechanisms and to substitute itself for them in the solution of life's principal problems.[1]

Since 1924 its history, under the leadership of the volcanic Breton, had been one of schisms and scandals. In particular, the surrealists had become increasingly preoccupied with their relationship with communism. The question was: could artistic radicalism be reconciled with the political variety? So much time and energy was wasted in controversy, that, by the time the war came, the movement was visibly in decline. Maurice Nadeau, in his authoritative history of the movement, remarks: 'The adherence to the political revolution required the adherence of all the surrealist forces, and consequently the abandonment of the particular philosophy which had constituted the movement's very being at its origin.'[2]

By the time the war came, it looked as if this, the most vigorous and important of the art movements of the period between the wars, had exhausted its impetus. But the 'particular

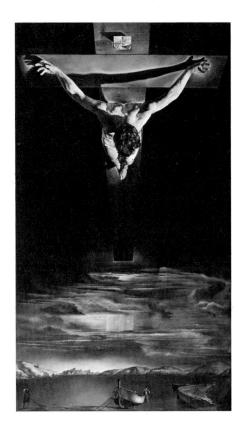

8 SALVADOR DALI
Christ of St John of the Cross
1951

philosophy' of which Nadeau speaks was still very much alive
when the surrealist movement arrived, almost *en bloc*, in New
York shortly after the outbreak of war. The exiles included not
only Breton himself but also some of the most famous surrealist
Ills 8, 10 painters: Max Ernst, Roberto Matta, Salvador Dali, and André
Ill. 9 Masson. Peggy Guggenheim, then married to Ernst, supplied
the group with a centre for their activities by opening the Art
of This Century Gallery in 1942. Many of the most important
American painters of the 1940s were later to show there.

The situation of the surrealist exiles was governed by several
factors. For example, in the midst of the conflict, the old,
rending political arguments were no longer relevant. New York
provided a fresh and challenging territory for their activities,
and they began to make converts among American artists.

As I have said, the United States had long been hospitable to the *avant-garde* art of Europeans. New York had a tradition of intermittent avant-gardism which stretched back to the Armory Show of 1913, and, beyond that, to the pre-First World War activities of Alfred Stieglitz, who presented a series of exhibitions by artists such as Rodin, Matisse, Picasso, Brancusi, Henri Rousseau, and Picabia in a small gallery at 291 Fifth Avenue. During the First World War there had been an active group of dadaists in the city, among them Marcel Duchamp, Picabia, and Man Ray. But the Depression years of the 1930s turned American art in upon itself. American critics, for instance Barbara Rose in her classic book *American Art since 1900*, stress the fact that this period of introspection and withdrawal was crucial for American artists. They point to the effect, in particular, of the Federal Art Project, the measure by which the American government sought to give relief to artists suffering from the prevailing economic conditions. Miss Rose contends that 'by making no formal distinction between abstract and representational art',[3] the Project helped to make abstract art respectable, and that the *esprit de corps* which the scheme created among artists carried over into the 1940s. Nevertheless, in 1939

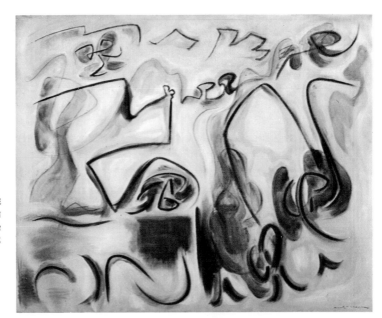

9 ANDRÉ
MASSON
*Landscape with
precipices* 1948

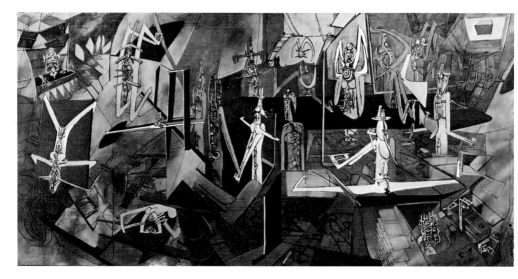

10 ROBERTO MATTA *Being With* 1945–6

American art counted for little where the European *avant-garde* was concerned, though a few distinguished *émigrés*, such as *Ills 16, 70* Josef Albers and Hans Hofmann, were already preparing the ground through their teaching for the change that was to come. Albers taught at Black Mountain College in North Carolina, Hofmann at the Art Students' League in New York and at his own schools on 8th Street and in Provincetown, Mass.

Yet it was not these, but the more-recently arrived surrealists who provided the decisive stimulus. Without their presence in New York, abstract expressionism would never have been born.

The transitional figure, the most important link between European surrealism and what was to follow, was Arshile *Ill. 11* Gorky. Gorky was born in Armenia in 1904, and did not arrive in America until 1920. His early work (undertaken in conditions of the bitterest poverty) shows a steady progression through the basic modernist styles, typical of an artist in a provincial environment who is conscious of his own isolation. He absorbed the lesson of Cézanne, then of cubism. In the 1930s, under the spell of Picasso, he was already veering towards

28

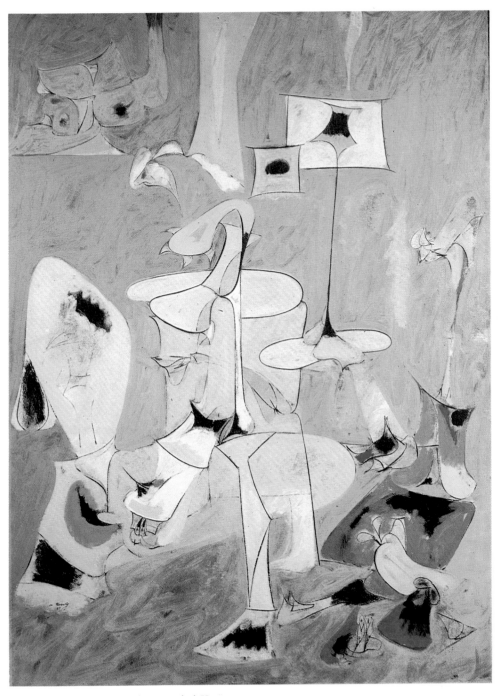

11 ARSHILE GORKY *The Betrothal II* 1947

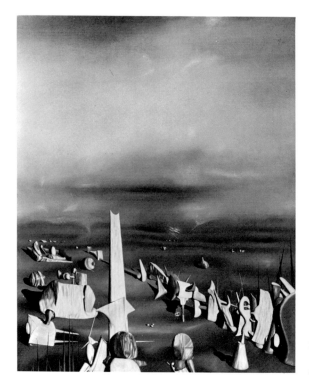

12 YVES TANGUY
*The Rapidity of
Sleep* 1945

surrealism. Then came the war, and he started to explore more
boldly. Basically, the surrealist tradition seemed to offer the
convert two choices. One was the meticulously detailed style of
Ills 8, 13   Magritte or Salvador Dali. Even in those of Dali's pictures
where the distortions are most violent, objects to some extent
retain their identity. The other choice was the biomorphic style
Ill. 12   of artists such as Miró or Tanguy, where the forms merely
hint at a resemblance to real objects, usually parts of the human
body – breasts, buttocks, the sexual organs. Gorky adopted this
method, and used it with increasing boldness. Harold Rosenberg
speaks of the characteristic imagery of Gorky's developed
style as

> ... overgrown with metaphor and association. Amid strange,
> soft organisms and insidious slits and smudges, petals hint of
> claws in a jungle of limp bodily parts, intestinal fists, pudenda,
> multiple limb folds.[4]

30

The painter himself, in a statement written in 1942, declared:

> I like the heat the tenderness the edible the lusciousness the song of a single person the bathtub full of water to bathe myself beneath the water. . . . I like the wheatfields the plough the apricots those flirts of the sun. But bread above all.[5]

Gorky was especially influenced by the Chilean-born painter Roberto Matta, and his work is often close to that which was *Ill. 10* being done by the veteran French surrealist André Masson, *Ill. 9* during the years the latter spent in America. He did not finally come into contact with Breton until 1944, and this completed his liberation as an artist. By 1947 he had begun to outstrip his masters, and the way in which he outstripped them was through the freedom with which he used his materials. The boldness of his technique can be seen in the second version of *The Betrothal*, which dates from 1947. The philosophy of art which Gorky

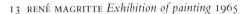

13 RENÉ MAGRITTE *Exhibition of painting* 1965

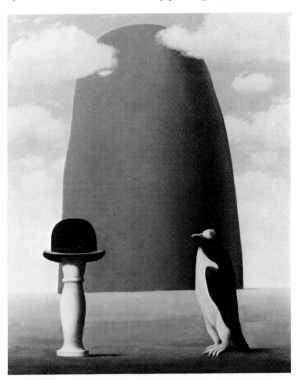

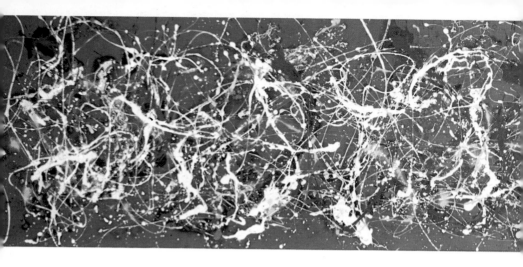

put forward in an interview with a journalist the same year had important implications for the future of American painting:

> When something is finished, that means it's dead, doesn't it? I believe in everlastingness. I never finish a painting – I just stop working on it for a while. I like painting because it's something I never come to the end of. Sometimes I paint a picture, then I paint it all out. Sometimes I'm working on fifteen or twenty pictures at the same time. I do that because I want to – because I like to change my mind so often. The thing to do is always to keep starting to paint, never finishing painting.[6]

This idea of a 'continuous dynamic' was to play an important part in abstract expressionism, and especially in the work of Jackson Pollock. Gorky himself was unable to press it further. After a long series of misfortunes, he committed suicide in 1948. He was perhaps the most distinguished surrealist that America has produced.

Far less 'European' was the work of Jackson Pollock, though it was Pollock who became the star of the Art of This Century Gallery. Like Gorky, Pollock developed very slowly. He was

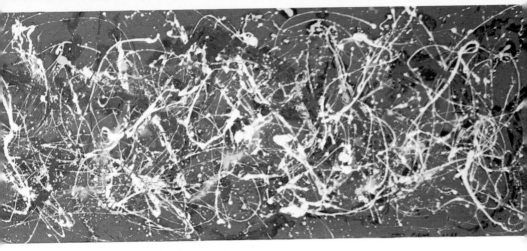

14 JACKSON POLLOCK *Number 2* 1949

born in 1912, and spent his youth in the West, in Arizona, northern California, and (later) southern California. In 1929 Pollock left Los Angeles and came to New York to study painting under Thomas Benton, a 'regionalist' painter. During the 1930s, like many American artists of his generation, he fell under the influence of the contemporary Mexicans. Diego Rivera's enthusiasm for a public art 'belonging to the populace' may well have helped to develop Pollock's sense of scale. Later he fell under the influence of the surrealists, just as Gorky had done, and Miss Guggenheim put him under contract for her gallery. By 1947, Pollock had broken through to the style for which he is now best known: free, informal abstraction, based on a technique of dripping and smearing paint on to the canvas. *Ill. 14*

Here is Pollock's own description of what took place when he worked on such pictures:

My painting does not come from the easel. I hardly ever stretch my canvas before painting. I prefer to tack the un-stretched canvas on the hard wall or floor. I need the resistance of a hard surface. On the floor I feel more at ease. I feel nearer, more part of the painting, since this way I can walk around it, work from the four sides and literally be *in* the painting. This is akin to the Indian sand painters of the West.

I continue to get further away from the usual painter's tools such as easel, palette, brushes, etc. I prefer sticks, trowels, knives and dripping fluid paint or a heavy impasto with sand, broken glass or other foreign matter added.

When I am *in* the painting I'm not aware of what I'm doing. It is only after a sort of 'get acquainted' period that I see what I have been about. I have no fears about making changes, destroying the image, etc., because the painting has a life of its own. I try to let it come through. It is only when I lose contact with the painting that the result is a mess. Otherwise there is pure harmony, an easy give and take, and the painting comes out well.[7]

Ill. 15

Compare this to Breton's instructions as to how to produce a surrealist text, as given in the manifesto of 1924:

Have someone bring you writing materials after getting settled in a place as favourable as possible to your mind's concentration on itself. Put yourself in the most passive, or receptive, state you can. Forget about your genius, your talents, and those of everyone else. Tell yourself that literature is the saddest path that leads to everything. Write quickly, without a preconceived subject, fast enough not to remember and not to be tempted to read over what you have written.[8]

I think it is clear that in many ways Pollock's and Breton's attitudes correspond. It is important, for example, to remember that even in so-called 'gestural' or 'action' painting there is a large element of passivity.

One of the more radical consequences of Pollock's method of working, so far as the spectator was concerned, was the fact that it completely changed the treatment of space. Pollock does not ignore spatial problems; his paintings are not flat. Instead, he creates a space which is ambiguous. We are aware of the surface of the picture, but also of the fact that most of the calligraphy

34

seems to hover a little way behind this surface, in space which has been deliberately compressed and robbed of perspective. Pollock is thus linked not only to the surrealists, but to Cézanne. Indeed, when we think of the illusionist perspective used by Dali and even by Tanguy, it will be clear that this is one of the points where Pollock differs most strikingly from his mentors. The shuttling rhythms which Pollock uses tend to suggest a spatial progression across the canvas, rather than directly into it, but this movement is always checked, and in the end returns towards the centre, where the main weight of the picture lies. As will be seen from his own description, these characteristics reflect Pollock's method of work. The fact that the image was created before the actual boundary of the canvas was settled (it was trimmed afterwards, to fit what had been produced) tended to focus attention on lateral motion. This rather primitive method of organization was to have important consequences.

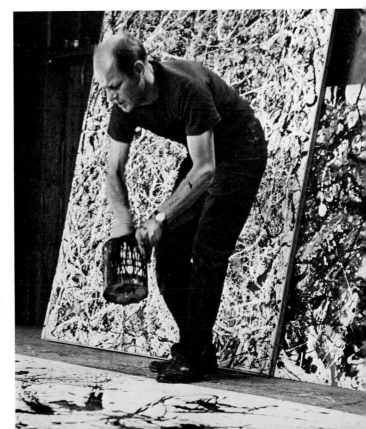

15 Jackson Pollock at work

Both by temperament and by virtue of the theories he professed – themselves largely the product of his temperament – Pollock was an intensely subjective artist. For him, inner reality was the only reality. Harold Rosenberg, the chief theorist of abstract expressionism, describes the style as a 'conversion phenomenon'. He goes so far as to call it 'essentially a religious movement'.[9] But it was a religious movement without commandments, as appears from Rosenberg's remark that 'the gesture on the canvas' was 'a gesture of liberation from Value – political, aesthetic, moral'.[10] One might add that in Pollock's case as in some others, it also seems to have been a gesture of estrangement from society and its demands. Frank O'Hara describes the artist as being 'tortured with self-doubt and tormented by anxiety'.[11]

Pollock would not, however, have made the impact he did, first in America and subsequently in Europe, if he had been completely isolated as a painter. The real father-figure of the New York school of painting during the post-war years was *Ill. 16* probably the veteran Hans Hofmann, who exercised great influence as a teacher, and whose late style shows how keen was his sympathy with what the younger men were doing. Hofmann was typical of the things which go to make up the American amalgam. He had lived in Paris from 1904 to 1914, and had been in contact with Matisse, Braque, Picasso, and Gris. It was Matisse's work that he particularly admired, and it is this which can be thought of as underlying the more decorative side of abstract expressionist painting. That the new painters were not without roots in the past is something that can be judged from Hofmann's own career. He had begun to teach in the United States in 1932, and had founded the Provincetown Art School in 1934. His last phase, upon which he embarked when he was over sixty, was both logical in the artistic climate of the time, and in human terms wonderfully unexpected: an example of a talent at last unfolding to its full extent when the right atmosphere was provided for it. Some of these late pictures are at least as bold as the work of younger men.

36

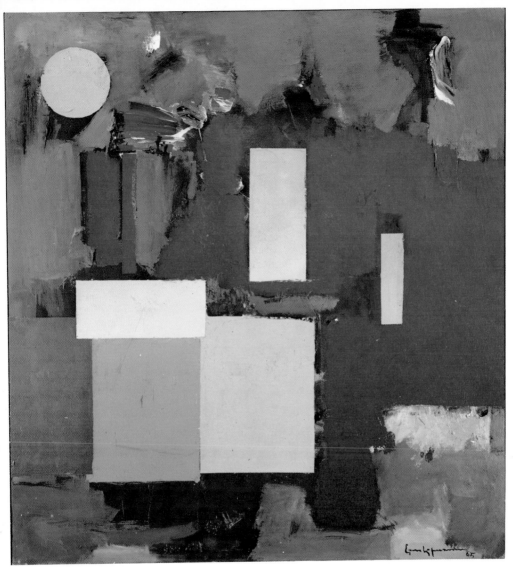

16 HANS HOFMANN *Rising Moon* 1964

The 'organizer' of the abstract expressionist movement, in so far as it had one, was neither Pollock nor Hofmann, but Robert Motherwell. Motherwell is an artist whose intellect and energies range wide. As a painter, he began his career under the influence of the surrealists, and, in particular, under that of Matta, with whom he made a trip to Mexico. He had his first one-man exhibition at the Art of This Century Gallery in 1944. As the abstract expressionist movement got under way, the range of Motherwell's activities continued to expand. He was co-editor of the influential but short-lived magazine *Possibilities* in 1947–8, and in 1948 founded an art school with three other
Ill. 17   important painters, William Baziotes, Barnett Newman, and Mark Rothko. In 1951 he published an anthology of the work of the dada painters and poets which was one of the earliest signs of the arrival of 'neo-dada'.

17 WILLIAM BAZIOTES *Congo* 1954

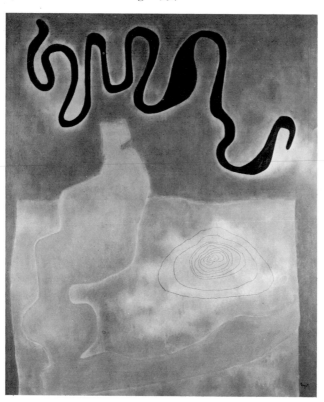

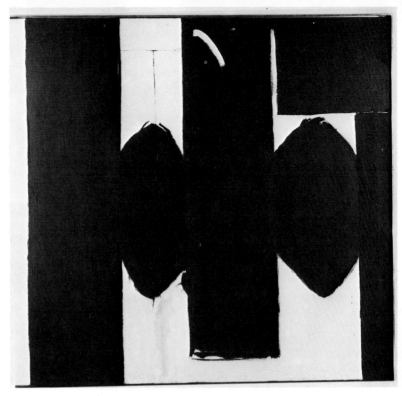

The variety of these activities did not prevent Motherwell
from having a large output as a painter. His best-known works
are the long series of canvases known collectively as the *Elegies
to the Spanish Republic*. These pictures serve to correct some *Ill. 18*
erroneous ideas about abstract expressionism. It's significant,
for instance, that Motherwell's theme is one drawn from the
recent history of Europe: recent, but not absolutely contemporary. Motherwell was in his early twenties when the Spanish
Civil War broke out, and is looking back with nostalgia on his
own youth. His choice of subject suggests that the 'subjective'
painting which flourished in America during the late 1940s and
early 1950s was by no means incapable of dealing with historical
or social issues, but that these issues had to be approached in
personal terms, and obliquely. The *Elegies* are certainly far
more oblique than *Guernica*. The nostalgic rhetoric of Mother-

39

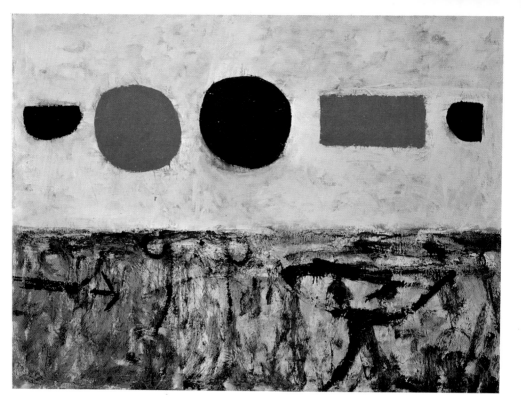

19 ADOLPH GOTTLIEB *The Frozen Sounds Number 1* 1951

well's paintings, sustained in painting after painting, is reminiscent of the tone to be found in a good deal of post-war American poetry: in that of poets as different from one another as Allen Ginsberg and Robert Duncan, for example. It is a mood which has few equivalents in the painting of post-war Europe, and which acts as a reminder both of the essentially American character of the style and of the fact that it was not necessarily the 'instantaneous' art which European painters at times mistook it for.

Essentially, there are two sorts of abstract expressionist painting, rather than one. The first kind, typified by Pollock, Franz Kline, and Willem de Kooning, is energetic and gestural. Pollock and de Kooning are much involved with figuration.

40

20 MARK ROTHKO *Orange Yellow Orange* 1969

The other kind, typified by Mark Rothko, is more purely
abstract and more tranquil. Rothko's work, in particular, serves
to justify Harold Rosenberg's use of the adjective 'mystic',
when describing the school. Rothko, like several other leading
American artists of the post-war period – Gorky, de Kooning,
Hofmann – was born abroad; he came to America from Russia
in 1913, when he was ten. He began as an expressionist, felt the
influence of Matta and Masson, and followed the standard
pattern by having an exhibition at the Art of This Century
Gallery in 1948. Gradually his work grew simpler, and by 1950
he had reached the point where the figurative element had been
discarded. A few rectangles of space are placed on a coloured
ground. Their edges are not defined, and their spatial position
is therefore ambiguous. They float towards us, or away, in a
shallow space of the kind that we also find in Pollock – it
derives, ultimately, from the spatial experiments of the cubists.
In Rothko's paintings the colour relationships, as they interact
within the rectangle and within this space, set up a gentle
rhythmic pulsation. The painting becomes both a focus for the
spectator's meditations and a screen before a mystery. The
weakness of Rothko's work (just as the subtlety of colour is its
strength) is to be found in the rigidity and monotony of the
compositional formula. The bold central image became one of
the trademarks of the new American painting – one of the
things that differentiated it from European art. Rothko was an
artist of real brilliance imprisoned in a straitjacket; he
exemplifies the narrowness of focus which many modern artists
imposed upon themselves.

The lesson is reinforced by the work of an artist who in many
ways resembles Rothko: Adolph Gottlieb. He is also linked to
Motherwell, in that he is a rhetorician – by 'rhetoric' in painting,
I mean the deliberate use of vague, expansive, generalized
forms. An interest in Freud led Gottlieb towards an art which
he deliberately filled with cosmic symbolism. The likeness
between Gottlieb's most characteristic style and the paintings
done by Joan Miró in the late 1930s is something that bears

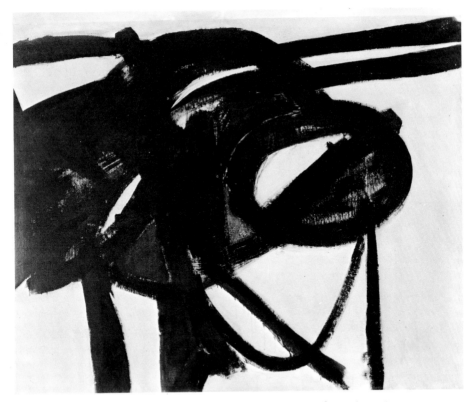

21 FRANZ KLINE *Chief* 1950 (Collection The Museum of Modern Art, New York)

investigation. Miró, too, is fond of cosmic symbols, but paints them more lightly and crisply, without too much stress on their deeper meanings. Gottlieb's work makes me feel that I am being asked to take a weighty significance on trust. This significance is not inherent in the colour or the brushwork; one has to recognize the symbol and make the historical connection.

The limitations I find in the work of Rothko and Gottlieb seem to me to be shared by the earlier work of Philip Guston, *Ill. 21* and by that of Franz Kline. Guston (d. 1980) typified the *Ill. 24* boneless aspect of abstract expressionism, when too often his pictures were no more than a riot of lush paint and sweet colour, until he reversed direction at the end of his life and started *Ill. 238* painting in a gritty 'cartoon' style which makes a bridge

43

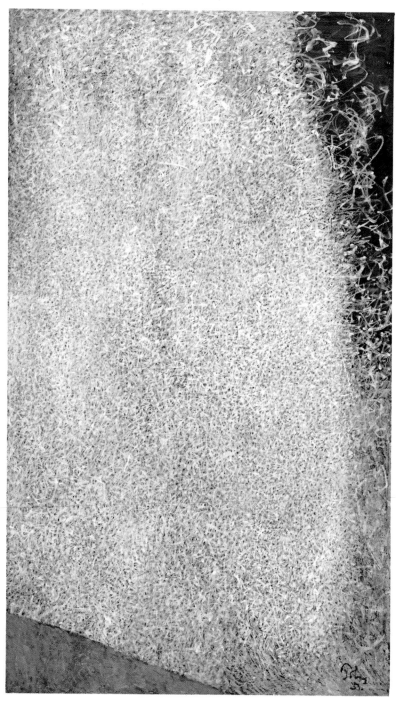

22 MARK TOBEY *Edge of August* 1953 (Collection The Museum of Modern Art, New York)

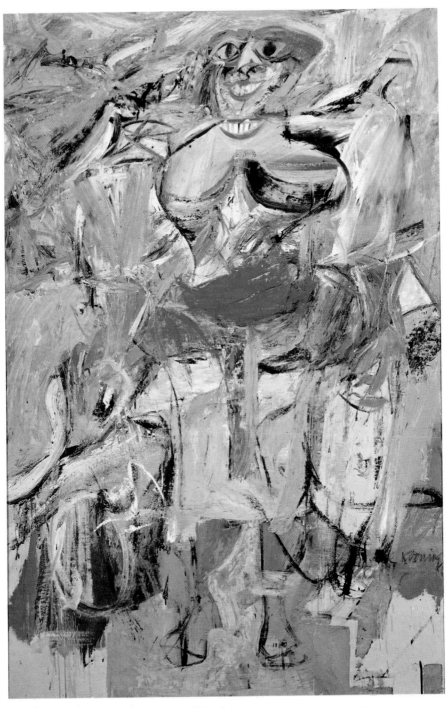

23 WILLEM DE KOONING *Woman and bicycle* 1952–3

between pop art and neo-expressionism. Kline, like Rothko, is an artist who runs to rather sterile extremes, and he is speeded on his way to them by abstract expressionist doctrine. Unlike Rothko's, his work is gestural, and his technical affiliations are with Pollock. What he most frequently did was to create on the canvas something which looked like a Chinese character, or part of one, enormously magnified. These strong, harsh ideograms relied for their effect on the stark contrast of black strokes on a white ground. Paint seems to be used only for reasons of breadth and scale: there is little in most of the paintings that could not have been said with Indian ink and paper. When, in the last years of Kline's life (he died in 1962), colour began to play a part in his work, the results were not usually happy because we are never made to feel that colour is essential to the statement. Its purposes are cosmetic.

Kline was always very wary about admitting to any sort of Oriental influence in his work, yet influences of this kind have undoubtedly been important in American painting since the war. Not only is there an element of passivity which grows increasingly powerful with each successive stylistic revolution – Rothko invites the spectator to contemplation, Morris Louis collaborates almost passively with the demands of his materials, Andy Warhol accepts the image and refuses to edit it – but the techniques of Oriental artists, as well as their philosophies, have made an important impact.

It is interesting to compare Kline's big gestural symbols with the work of an artist who had a very different sense of scale: Ill. 22 Mark Tobey. Mark Tobey was not, strictly speaking, an abstract expressionist painter. Rather, he pursued a parallel development, modified by different experiences and a different context. Tobey's career was centred not on New York but on Seattle – that is, until a final move to Switzerland. He visited the Near East and Mexico, besides making several visits to China and Japan. In Japan he stayed for a while in a Zen monastery, and became a convert to Buddhism (thus anticipating a similar conversion on the part of one of the most important of the

American Beat poets, Gary Snyder). Tobey's journeys to the Orient were made with the specific purpose of studying Chinese calligraphy, and they had an avowed and decisive effect on his painting. He adopted a technique which he labelled 'white writing', a way of covering the picture surface with an intricate network of signs which are like Kline's hieroglyphs writ small. In many ways Tobey's work is a critique of Kline's, and of abstract expressionism as a whole. The thing which is impressive about Tobey's paintings, however tenuous his formal devices may sometimes appear, is the fact that what he produces is always complete in its own terms. Tobey's discoveries reinforced those of Pollock: in his later work, the canvas, or 'field', is articulated from end to end by the rhythmic marks of the brush. But he, more than the true abstract expressionists, gives the spectator a feeling of possibility. The marks, one feels, might at any moment rearrange themselves, but would retain a sense of ordered harmony. This is not an art straining against its own limitations, but one which is exploring a newly discovered and infinitely flexible means of expression.

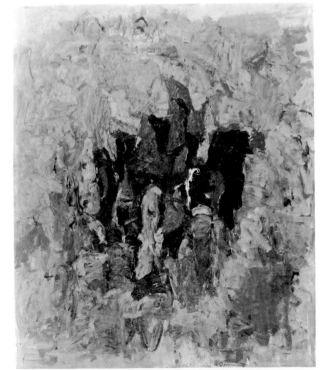

24 PHILIP GUSTON *The Clock* 1956–7 (Collection The Museum of Modern Art, New York)

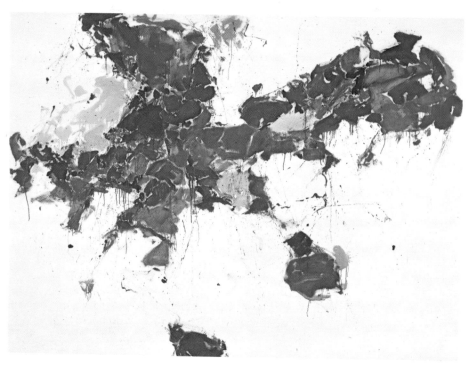

25 SAM FRANCIS *Blue on a point* 1958

Ill. 23

Yet it would be a mistake to assume that abstract expressionism itself was entirely inflexible. The school was at any rate flexible enough to incorporate the art of Willem de Kooning, an artist who, in his best pictures, stands next to Pollock in force and originality of talent. De Kooning was born in Holland, and did not arrive in America until he was already an adult. His style tends to emphasize the expressionist component of abstract expressionism, at the price of abstraction. He deals with imagery which seems to rise up out of the texture of the paint, and then to relapse again into the chaos which momentarily gave it form. What marks him off from contemporary European expressionists is the characteristically American boldness – one might even say rawness – and sense of scale that appear in his pictures. When de Kooning bases himself on imagery taken from landscape, the work is so broad that it

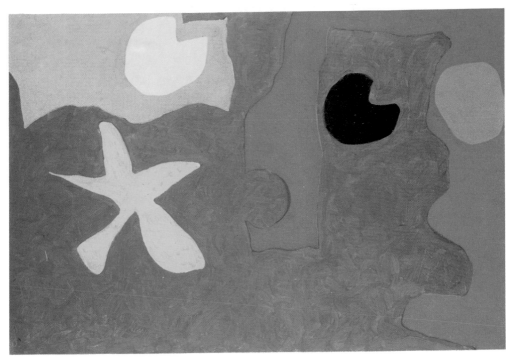

26 PATRICK HERON *Manganese in deep violet: January 1967*

seems as if he has discovered a way of using oil-paint as the boldest Chinese and Japanese scholar-painters used ink: yet his grip on the original source of the image is never quite broken. When he paints in a more directly figurative way, as in the series of *Women*, the whole force of the sexual impulse is there in the painting. These Kali-like figures correspond to the kind of work which Jean Dubuffet did in his earliest period, and again in the *Corps de Dame* series of 1950. De Kooning's work is an important point of contact, therefore, between European and American art. In addition to this, it predicts certain aspects of pop art. De Kooning's *Women* are the forerunners of Warhol's *Marilyns*.

The enormous success scored by abstract expressionism was to have important consequences for the arts on both sides of the Atlantic. Pollock's legend grew with tremendous rapidity in the years between the first European showing of his work in 1948 and his death in a car crash in 1956. Some of the effects of this success were all too predictable. An attempt was made to set up abstract expressionism as the only conceivable kind of art. A rapid succession of yet newer and more radical adventures seemed to disprove this claim almost immediately. Ironically enough, there was something in it. Abstract expressionism looked both forward and back. Despite the huge scale on which they worked, Pollock and Kline seem to have had perfect faith in canvas and paint as a viable means of communicating something. That faith has since been questioned, and one reason for the questioning is the degree to which the abstract expressionist painters strained traditional categories of art; nothing further evolved from what they did. If one compares the work of a painter such as Clyfford Still to the superficially very similar work of Sam Francis, one gets some idea of the extent to which abstract expressionism was at home only in America. Francis, as a Paris-domiciled American, introduces the European element of 'taste', which immediately compromises the rigour of the style. And again, if one compares the work of one of the few good abstract expressionists of the second generation, Helen

Ill. 65

Ill. 27
Ill. 25

50

Frankenthaler, with that of the pioneers, one sees how difficult Ill. 77
it was to build on what those pioneers had achieved. This least
academic of styles made an astonishingly rapid descent into
academicism. The art boom of the middle and late 1950s
created a spate of bubble-reputations.

The effect of the new American art on Europe was not
altogether happy. One reason for this was that Europeans mis-
understood it, and tried to make use of criteria which had been
suddenly outgrown. In England, for example, one still
encounters a certain bitterness among early supporters of
abstract expressionism. The British painter-critic Patrick Heron, *Ill. 26*
who welcomed his American colleagues very generously when
they first appeared, has complained of their ingratitude.[12]
He too suggests that the monotony of the central, heraldic
image to be found in much abstract expressionist painting
could be remedied by a resort to more sophisticated European
methods of composing the picture space. This shows that his
initial enthusiasm was based on a misapprehension, as such
methods of composition were just what the Americans had
been most concerned to reject from the very beginning, even
at the price of losing their freedom to develop and manœuvre.

The importance of abstract expressionism was arguably more
to culture as a whole than to painting in particular. The success
made by the new painting, and its attendant publicity, drew the
attention of writers and musicians who were discontented with
their own disciplines. Earle Brown, one of the most radical of
the new composers, claimed to have found new inspiration for
his own work in that of Pollock. At first, it was the gesture of
liberation which counted, rather than any specific resemblance
between the disciplines of the various arts. The so-called 'mixed
media' and 'intermedia' were to come later, partly as a result of
experiments with assemblage and collage.

CHAPTER THREE

The European scene

The course of events in France, and on the Continent as a whole, was very different to that in America. Paris was naturally the place towards which Europeans looked as soon as peace was restored. Equally naturally, it was the artists of the 'great generation' who began by attracting the most attention. Indeed, the six-year gap had served to establish these artists more, rather than less, firmly in the public mind. They were no longer outsiders; they had come to seem like representatives of the civilization which the Allies had been fighting for; and the Nazi condemnation of 'decadent art' was now of some considerable service to their reputations. Picasso became as much an object of pilgrimage to American GI's in liberated Paris as their own compatriot, Gertrude Stein.

On the other hand, there was a sense in which these senior artists found themselves cut off from their roots by what had happened. A feeling of change was in the air, and they, who had been the instigators of so many changes, were not the promoters but the victims of this one. The new eminence they were accorded often brought a certain aridity to their work.

This verdict seemed to apply particularly to Picasso. Immediately after the war he was awarded his final status as a mortal god: the most universally acclaimed and celebrated artist since Michelangelo. It says something for Picasso's furious creativity that, even when he had been placed in this uneasy situation, it showed no sign of slackening. His production after 1945 was prodigious, and new aspects of it were almost constantly revealed to the public. In 1966, for example, his extensive but previously almost unknown production as a sculptor was shown in exhibitions in London, Paris and New York. Despite his immense celebrity, however, Picasso's work

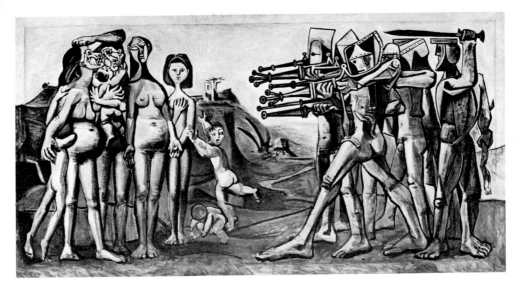

28 PABLO PICASSO *Massacre in Korea* 1951

gradually fell from favour with the leaders of taste in modern art. They were encouraged to downgrade him both by his Arcadian visions of nymphs and fauns, which seemed not only frivolous, but curiously 'thirties' in style – part of the repertoire of Art Deco (then still very much out of favour) – and by the occasional propaganda pictures which expressed the painter's Communist sympathies. One such was his *Massacre in Korea*, painted at the time of the Korean war. Most people saw it as a rather barren paraphrase of Goya's *Dos de Mayo*. *Ill. 28*

Paraphrase was a habit which increasingly grew on the artist. Among the most characteristic works of the 'late' – but not the latest – period of his production were the series of variations on famous paintings by the great masters of the past, such as the *Las Meninas* of Velásquez, or the *Women of Algiers* by Delacroix. *Ill. 6* Picasso applied to these Monet's habit of working in series, conducting a kind of unpacking process, taking from the original work various ideas and qualities, and holding these up for our inspection, adding at the same time comments of his own. Often the spectator is conscious of a sort of hostility

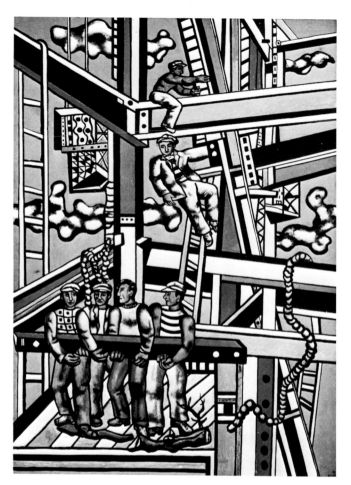

29 FERNAND LÉGER *The Constructors* 1950

towards the achievements of the past; some of the versions might almost be described as rapes or dismemberments.

Picasso turned the same baleful eye on the effects of the ageing process as it applied to himself, and some of his most personal late works are a series of prints on this theme, often including self-portraits showing the artist as an aged voyeur or else as a monkey. They were produced in a great burst of creative energy between 16 March and 5 October 1968. Even more extraordinary are the very late paintings, done in the final years before the artist's death in April 1973. Painted with tremendous boldness, and even with a certain crudity, they met with incomprehension when they were first shown, but have since been hailed as the most important precursors of the new expressionist figuration. Certainly there is a wild sense of risk about them which makes them exciting. Images are radically simplified, yet retain legibility thanks to Picasso's unsurpassed skill as a draughtsman.

Several other painters of the great generation continue to seem isolated from the main current of post-war events, though the work they did was often impressive. Georges Braque, for example, painted some undoubted masterpieces in his old age, such as the series of pictures devoted to the theme of the studio. These tranquil, monumental paintings sum up all the lessons of the painter's long lifetime. Yet it is surely significant that they are inward-turned without being truly introspective. They look, not at the world outside, nor at the psyche, but at the familiar paraphernalia of the artist's workshop. Their greatness comes, not from new invention, but from refinement of invention. Braque is giving a final polish to ideas which he first began to use in the days of cubism, and he deploys these ideas less radically in the late than in the early work.

More willing to get to grips with the world around him was another veteran, Fernand Léger. In a picture such as *The Constructors*, painted in 1950, we see an attempt to bring a *Ill. 29* Poussinesque classicism to terms with properly modern and Marxist subject-matter. The results have been duly admired by Marxist critics. Nevertheless, a reversion to Poussin seems curiously eccentric and wilful even in the wilful world of post-war art.

Even the two acknowledged masters whose work seems most relevant to the post-war scene seem to have achieved this relationship almost by accident. The most conspicuous triumph was that of Matisse, who became in his old age almost as radical an artist as he had been at the time of the fauves. Between the wars Matisse had specialized in a fluent hedonism which made increasingly few demands on his talent. In 1941 he underwent a series of operations, and emerged from them a permanent invalid. In some ways this ordeal and even the war itself seem to have sharpened his perceptions. In the late 1940s he painted a series of splendid interiors, flooded with light and colour,

Ill. 34   which form a parallel to the *Studios* of Braque. But he was to go beyond this. By 1950, the patches of colour in his pictures (for

Ill. 30   example, the *Zulma* in Copenhagen) had begun to enjoy an autonomy of their own. It was at about this time that, because of his increasing feebleness, Matisse began to use the *papier découpé* technique which was the chief creative resource of his last years. Pieces of paper were coloured to the artist's specification, and these were then cut and used to form designs. Thus

31 HENRI MATISSE ▶
The Snail 1953

30 HENRI MATISSE *Zulma*
1950

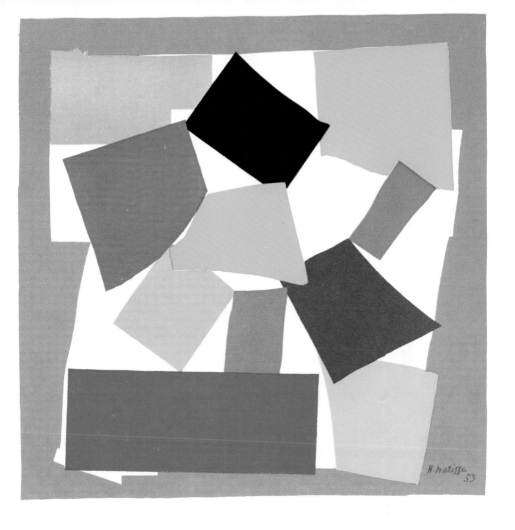

the old man could create works of considerable size without too much strain. The method encouraged extreme simplification, and helped to discipline Matisse's decorative gift. *The Snail* is _Ill. 31_ one of the most abstract of all the designs of this period, severer even than the work which Matisse did around 1910. The activation of colour which Matisse achieved in these works was to mean something important to painters much younger than himself.

57

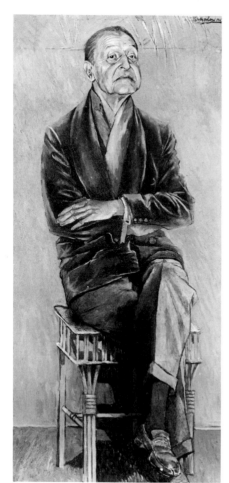

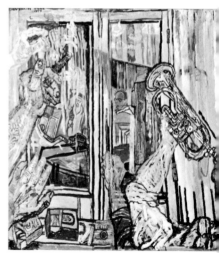

33 JOHN BRATBY
*Window, self-portrait, Jean
and hands* 1957

32 GRAHAM SUTHERLAND
Somerset Maugham 1949

Ill. 36

Ill. 35

The other painter who had something to contribute was Miró, whom I have already mentioned while discussing abstract impressionism. Miró's great simple canvases of the Fifties were certainly close to the abstract expressionists, and even to some of the 'colour painters' whom I have yet to discuss. His sculpture, too, has links with Dubuffet. But Miró remains strangely elusive as an artistic personality: an artist who kept so many options open is difficult to interpret satisfactorily.

Other major artists, such as Max Ernst, continued their careers, but producing work which seems increasingly remote

58

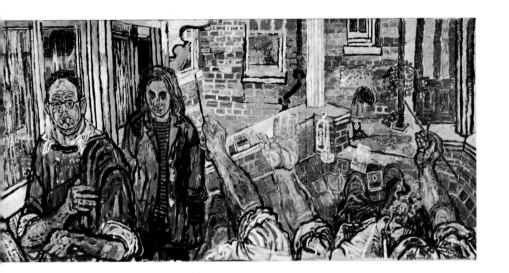

from the current scene. Some important painters acknowledged this dilemma quite openly. One seems to find a
confession of it in the powerful realistic portraits which the
British painter Graham Sutherland produced after the war,
numbering Sir Winston Churchill and Somerset Maugham
among his sitters. These seem a surprising development of style
for an artist who certainly began in the surrealist tradition, and
who continued, in other paintings, to produce work which was
reminiscent of surrealism.

Ill. 32

'Realism' itself is not, however, an irrelevant issue, where the
post-war painting of Europe is concerned. In fact, the sombre
mood of immediately post-war Europe did seem to produce at
least a theoretical leaning towards realist art. There was a
feeling that artists should now face up to their responsibilities,
that they should participate in building a new and better world,
and, in particular, that they should fall into line with film-
makers and authors, both of whom were attracted towards a
documentary style. In Italy, for example, Rossellini's early neo-
realist films, *Città Aperta* and *Païsa*, were important – infinitely
more so than the *Manifesto del Realismo* issued by leading Italian
artists in 1945.

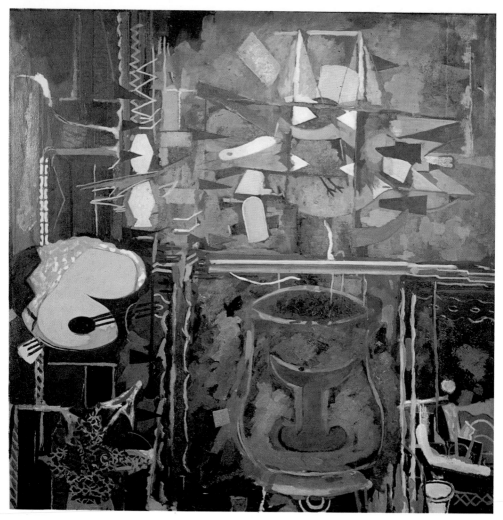

34 GEORGES BRAQUE *Studio IX* 1952–6

35 MAX ERNST *Cry of the seagull* 1953

36 JOAN MIRÓ *Blue II* 1961

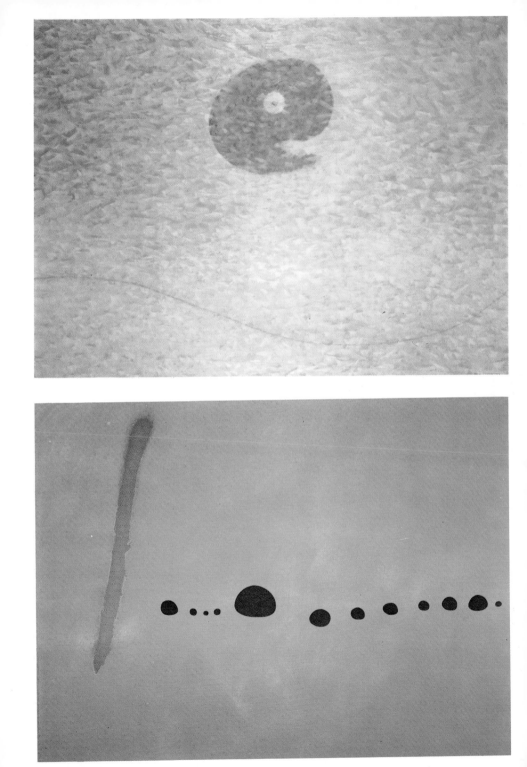

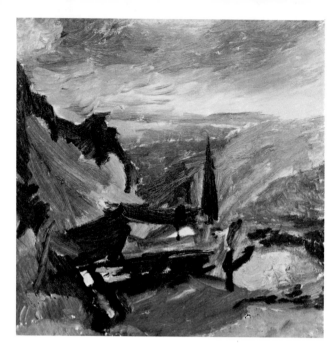

37 DAVID BOMBERG
*Monastery of Ay
Chrisostomos, Cyprus* 1948

38 FRANK AUERBACH
Head of Helen Gillespie III
1962–4

39 LEON KOSSOFF *Profile of
Rachel* 1965

On the whole, social realism took root only in those countries which could be counted as markedly provincial. In England, for example, the so-called 'Kitchen Sink' painters enjoyed a considerable vogue. Their leader, David Bomberg, had begun his career as a pioneer modernist, under the influence of vorticism, but later developed in a way which showed that his true masters were the German expressionists. Bomberg tried to create a balance: he wanted the spectator to be able to enter into his work, both in its role as a representation and in its role simply as paint. His followers tended to emphasize one of the terms of this occasion at the expense of the other. The work of Frank Auerbach and of Kossoff, for example, is concerned with a reality that is achieved literally: by means of the solidity of paint, which is piled up on the canvas in ropes and mounds. Though the approach is different, the final result has something in common with the French 'matter painters' whom I shall discuss in a moment.

Ills 38, 39

62

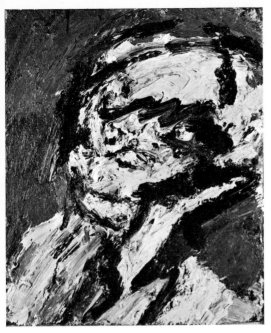
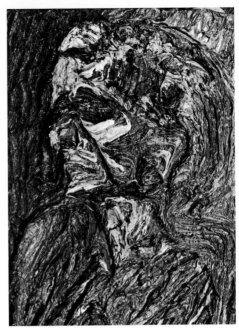

The realism of the other 'Kitchen Sink' painters (those to whom the term more properly applies) was more descriptive, and their allegiance to it proved more fragile. The early work of artists such as Jack Smith, Edward Middleditch, and John *Ills 33, 43* Bratby dates only from the middle 1950s, and is the equivalent of the kind of realism which was then dominant in English literature and on the London stage: Kingsley Amis's novel *Lucky Jim*, John Osborne's play *Look Back in Anger*. None of these English painters produced work of the strength of that done by the Italian realist Renato Guttuso, who discovered a *Ill. 42* kind of neo-baroque idiom in which to describe the lives of 'ordinary people' – workers, people on the beach. Where Léger, in his late years, looked back towards the baroque of Poussin, in trying to create an 'art of the people', Guttuso based himself on the more tactile art of the Carracci, and of Caravaggio.

There is, however, one British figurative painter who ranks among the more distinguished European contemporary artists:

63

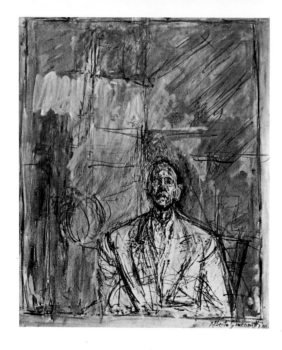

40 ALBERTO
GIACOMETTI *Portrait of
Jean Genet* 1959

Ills 41, 44,
45 Francis Bacon. Bacon and the Frenchman Balthus seem to me,
in fact, to be the only two artists who have managed to make
figuration work in a contemporary European context. Both are
so strange and individual that it is worth considering them side
by side.

Bacon seems to me to represent the degree to which the
demands of traditional figurative painting can be forced into a
compromise with those of modernism. By the standards of
many of the artists whose work is described in this book, he is
an extremely traditional figure. He works with the old materials,
oil-paint on canvas, and he accepts the discipline of the old
formats. In other ways he is far from orthodox. This is the way
in which he described his method of work in a television
interview with David Sylvester:

I think that you can make, very much as in abstract painting,
involuntary marks on the canvas which may suggest much
deeper ways by which you can trap the facts you are obsessed
by. If anything ever does work in my case it works from that

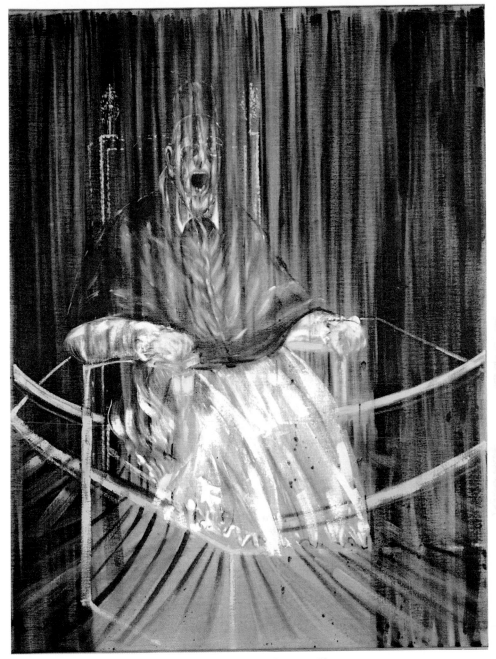

41 FRANCIS BACON *Study after Velázquez: Pope Innocent X* 1953

moment when consciously I didn't know what I was doing. . . . It's really a question in my case of being able to set a trap with which one would be able to catch the fact at its most living point.[1]

This leaves open at least two questions: the precise one of the 'facts' the painter feels attracted towards, and the more general one of the future of figurative art. In Bacon's case the facts seem to be mostly those of terror, isolation, and anguish. A visit to any large retrospective exhibition of Bacon's work is an oppressive experience. Bacon has been through a number of stylistic changes: the screaming popes and businessmen that made him famous have now given way to harder, clearer, and in a way more disturbing images. Distorted figures cower in glaringly lit rooms, which suggest both the luxury apartment and the execution chamber. These figures are not merely isolated, they are abject: man stripped of his few remaining pretensions.

Bacon's consistent, narrow art represents at least one of the positions that it is possible to take up, *vis-à-vis* mid twentieth-

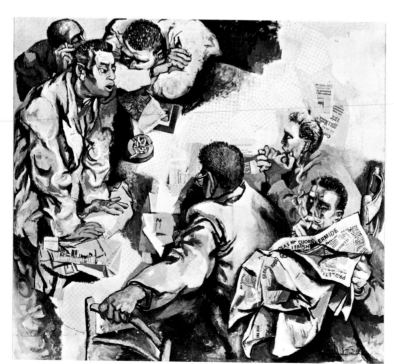

42 RENATO GUTTUSO *The Discussion* 1959–60

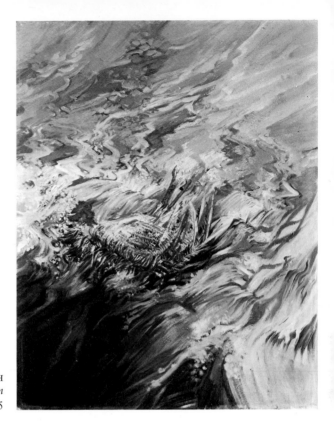

43 EDWARD MIDDLEDITCH
Dead chicken in a stream
1955

century experience. But, though the unease of his work has impressed both the ordinary spectator and his fellow artists, there is no such thing as a 'school of Bacon', even in England. The attitudes he has taken up preclude membership of any group or movement.

Easier to assimilate psychologically, but still isolated from the main current, is the work of Balthus. He differs from Bacon in being more naturalistic, in eschewing improvisation, in being influenced by artists such as Courbet and Piero della Francesca who could never be described as Bacon's masters (Bacon's debts are mostly to Velázquez). But they still have much in common. Like Bacon, Balthus broods on private obsessions; like Bacon, he often uses the symbolism of figures in a room which claustrophobically contains and shuts them in. If Bacon

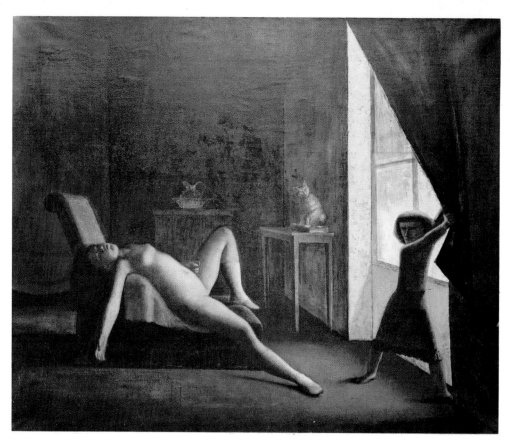

44 BALTHUS *The Bedroom* 1954

Ill. 44 occasionally seems to depict the aftermath of rape, Balthus gives
its foretaste. Nude, adolescent girls sprawl in abandoned poses,
inviting sexual violence. Light gilds their contours, with a hand
which is secretive and loving.

Bacon and Balthus stand out among their contemporaries
because each is endowed with a very special temperament, one
which overrides all considerations of style. Few artists are
endowed with the perhaps burdensome qualities which these
two seem to possess, and the development of European painting
was to go a very different way.

68

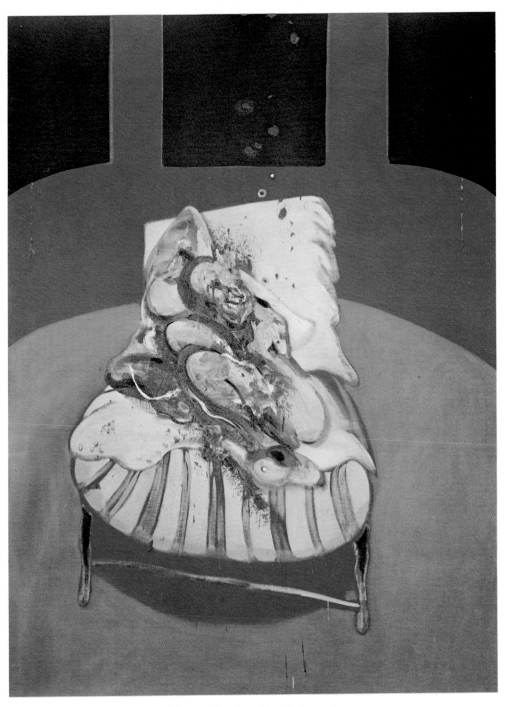

45 FRANCIS BACON *One of three studies for a Crucifixion* 1962

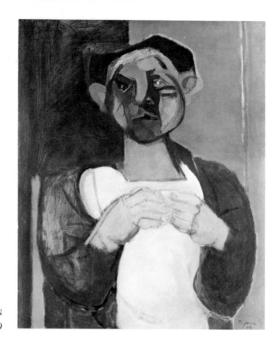

46 ÉDOUARD PIGNON
The Miner 1949

47 MAURICE ESTÈVE *Composition 166* 1957

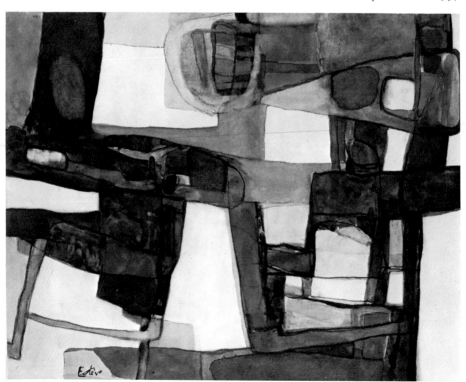

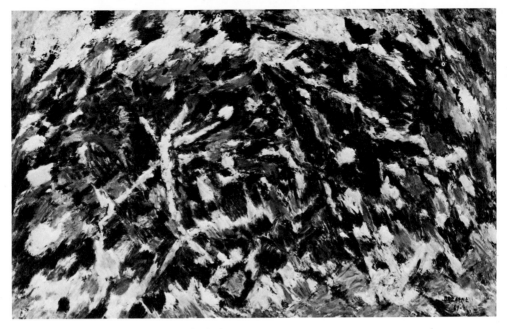

48 JEAN BAZAINE *Shadows on the hill* 1961

I have spoken of the sudden attention which was devoted to the great names of the Ecole de Paris immediately following the war. For younger artists in France, the process of growing up under the shadow of these giant reputations was bound to be a difficult one. Those artists most spoken of as 'promising' in Paris at this time were the so-called 'middle generation', which consisted of Jean Fautrier, Maurice Estève, Edouard Pignon, and Jean Bazaine among others. These men were expected to do several entirely contradictory things at the same time. It was their duty to maintain the impetus of the modernist revolution; it was equally their duty to maintain the prestige of Paris, and the whole apparatus of dealers and critics that went with Paris as a centre. Naturally they found themselves in two minds. Their development was not made any easier by the vigorous promotion they received.

Ills 46–8

Of the painters whom I have just mentioned, Fautrier is without question the most original and important, as well as

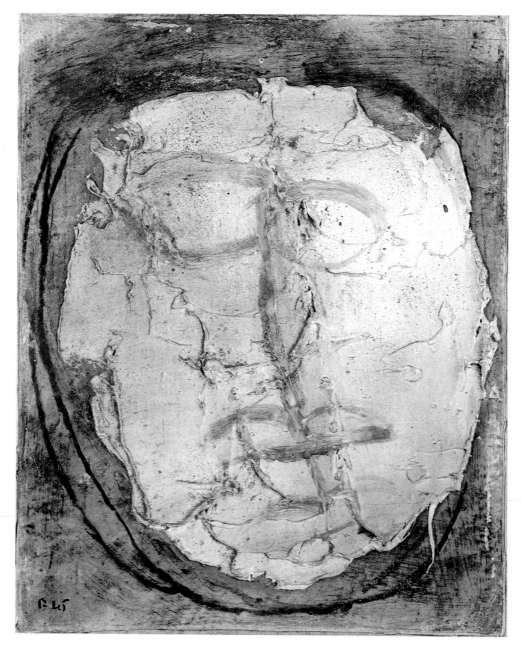

49 JEAN FAUTRIER *Hostage* 1945

50 WOLS *The Blue Pomegranate* 1946

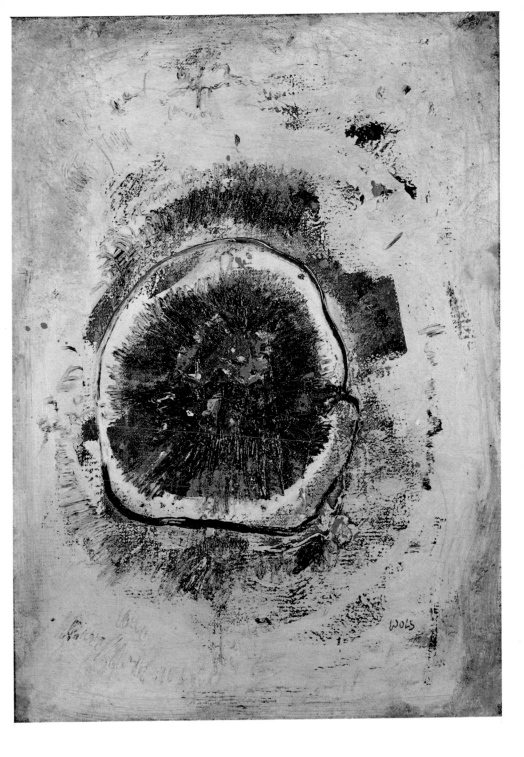

being the oldest. He was born in 1898, the other three in the middle of the next decade. Fautrier's first post-war show, at the Galerie Drouin in 1945, which consisted of the series of pictures *Ill. 49* called *Hostage*, did have a significance for the future. The ostensible subject was the mass deportations during the war, but the paintings put great stress upon the tactility of the painter's materials, the evocative quality of the surface itself. There is a narcissism in this which tells us something about the waning vitality of French painting, but it was also a genuine innovation. One sees in these pictures the first steps being taken towards *art informel* – art 'without form' – the style which was to dominate the next decade; and it is interesting to note that the step was made before the influence of the American abstract expressionists had reached France. Bazaine, Estève, and Pignon are lesser figures. In their work, fauvism, cubism, and expressionism jostled together to make an amalgam that had little that was new in it, save the fact of the mixture.

There were, however, better artists than these at work in the Paris of the late 1940s and the 1950s: men who did something, if not enough, to justify the critic Michel Tapié's claim, in his book *Un Art autre*, that there was now a kind of painting which started from premisses wholly different from the traditional ones. Most of the painters whom Tapié supported were working in a direction which paralleled that being taken by the abstract expressionists in America. The pioneer, almost the Arshile Gorky of this group, was the short-lived German artist Wols. *Ill. 50* Wols began by training as a violinist, then went to study at the Bauhaus in Berlin under Moholy-Nagy and Mies van der Rohe. In the early 1930s he moved to Paris, and formed links with the surrealists. The rest of the decade was divided between France and Spain: at this period Wols worked mostly as a photographer. In 1939–40 he was interned, and began to achieve his mature style in a series of drawings. These were successfully shown at the Galerie Drouin in 1945, and Wols began to exercise a real influence over his contemporaries. The paintings he made in the few years that remained to him (he died in 1951) seem to blend the graphic sensibility of Klee with the new and more freely abstract way of seeing things. Wols's fascination with the actual substance of which the picture is made, the thick impasto which can be scratched and carved, prompts a comparison with Fautrier.

Hans Hartung was a compatriot of Wols. During the art Ill. 51 boom of the mid 1950s, he was to score a resounding success, thanks to a rather limited formula for picture-making which is correspondingly easy to recognize. Like Wols, Hartung left Germany in the 1930s, and settled in Paris, where he was encouraged by the sculptor Julio González. What he had to show now, in the years immediately following the war, was a vigorous calligraphy of bundled sheaves of lines. No picture of Hartung's is wholly without energy, but, once one has seen a group of them, it is certainly possible to wonder why a given mark, a given brushstroke, appears in one canvas and not in another.

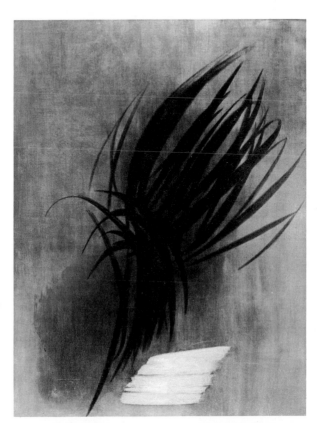

51 HANS
HARTUNG
*Painting T
54-16* 1954

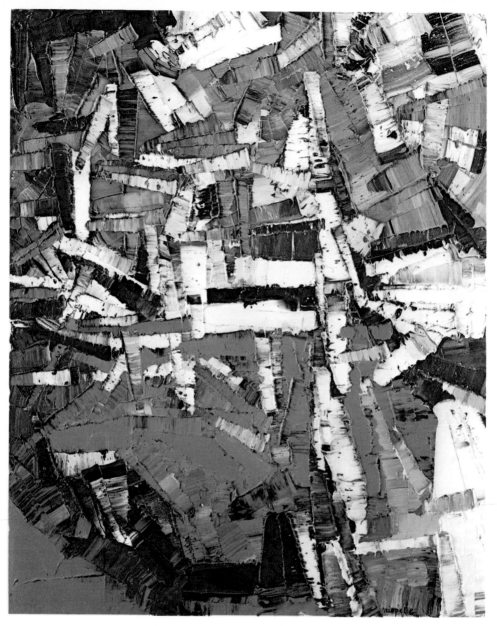

52 JEAN-PAUL RIOPELLE *Encounter* 1956

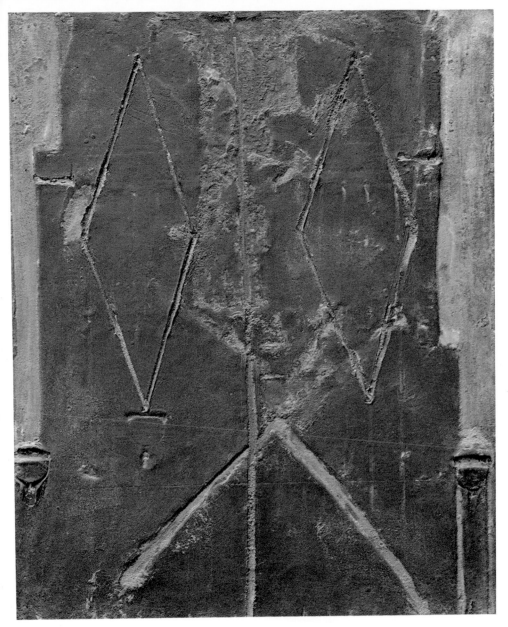

53 ANTONIO TAPIÉS *Black with two lozenges* 1963

Another very fashionable painter in the 1950s was the French-
Ill. 52 Canadian Jean-Paul Riopelle. Riopelle, too, has an effective but
limited formula. His work is an attempt to marry the spontaneity of 'informal' abstract painting to the rich texture and
colour which are to be obtained from a heavy impasto. Here,
as in Hartung's paintings, there is vigour of rather an obvious
sort. The bright colour emphasizes the mechanical roughness
of the surface, but the two elements – colour and texture – do
not quite coalesce.

A stronger artist, whose work is akin to informal abstraction,
but stands somewhat apart from it, is the poet-draughtsman
Ill. 55 Henri Michaux. Michaux seems to have turned to making
drawings as a means of conveying meanings which it was
impossible to catch in writing (he had been a prominent
literary figure since the 1930s). Many of these meanings were
connected with the altered states of consciousness induced by

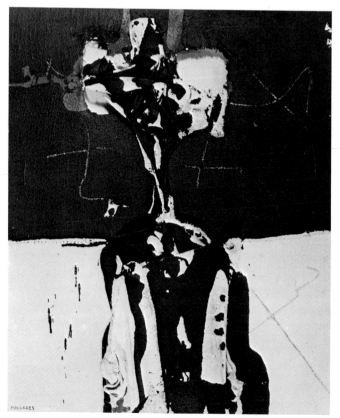

54 MANOLO MILLARES
No. 165 1961

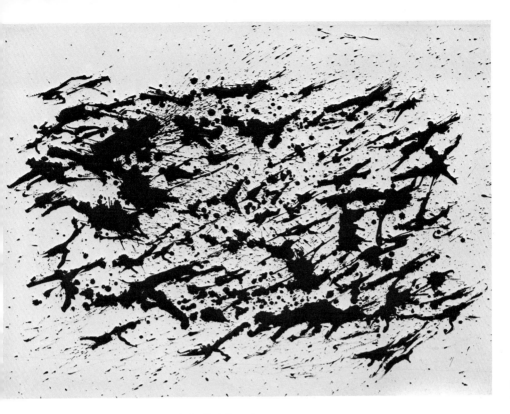

55 HENRI MICHAUX *Painting in india ink* 1960–7

hallucinogenic drugs. Michaux's drawings are so alike that, when they are seen in bulk, the effect becomes monotonous; but the best of them come surprisingly close to some of Pollock's work.

The new abstraction scored an enormous success not only in Paris, but in the rest of Europe. Painters such as Antonio Tapiés in Spain, and Alberto Burri in Italy are recognizably part of the same impulse. Both are interesting because of the way in which they relate an international tendency to a national situation. Tapiés, who is self-taught, began to paint in 1946, and had his first one-man show in Barcelona in 1951. His work shows a fascination with surfaces, textures, and substances which links him closely to the French 'matter painters', such as Fautrier,

Ill. 53

79

who directly influenced him. Tapiés brings the spectator face to face with one of the paradoxes of the radical art of the post-war epoch. He is in politics a liberal, and it is not without significance that he comes from Barcelona, traditionally the centre of left-wing sentiment in Spain. Yet his work was by its nature and concepts too ambiguous to give much uneasiness to the Franco government. With its 'hand-made' textures, it tended to align itself with the products of the Spanish luxury crafts, such as fine leatherwork. This may give us the reason why Tapiés, and other Spanish artists whose work in a general *Ill. 54* way resembles his, such as Manolo Millares, enjoyed a certain degree of favour in the eyes of the authorities in Franco's day. What they created became a form of prestige export, better known abroad than in its country of origin.

Burri is a rather similar case. He was a doctor during the war, and first began to paint in 1944, in a prison camp in Texas. When he was set free, he gave up his practice in order to continue painting. His first exhibition was held in 1947. Burri *Ill. 56* is best known for works made of sacking and old rags: his reason for using these materials was that they reminded him of the blood-soaked bandages he had seen in wartime. He has also made use of charred wood, of plastic foil burned and melted with a blow-lamp, and of battered plates of tin. The programme put forward to justify these works is the existentialist one of metaphysical anguish, but what strikes one instead is their good taste, their easy sensuousness.

Indeed, it is possible to feel that nearly all the European free abstractionists of the late 1940s and early 1950s suffer from a thinness of emotion and a restriction of technical means. At the same time, one must sympathize with their predicament. As can be seen from the work of Wols and Fautrier, they were explor-ing a kind of painting which had also attracted the leading Americans. The European experiments were, however, less radical and less sure of their direction than those being made in New York. The long-standing European (and especially French) tradition of *belle peinture* – of the painting as a beautiful

80

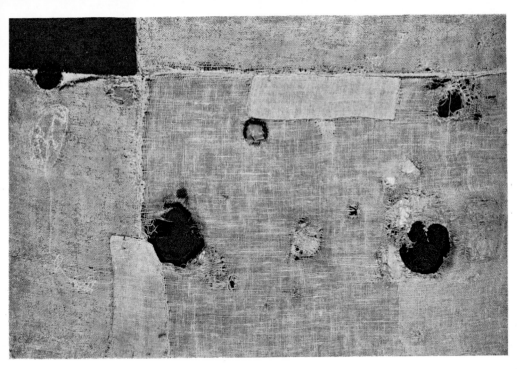

56 ALBERTO BURRI *Sacco 4* 1954

and luxurious object, a bed of delight for the senses – stood in
the way of radicalism. The American worship of 'rawness' is
to be found, although in another form, in Picasso's *Demoiselles
d'Avignon*, but it is not visible in the art which was being
produced in France some forty years later. When the new
Americans began to be exhibited in Europe, as when Peggy
Guggenheim's collection made a tour of European cities in
1948, the effect was overwhelming. One reason that the
Americans triumphed so easily was to be found in the fact that
their European colleagues were already partly converted –
enough so to understand what they were being offered – but
had not yet achieved so spectacularly radical a stance. Yet
European artists found it difficult to use abstract expressionism
as a starting-point, because the American statement had a
completeness of its own.

81

Ill. 57

The dilemma is clearly shown in the work of Pierre Soulages, and in that of Georges Mathieu. Soulages can, on occasion, look like a sweeter and less committed version of Franz Kline, but his broad strokes of the brush do not have the energy or the constructional quality which one finds in the American artist.

Ill. 58

Mathieu is a more interesting figure than Soulages. His work has affinities with that of Pollock, though he started painting in a freely calligraphic way so early (1937) that there can be no question of direct derivation. Rather, his has been an independent development along similar lines: which does not amount to a claim that Mathieu is an artist of the same stature as Pollock. For instance, his pictures, even the very large ones, are always far less complex than those painted by the American. Image and background have separate identities, which is not the case with Pollock; and there is in Mathieu's work little real feeling for space, even for the shallow, flattened version of it that Pollock uses. Mathieu writes on the canvas in a series of bravura scribbles. These scribbles do not blend with the ground; they dominate it. Rhythmical as they are, they express little beyond a delight in their own ease and dash. Mathieu seems very much the virtuoso, satisfied with his own tricks.

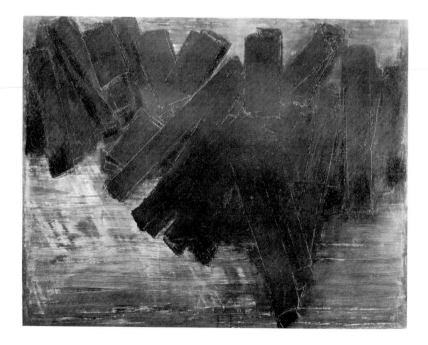

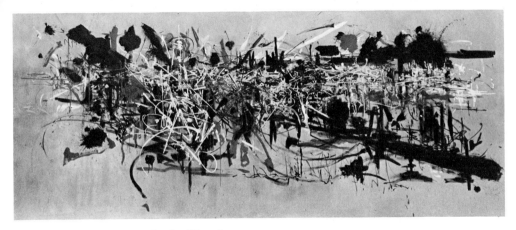

58 GEORGES MATHIEU *Battle of Bouvines* 1954

Nevertheless, he has an importance which is unconnected with the flashy triviality of so many of his pictures. He has been an efficient and intelligent publicist and organizer: it was he who arranged the exhibition in which the new French and American painters were shown together for the first time. More, he has been in all senses a forerunner, a man keenly attuned to the seminal ideas of the time. When, in 1956, Mathieu painted a twelve-foot canvas in the presence of a large audience at the Théâtre Sarah Bernhardt, he anticipated the 'Happenings' which American artists were to make fashionable a few years later, as well as recalling some of the antics of the dadaists and surrealists. Modern art has produced a crop of dazzling show-men, and Mathieu, like Salvador Dali, has been one of these.

Art informel, though the best publicized of the European developments after the war, was by no means the only new beginning. Even more significant, in many ways, was the short-lived Cobra Group of 1948–50. The name is taken from the names of the cities which the various participants hailed from: Copenhagen, Brussels, Amsterdam. Among its members were the Dane Asger Jorn, the Dutchman Karel Appel, and the Belgians Corneille and Pierre Alechinsky. Like the abstract expressionists, the artists of the Cobra Group were interested in giving direct expression to subconscious fantasy, with no

Ills 59, 61
Ills 62, 63

83

57 PIERRE SOULAGES *Painting* 1956
(Collection The Museum of Modern Art, New York)

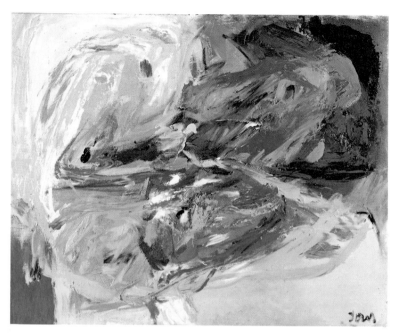

59 ASGER JORN *You never know* 1966

60 ALAN DAVIE *The Martyrdom of St Catherine* 1956

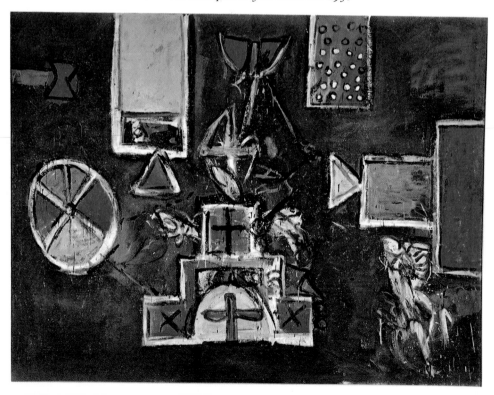

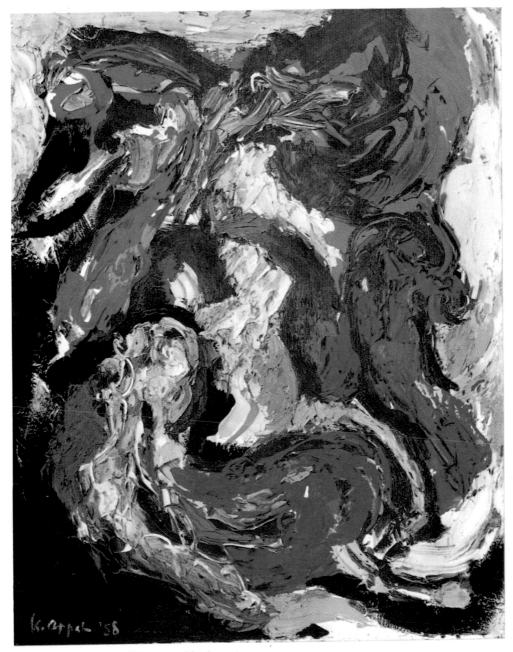

61 KAREL APPEL *Women and birds* 1958

censorship from the intellect. But they did not rule out figuration: in this they resembled Fautrier and Wols, rather than Hartung, Soulages, and Mathieu. Expressionism had struck deep roots both in Scandinavia (with Munch) and in Holland and Belgium. The Dutch-American de Kooning shows its impress just as clearly as Karel Appel, a Dutchman who has remained a 'European'. In one sense, therefore, the Cobra Group revives and continues an old tradition, rather than making a completely fresh start. This led to a greater complexity of reference than we usually find in the art of the immediately post-war period. Jorn, for example, veered from the cheerful to the sinister. His pictures incorporated a wide range of references; thanks to his interest in myths and magic, Jorn had access to a great range of signs and symbols. He was also a notably bold colourist. Yet he and his colleagues had less impact than one might have predicted, and the same is true of an English artist whose work in some respects resembles theirs,

Ill. 60   Alan Davie. Davie formed one of the few real bridges between

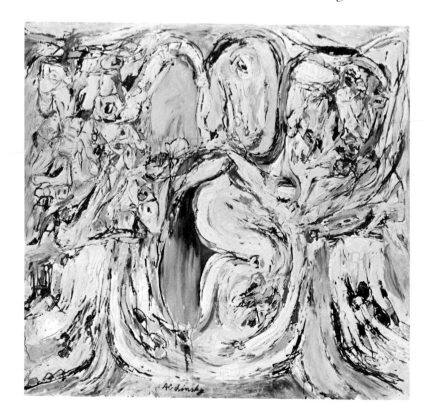

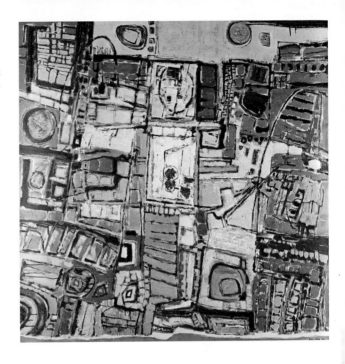

English and Continental art at this period, and was exhibited in European exhibitions where English painters were seldom seen.

More loosely linked to the Cobra group than Davie, yet working in a parallel style, is the Austrian Hundertwasser. In his work, expressionism becomes formal and decorative, under the influence of Art Nouveau.

Ill. 64

Yet there is one European artist of crucial importance who is related to the Cobra Group painters, as well as to Wols and to Fautrier. Jean Dubuffet is one of the few really major artists to have appeared in France since the war, though 'since the war' is perhaps the wrong phrase, for Dubuffet was at work as a painter long before 1945. But his first one-man show was held in 1945, a few months after the Liberation.

The picture illustrated contains the clues to many of Dubuffet's preoccupations. He is interested in child art, in the art of madmen, in graffiti on walls and pavements, and in the accidental markings and maculations to be found on these surfaces. Dubuffet is the most persistent explorer of the possibilities

Ill. 65

87

62 PIERRE ALECHINSKY *The Green Being Born* 1960

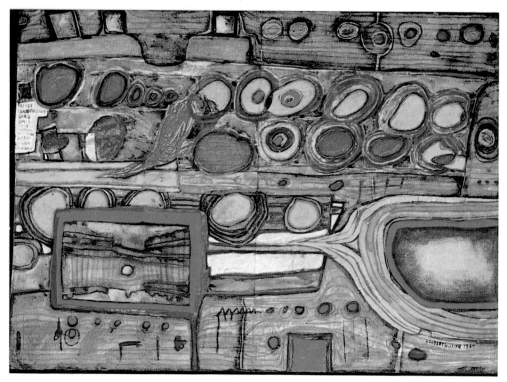

64 HUNDERTWASSER *The Hokkaido Steamer* 1961

offered by materials and surfaces to have appeared during the
post-war period. He says:

> In all my works . . . I have always had recourse to one never-
> varying method. It consists in making the delineation of the
> objects represented heavily dependent on a system of
> necessities which itself looks strange. These necessities are
> sometimes due to the inappropriate and awkward character
> of the material used, sometimes to the inappropriate manipu-
> lation of the tools, sometimes to some strange obsessive
> notion (frequently changed for another). In a word, it is
> always a matter of giving the person who is looking at the
> picture a startling impression that a weird logic has directed
> the painting of it, a logic to which the delineation of every

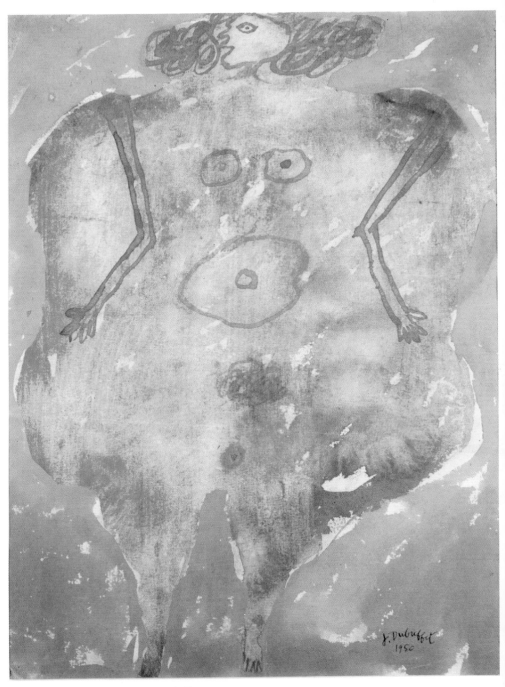

65 JEAN DUBUFFET *Corps de Dame* 1950

object is subjected, is even sacrificed, in such a peremptory way that, curiously enough, it forces the most unexpected solutions, and, in spite of the obstacles it creates, brings out the desired figuration.[2]

The artist here proclaims himself the ally of certain important creators in the other arts. There seems to be a real affinity, for example, between Dubuffet's methods and those adopted by the dramatist Eugène Ionesco. Dubuffet and Ionesco alike are heavily permeated with the idea of 'the absurd', perhaps more thoroughly so than Sartre, with whom it originated. Dubuffet appears in his statements about art as a man of culture who is sophisticatedly obsessed with the anti-cultural. His work shows how hard it is for the modern artist to break out of the prison of 'taste'. His remarks about the *Corps de Dame* series, which I have already mentioned in connection with de Kooning, show just how such considerations creep into his work, more or less by the back door:

> It pleased me (and I think this predilection is more or less constant in all my paintings) to juxtapose brutally, in these feminine bodies, the extremely general and the extremely particular, the metaphysical and the grotesquely trivial. In my view, the one is considerably reinforced by the presence of the other.[3]

Dubuffet has spent his life, not so much in breaking new ground, as in trying to see what could be done with the existing heritage of the Ecole de Paris, by misusing it as well as using it. He has made sculpture out of clinker, foil, and papiermâché, and pictures from leaves and butterfly-wings. The result is an *œuvre* in which the individual works are nearly always fascinating, either in their grossness or their intricacy, or some intermingling of these two qualities. Dubuffet's creative limits are to be found in his selfconsciousness, and the degree to which his work is an exegesis rather than a truly original contribution to modernism. It comments both wittily and pertinently, but we are aware that, to savour these comments fully, we must

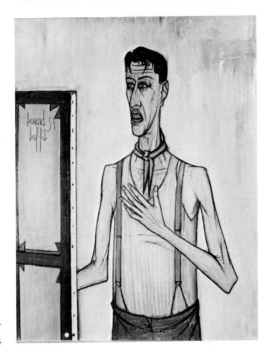

66 BERNARD BUFFET
Self-portrait 1954

have at least some knowledge of modern art, its theories and its controversies.

Nevertheless, Dubuffet seems to me to sum up many of the leading tendencies to be found in the visual arts in the period immediately following the war. The priority given to the inner world of the artist, and the rejection of the traditional claims of art to be more coherent, more organized, and more homogeneous than 'non-art', or 'reality', were pointers to the future.

The difficulties of a more traditional approach can be judged from the work of two other painters who made their reputations at about the same period. One of them need not detain us long, however. Dubuffet's near-namesake Bernard Buffet *Ill. 66* had a spectacular success in the 1940s and 1950s with schematic figurative paintings which were literal interpretations of the gloomier and more superficial aspects of Sartre's existentialist philosophy. Buffet's interest really lies in the fact that quite a large section of the public received him so eagerly as an acceptable representative of modern art.

Another, equally popular and far more gifted painter was
Ill. 67 the tragic Nicolas de Staël. In terms of natural endowments
for painting, de Staël is the only French painter of the
immediately post-war generation with serious claims to rival
Dubuffet. The two artists pursued opposite courses. Instead of
accepting absurdity and fragmentation, and exploiting them,
as Dubuffet did and does, de Staël looked for a synthesis, and in
particular for a synthesis between the claims of modernism and
those of the past. He began as an abstract painter, with certain
affinities to Riopelle. Abstraction dissatisfied him, and gradually
he came closer and closer to figuration, first through a series of
Football players, and then in the late landscapes and still-lifes for
which he is best known. These extremely simplified paintings
can be seen both in abstract terms and as representations. A
skilful, delicate balancing-act is going on in them; the various
planes must be made to advance and recede in such a way that
the 'abstract' paint surface is never broken; so that we never
feel that the representation is being forced on us, but rather, that
it has come about naturally as the result of the play of form
against form and colour-area against colour-area. In his best
pictures, de Staël achieves his aim: the paint surface is placidly,
creamily delicious; the colours have a sonority that reminds
us of the painter's Russian ancestry.

But is this an art which lives up to the great claims that have
been made for it since the painter's suicide in 1955? De Staël
has been compared to Poussin (that high compliment of the
academic art critic), has been called the greatest of post-war
painters, and so forth. True, with his piquant combination of
the traditional and the original, he appeals to many spectators:
to find a Poussin-like scheme of forms under an apparently
abstract and arbitrary surface is strangely reassuring. The
question is if the power to reassure is enough to make a genius.
De Staël's compromise between figuration and abstraction
pales beside the obsessive force of Bacon or Balthus. The abrasive
style of Bacon makes an especially interesting contrast, because
Bacon, too, owes something to the arbitrary procedures of

67 NICOLAS DE STAËL *Agrigente* 1954

abstraction but tries to yoke them to a figurative vision. While it would be foolish to deny the calm beauty of de Staël's best work, it seems obsessed with a perfectionism which in the end becomes sterile. As a painter, he succeeds rather as Whistler did before him, not through the invention of new forms, but through tact and taste in the manipulation of pre-existing ones.

The path of tact and taste was certainly not the one which the post-war arts were to pursue. Abstract expressionism and *art informel* were to be followed by a rapid succession of other styles, none of them owing much to traditional ideas about *belle peinture*.

CHAPTER FOUR

Post-painterly abstraction

As it turned out, however, there was one style which held its own in the wake of abstract expressionism, and which, while owing something to the abstract expressionist example, had deep roots in the European art of the 1920s and 1930s. 'Hard edge' abstraction never completely died out, even in the palmiest days of Pollock and Kline. By 'hard edge' I mean the kind of abstract painting where the forms have definite, clean boundaries, instead of the fuzzy ones favoured, for example, by Mark Rothko. Characteristically, in this kind of painting, the hues themselves are flat and undifferentiated, so it is perhaps better to talk of colour-areas and not forms.

Ill. 70   One of the progenitors of this kind of painting in America was Josef Albers, who has already been referred to because of his importance as a teacher. Albers had been closely connected with the Bauhaus during the 1920s: in fact, as student and teacher, he worked there continuously from 1920 to 1933, when it was closed, a longer period of service than any other *Bauhäusler*. During the 1930s, when he was already living in America, Albers took part in the annual shows mounted by the Abstraction-Création group in Paris. He was thus thoroughly cosmopolitan. Albers's cast of mind is very typical of the Bauhaus atmosphere: systematic and orderly, but also experimental. He was, for instance, very much interested in Gestalt psychology, and this led him towards an exploration of the effects of optical illusion. Later he was drawn towards a study of the ways in which colours act upon one another. The pictures and prints of the *Homage to the Square* series, Albers's best-known works, are planned experiments with colour.

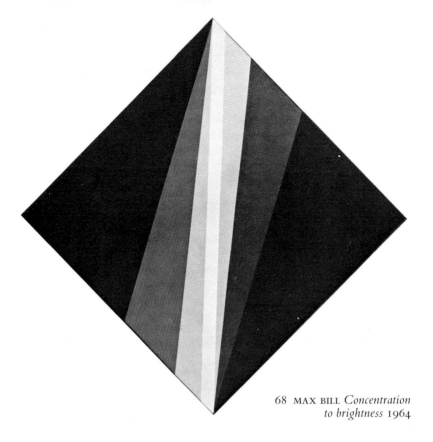

68 MAX BILL *Concentration to brightness* 1964

Albers is interesting not only in himself, but because he seems to stand at the point where several attitudes towards painting converge. The systematic element in his work relates it to that of two Swiss artists, Max Bill and Richard Lohse: Bill is also a Bauhaus alumnus, and, in his subsequent career, has become a sort of universal genius, at once artist, architect, and sculptor. The serial development of colour has been one of his interests throughout his career. Bill and Lohse are usually spoken of as exponents of 'concrete art', and Albers is lumped in as a third member of the triumvirate. On the other hand, Albers's interest in optical illusion relates him to the so-called op artists, while his particular treatment of form brings him into relationship with what critics have now labelled 'post-painterly abstraction'.

Ills 68, 69

95

If one looks for a difference between Albers and his two Swiss colleagues, it seems to lie in the treatment of form. Albers's squares are free, passive, unanchored, floating, and it is this passivity which has come to seem particularly typical of a great deal of post-abstract expressionist painting in America. The difference between 'hard edge' and 'post-painterly abstraction' is precisely that it is not the hardness of the edge that counts, one colour abutting firmly upon another, but the quality of colour. It does not matter whether the colour melts into a neighbouring hue, or is sharply differentiated from it: the meeting is always passive. Albers's squares are crisp enough, but generate no energy from this crispness of outline.

Another painter whose work has something of this quality, without qualifying as post-painterly abstraction in the strictest

69 RICHARD LOHSE *Fifteen systematic colour scales merging vertically* 1950–67

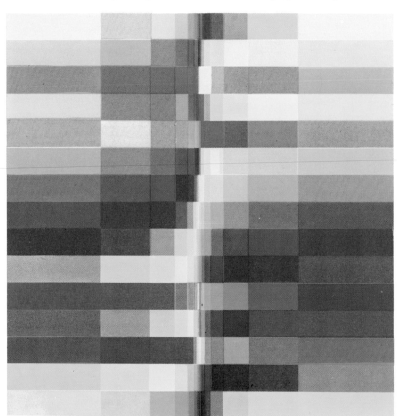

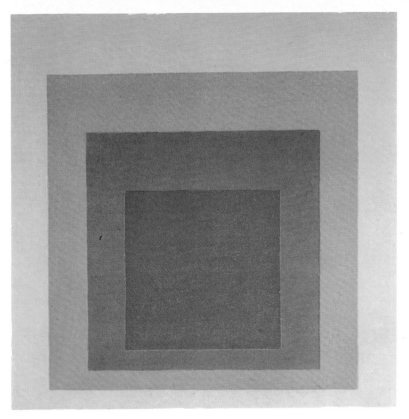

70 JOSEF ALBERS *Homage to the Square 'Curious'* 1963

sense, is Ad Reinhardt, who made a reputation as *the* profes- *Ill. 75*
sional nonconformist of the New York art world during the
1950s, and succeeded in retaining it until his death in 1967.
Influenced by the abstract decorative art of Persia and the
Middle East, Reinhardt went through a phase in the 1940s when
his work came close to the calligraphy of Tobey. But these
'written' marks drew together, and became rectangles which
covered the whole picture surface. From an orchestration of
intense colours, Reinhardt moved towards black. The characteristic paintings of his last phase contain colours so dark, and so
close in value to one another, that the picture appears to be

97

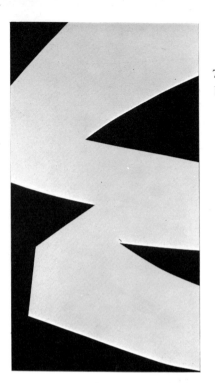

71 ELLSWORTH KELLY
White – Dark Blue 1962

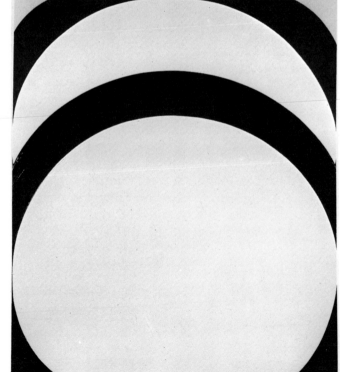

72 AL HELD *Echo* 1966

98

black, or almost black, until it is closely studied, at which point the component rectangles slowly emerge from the surface.

It is interesting to contrast Albers and Reinhardt with 'hard edge' painters who have a more conventional, but still very American, attitude towards composition. Among these are Al Held, Jack Youngerman, and Ellsworth Kelly. Of these, *Ills 71–3* Kelly is probably the best known. His painting consists of flat fields of colour, rigidly divided from one another. Sometimes one colour will contain another completely, so that the picture consists of an image placed upon a ground. These are usually Kelly's weakest works, especially when the image itself is derived from some natural form, such as a leaf. At other times it seems as if the canvas, already very large, has not been big enough to accommodate the form, which is arbitrarily sliced by the edge, and continues itself in the mind's eye of the

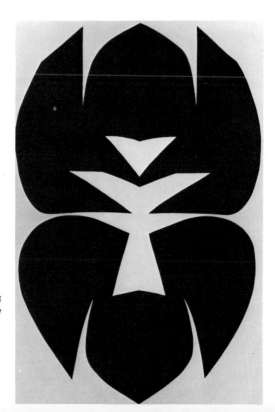

73 JACK YOUNGERMAN
Totem black 1967

·74 BARNETT NEWMAN *Tundra* 1950

spectator. As a device to impart energy and interest to the painting, this is quite successful, but there is something rather gimmicky and tricky about it. There is also the fact that 'energy' and 'interest' are traditional pictorial concepts which, in the sense in which I have just used them, Albers, Reinhardt, and the post-painterly abstractionists seem alike determined to reject.

What links Albers and Reinhardt with the so-called post-painterly abstractionists is, in part, the fascination not with pictorial means, but with aesthetic doctrine. The doctrinaire nature of post-painterly abstraction is striking. Rather as the logical positivists have concentrated on the purely linguistic aspects of philosophy, so the painters who adhere to the move-

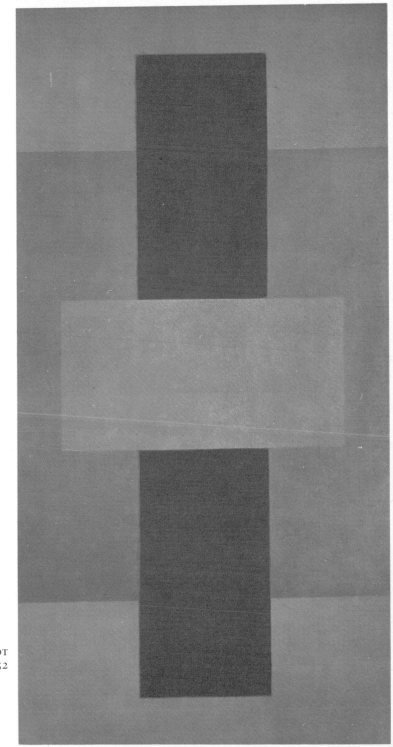

75 AD REINHARDT
Red painting 1952

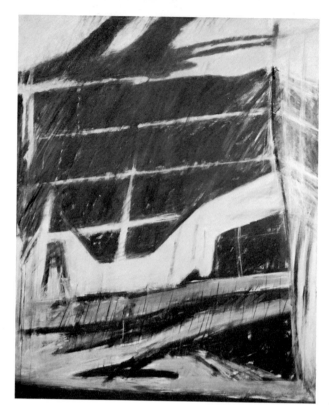

76 JACK
TWORKOV
*North
American* 1966

ment have been concerned to rid themselves of all but a narrow range of strictly pictorial considerations. The American critic Barbara Rose notes that

> in the process of self-definition, an art form will tend toward the elimination of all the elements which are not in keeping with its essential nature. According to this argument, visual art will be stripped of all extravisual meaning, whether literary or symbolic, and painting will reject all that is not pictorial.[1]

Rising out of what Jacques Barzun on one occasion described as the 'abolitionist' nature of abstract expressionism (referring to its apparent desire to do away with the art of the past), the new style rejected stratagems even more completely than Albers and Reinhardt.

The two painters who can be thought of as its real originators are Morris Louis and the veteran abstract expressionist Barnett Newman, though other abstract expressionists, such as Jack Tworkov, also show some characteristics of post-painterly abstraction in their later work; an example is the use of thinned paint, which gives a 'flat' look to the canvas. *Ills 74, 78, 80*

Ill. 76

By 1950 – that is, while abstract expressionism was at the height of its success – Newman's aims were already clear. He wanted to articulate the surface of the painting as a 'field', rather than as a composition – an ambition which went considerably beyond Pollock. Newman's way of achieving the effect he wanted was to allow the rectangle of the canvas to determine the pictorial structure. The canvas is divided, either horizontally or vertically, by a band, or bands. This line of division is used to activate the field, which is of intense colour, with some small variations of hue from one area to another. The American critic Max Kozloff declares that, in Newman's work, 'the colour is not used to overwhelm the senses, so much as in its curious muteness and dumbness, to shock the mind'. He adds: 'Newman habitually gives the impression of being out of control without being in the least bit passionate.'[2] Whether one agrees with this verdict or not, muteness and lack of passion – 'coolness' in the slang sense of the term – were certainly to be characteristic of the new phase of American art.

With Newman, however, we still get the sense that the canvas is a surface to which pigment has been applied. Morris Louis differs from this, in being not so much a painter as a stainer. The colour is an integral part of the material the painter has used, and colour lives in the very weave of it.

More even than the leading abstract expressionists, Louis was an artist who arrived at his mature style by means of a sudden breakthrough. This suddenness is one of the things which has to be taken into account when discussing his work. Louis was not a New Yorker. He lived in Washington, and New York was a place he was notoriously reluctant to visit. In April 1953, Kenneth Noland, a friend and fellow painter, persuaded him to

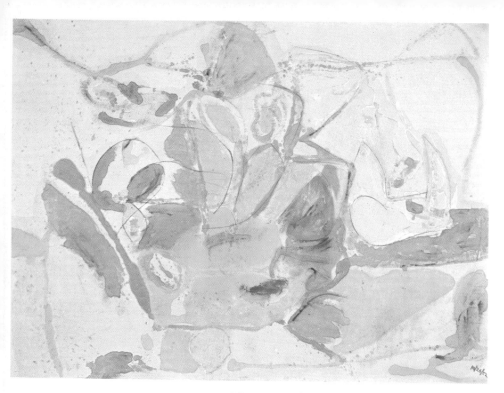

77 HELEN FRANKENTHALER *Mountains and sea* 1952

make the trip, both to meet the critic Clement Greenberg and to see something of what was currently being done by the New York artists. Louis was then aged forty-one, and had produced no work of more than minor significance up to that point.

Ill. 77   The trip was a success, and Louis was especially impressed by a painting by Helen Frankenthaler, *Mountains and sea*, which he saw in her studio. The effect on his work was to draw him towards both Pollock and Frankenthaler as influences. Some months of experiment followed, but by the winter of 1954 he had suddenly arrived at a new way of painting. One aspect of its novelty was its technique, which Greenberg later described in this way:

> Louis spills his paint on unsized and unprimed cotton duck canvas, leaving the pigment almost everywhere thin enough,

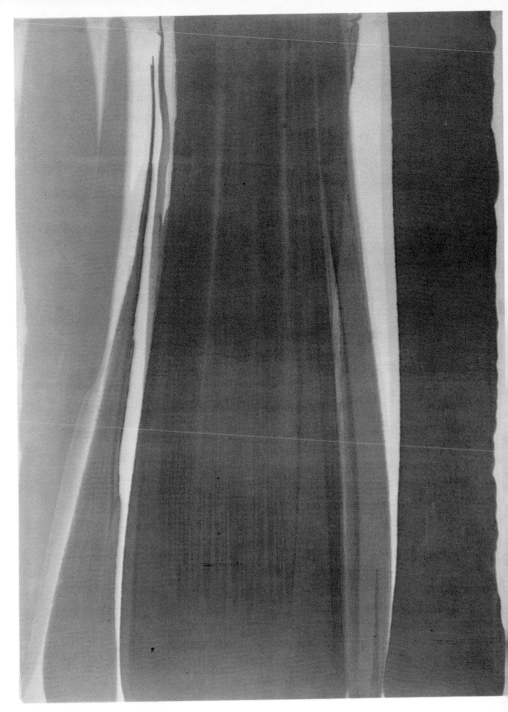

78 MORRIS LOUIS *Untitled* 1959

no matter how many different veils of it are superimposed, for the eye to sense the threadedness and wovenness of the fabric underneath. But 'underneath' is the wrong word. The fabric, being soaked in paint rather than merely covered by it, becomes paint in itself, colour in itself, like dyed cloth; the threadedness and wovenness are in the colour.[3]

In fact, Louis achieved his originality partly through the exploitation of a new material, acrylic paint, which gave his paintings a very different physical make-up from those of the abstract expressionists. The staining process meant a revulsion against shape, against light and dark, in favour of colour. As Greenberg remarked: 'His revulsion against cubism was a revulsion against the sculptural.' Even the shallow space which Pollock had inherited from the cubists was henceforth to be avoided.

One of the advantages of the staining technique, so far as Louis was concerned, was the fact that he was able to put colour into colour. His early paintings after the breakthrough are veils of shifting hue and tone: there is no feeling that the various colour configurations have been drawn with a brush. Indeed, Louis did not 'paint' even in Pollock's sense, but poured, flooded, and scrubbed the colour into the canvas. This departure from the process of drawing was in some ways rather a reluctant one. In later experiments, Louis was to try and recover some of the advantages of traditional drawing for the stain medium.
Ill. 80 This is particularly true of the series of canvases called *Unfurleds*, which were painted in the spring and summer of 1961. Irregularly parallel rivulets of colour now appear in wing-like diagonals at the edges of large areas of canvas which are otherwise left unpainted. Michael Fried remarks:

The banked rivulets . . . open up the picture-plane more radically than ever, as though seeing the first marking we are for the first time shown the void. The dazzling blankness of the untouched canvas at once repulses and engulfs the eye, like an infinite abyss, the abyss that opens up behind the least

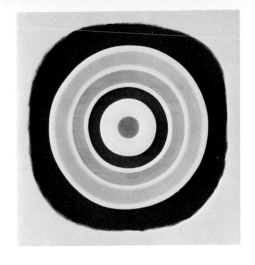

79 KENNETH NOLAND
Cantabile 1962

mark that we make on a flat surface, or *would* open up if innumerable conventions both of art and of practical life did not restrict the consequences of our act within narrow bounds.[4]

Louis's final period of activity (he died of lung cancer in 1962) resulted in a series of stripe paintings, in which stripes of colour, usually of slightly different thicknesses, are bunched together some distance from the sides of the canvases. Fried feels that these show, as compared to the *Unfurleds* which preceded them, a further strengthening of the impulse to draw. Yet, in their strict, undeviating parallelism, the lines of colour seem inert, and this is true even where, in three paintings of this series, the stripes run diagonally across the canvas. Inertia, strict parallelism, and the constructive impulse (as shown by the paintings with diagonal stripes) were all characteristics which Louis shared with the other post-painterly abstractionists.

Louis's friend and associate Kenneth Noland was slower in making his own breakthrough, and therefore belongs to a later stage of the development of this new kind of abstract painting. Noland, like Louis, adopted the new technique of staining, rather than painting, the canvas. And like Louis, he tends to paint in series, using a single motif until he feels that he has exhausted its possibilities. The first important motif in Noland's work is a target shape of concentric rings. The pictures composed on this principle belong to the late 1950s and early 1960s. The target pattern was used, not as Jasper Johns used it contemporaneously, with the deliberate intention of alluding to its banality, but as a means of concentrating the effect of the colour. Often the targets seem to spin against the background of unsized canvas, an effect produced by the irregular staining at their edges. Fried notes:

Ill. 79

> The raw canvas in Noland's concentric-ring paintings . . . fulfils much the same function as the coloured fields in Newman's large pictures around 1950; more generally, Noland in these paintings seems to have managed to charge the entire surface of the canvas with a kind of perceptual intensity which until that time only painters whose images occupy most or all of the picture-field – Pollock, Still, Newman, Louis – had been able to achieve.[5]

80 MORRIS LOUIS *Omicron* 1961

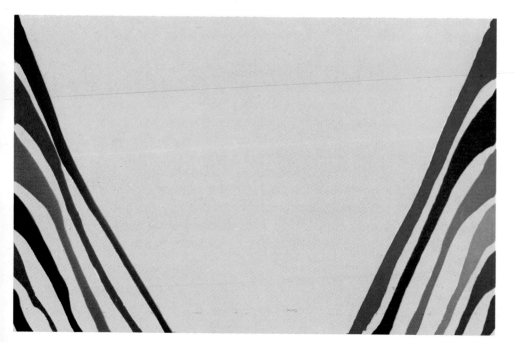

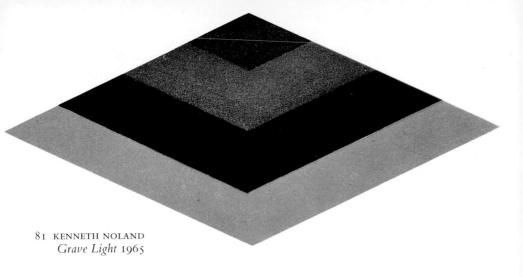

81 KENNETH NOLAND
    Grave Light 1965

After experimenting with an ellipsoid shape which was no longer, in every case, in the exact centre of a square canvas, Noland began, in 1962, a series which used a chevron motif. *Ill. 81* This was the signal for a growing concern with the identity of the canvas simply as an object. The framing-edge began to have an importance which, on the whole, had not been accorded to it since Pollock. At first, Noland allowed the raw canvas to continue to play its part. But the chevrons suggested the possibility of a lozenge-shaped support – a kind of picture which would be wholly colour, without any neutral areas, with the coloured bands moored to the bands of the frame. These canvases, like the late, diagonally striped paintings by Louis, have an obvious relationship to pictures by Mondrian, where the canvas is designed to be hung diagonally. The abstract expressionist and the constructivist traditions here begin to draw together.

After a while, Noland's lozenges grew narrower and longer, and eventually the chevron pattern was abandoned for stripes running horizontally on enormous canvases, some of them more than thirty feet long. Colour is thus reduced to its simplest relationship, as in the late paintings by Louis, and all pretence at composition is abandoned. These late pictures show the

109

extreme refinement of Noland's colour sensibility. As compared to his early work, the colour is paler and lighter. The tones are close together, which produces effects of optical shimmer, intensified by the sheer vastness of the field, which enfolds and swallows the eye. There is nothing painterly about the way in which the colour is applied; it does not even have the unevenness of Louis's stainings, and the colour-bands meet more crisply and decisively than Louis's stripes. Or, rather, they almost meet: on close examination they prove to be separated by infinitesimally narrow bands of raw canvas, an effect which Noland may have derived from the early paintings of Frank Stella.

Ills 82, 83 Stella, though his work is often grouped with Louis's and with Noland's, is more of a structuralist than a post-painterly abstractionist. His concern is not so much with colour-as-colour, as with the painting-as-object, a thing which exists in its own right, and which is entirely self-referring. His work, however, does have a direct link to that of Barnett Newman.

The paintings which established Stella's reputation were those which were shown in the Museum of Modern Art exhibition 'Sixteen Americans' in 1960. They were all black canvases, patterned with parallel stripes about $2\frac{1}{2}$ inches wide, a width chosen to echo the width of the wooden strips used for the picture support. Stella went on to execute further series of stripe paintings, in aluminium, copper and magenta paint. With the aluminium and copper paintings, Stella began to make use of shaped supports. These made the paintings not only objects to hang on the wall, but things which activated the whole wall-surface. There was then a period of experiment with paintings where the stripes were of different colours, followed by one where the shaped canvases fitted together in series to make serial compositions. Then came asymmetrical canvases painted in vivid colours which segmented the shapes, some of which were now curved. These works in turn developed into painted metal reliefs, with freely curved shapes attached to a background. Both these attached strips and the background

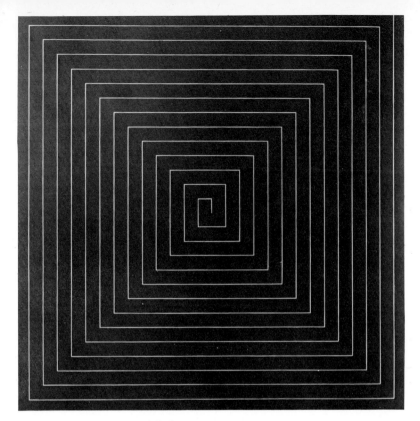

82 FRANK STELLA *New Madrid* 1961

itself were painted with a fluency which seemed to contradict the rigidity of Stella's earlier work, but the emphasis on structure as the subject of the painting was nevertheless still present.

If Stella seemed inclined to flirt both with the earliest modernism and with pop art, another colour painter, Jules Olitski, experimented with what was essentially a critique of abstract expressionism. Olitski covered huge areas of canvas with tender stainings; these stained areas are often contrasted *Ill. 85* with a passage at the edge of the canvas in thick, luscious brushwork, reminiscent not so much of Pollock as of a European such as de Staël. The paintings themselves are usually vast. The paradox in Olitski's work is the hugeness of scale

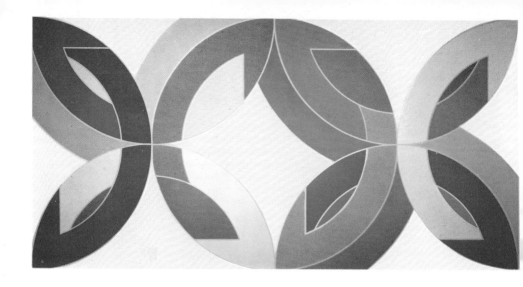

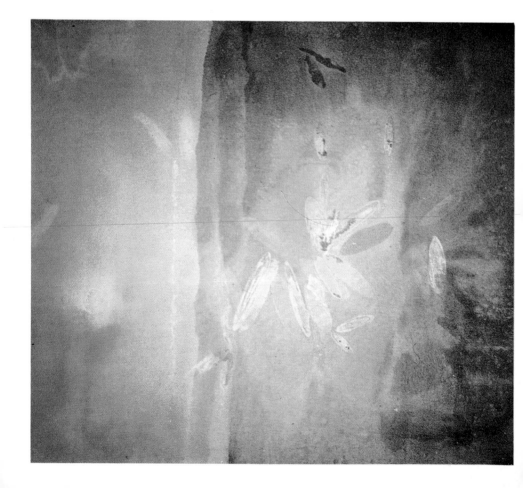

83 FRANK STELLA
Untitled 1968

84 LARRY POONS
Night Journey 1968

85 JULES OLITSKI
Feast 1965

compared with the limitation of content – the pictures hint at an aesthetic position in order to deny it. The sweetness and prettiness are ironic, and yet at the same time truly meant and felt. More even than Noland's and Stella's work, these paintings address themselves to an informed audience.

Ill. 84   The same might be said about the work of Larry Poons. Though Poons has sometimes been called an op artist, his typical work makes it plain where his true allegiance lies. Essentially, his paintings consist of a coloured field, scattered at random with spots of contrasting colour. The eye is offered a multitude of points of focus, and skims about among them, without coming to rest. In Poons's earlier work, the optical effect is enhanced by the choice of tone and hue. The tones are close together, the hues in sharp contrast, which generates an after-image in the eye. Later Poons enlarged the marks to eliminate this effect.

Similar comments could be made about the work of another American who was also a second-generation member of the post-painterly abstractionist group. Edward Avedisian's work has close links with that of Poons, and functions similarly.

It is interesting to note that, while both abstract expressionism and pop art scored very considerable triumphs in Europe, post-

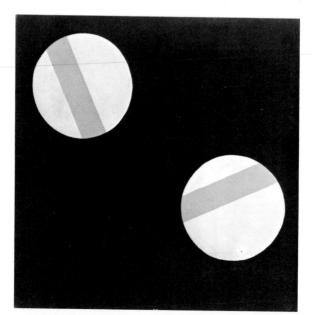

86 EDWARD AVEDISIAN
At Seven Brothers 1964

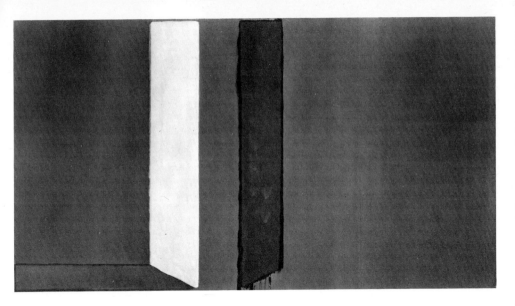

87 JOHN HOYLAND *28.5.66* 1966

painterly abstraction was not nearly so successful in making an impact on the European art scene. When Parisians spoke, sometimes rather bitterly, of the American rejection of 'our' painters, they were talking of the apparent dominance of post-painterly abstraction in New York. The one country outside the United States where its ideas have gained a considerable foothold is Britain, and this is something which symbolizes the transfer of influence over British art.

For example, John Hoyland, one of the few British artists *Ill. 87* with an American command of scale, is essentially in the tradition of Louis and Noland. His use of the acrylic paint medium is enough to affirm it. But Hoyland sometimes gets a hostile reaction from American reviewers for not being sufficiently *pur sang*, sufficiently reductionist. He seems to owe something important to Matisse and to Miró, and his paintings have clearly not abandoned all traditional ideas on the subject of composition. One can even detect references to de Staël, whom Hoyland at one time admired very much.

Ill. 90 Robyn Denny's paintings find their starting point in the work of Josef Albers, and especially in the painting Albers produced in the 1940s. The design tends to be bilaterally symmetrical, while the colours chosen are sharply contrasted in hue but carefully matched in tone. On a large scale, this produces a semi-optical effect, since the oblong colour-patches seem to move backwards and forwards in relationship to the main picture surface.

One of the things which seem to divide these British painters from their American colleagues is the fact that the British remain fascinated by pictorial ambiguity, and continue to juggle with effects of depth and perspective which are quite foreign to American art of the same kind. Work by painters *Ills 89, 91* such as John Walker, Paul Huxley, Jeremy Moon, and Tess *Ill. 88* Jaray all bears out this contention. Miss Jaray's work makes the

88 TESS JARAY *Garden of Allah* 1966

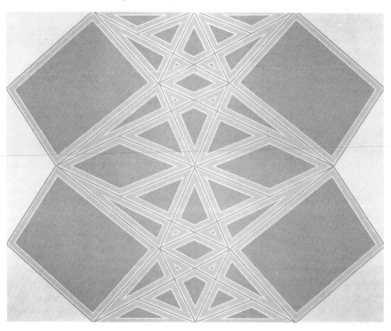

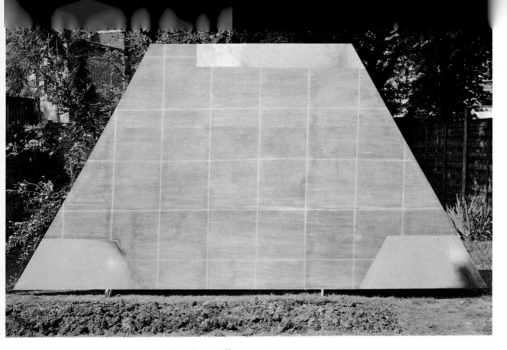

89 JOHN WALKER *Touch – Yellow* 1967
90 ROBYN DENNY *Growing* 1967

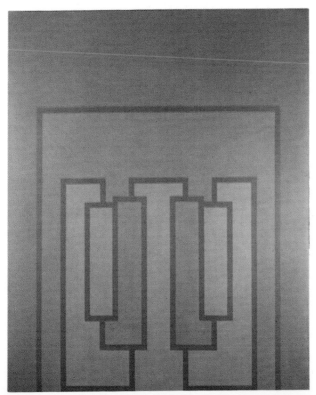

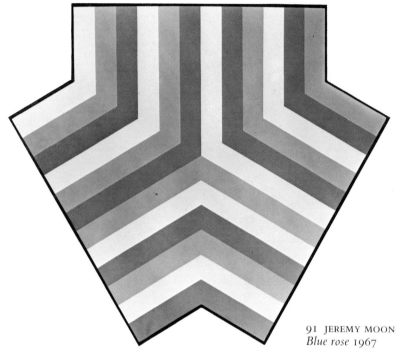

91 JEREMY MOON
Blue rose 1967

point particularly clearly, as one of its sources is perspective drawings of architecture.

For at least a decade, post-painterly abstraction represented a kind of modernist orthodoxy – it occupied the kind of position, in terms of intellectual prestige, that history painting enjoyed in the eighteenth century. Strong evidence of its success can still be seen in the work of certain minimalist painters of the 1970s, such as Brice Marden in the United States, and Bob Law and Alan Charlton in Britain. Because post-painterly abstraction seemed to bring the possibilities offered by pure painting to a kind of conclusion, artists who wished to find their way forward were for a while inclined to abandon the idea of the painted canvas as a vehicle for what they wanted to do or say. This resulted in a great swing of attention towards sculpture, and also led to an increasing number of experiments with mixed media.

CHAPTER FIVE

Pop, Environments and Happenings

Post-painterly abstraction, as I have described it, was a continuation of abstract expressionism, at least in part. Pop art was a reaction against it, and to begin with it was pop which caused a greater degree of uproar. As I have explained in my first chapter, pop basically sprang from a shift of sources. Surrealism with its appeal to the subconscious, was replaced by dada, with its concern with the frontiers of art. But this was not a purely intellectual choice. There were forces within abstract expressionism and *art informel* which propelled artists towards the new mode. For example, as abstract expressionism began to exhaust its impetus, the prevailing interest in texture led artists to ever-bolder experiments with materials. Some of these – with acrylic paint – were conducted by Morris Louis, and led to post-painterly abstraction. But most consisted of a re-exploration of the possibilities of collage. Using collage involved an important philosophic step for an artist already familiar with informal abstraction. There, an interesting texture was something which the artist *created*, but collage additions came to his hand *ready-made*; and Marcel Duchamp's idea of the 'ready-made' was one of the central innovations of dada. Collage had been invented by the cubists as a means of exploring the differences between representation and reality. The dadaists and surrealists had greatly extended its range, and the dadaists, in particular, had found it especially congenial, and in line with their preference for anti-art. In the hands of the post-war generation, collage now developed into the 'art of assemblage', a means of creating works of art almost entirely from pre-existent elements, where the artist's contribution was to be found more in making the links between objects, putting them together, than in making objects *ab initio*.

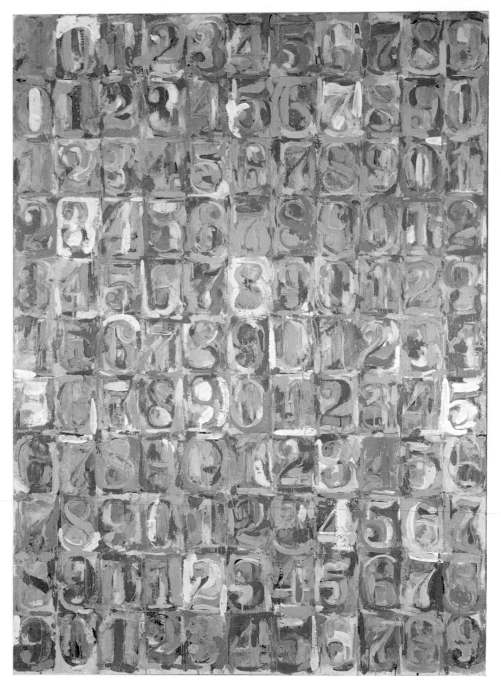

92 JASPER JOHNS *Numbers in colour* 1959

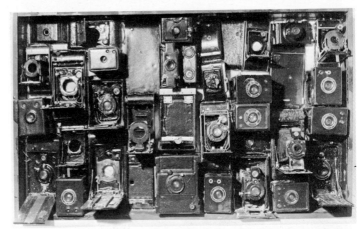

93 ARMAN
Clic-Clac Rate
1960–6

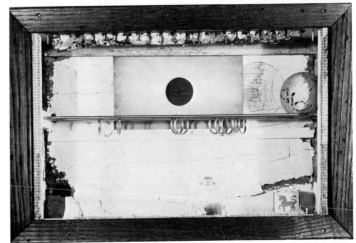

94 JOSEPH
CORNELL *Eclipse*
series c. 1962

In 1961, the Museum of Modern Art in New York staged an important exhibition under the title 'The Art of Assemblage'. William C. Seitz remarked in his introduction to the catalogue:

> The current wave of assemblage . . . marks a change from a subjective, fluidly abstract art towards a revised association with environment. The method of juxtaposition is an appropriate vehicle for feelings of disenchantment with the slick international idiom that loosely articulated abstraction has tended to become, and the social values that this situation reflects.[1]

121

Assemblage was important for another reason too. It was not only that it provided a means of transition from abstract expressionism to the apparently very different preoccupations of pop art, but it brought about a radical reconsideration of the formats within which the visual arts could operate. For example, assemblage provided a jumping-off point for two concepts which were to be increasingly important to artists: the environment and the happening.

Of course, some practitioners of assemblage did not move very far beyond their original sources. The exquisite boxes made by Joseph Cornell, with their poetic juxtapositions of objects, and the witty collages of Enrico Baj, are things which explore the resources of a tradition, without seeking to enlarge them very radically. Other artists were not content with this. Most of them fall into the category which has now been rather slickly labelled 'neo-dada'. One would prefer to say, rather, that they are often artists who want to explore the idea of the minimal, the unstable, the ephemeral in what they do.

In America, the two most-discussed exponents of neo-dada have undoubtedly been Robert Rauschenberg and Jasper Johns. Of the two, Rauschenberg is the more various, and Johns the more elegant; elegance has a genuine, if rather uneasy, part to play in any discussion of what these two represent.

Rauschenberg was born in Texas in 1925. In the late 1940s he studied at the Académie Julien in Paris, and then under Albers at Black Mountain College. In the early 1950s, Rauschenberg painted a series of all-white paintings where the only image was the spectator's own shadow. Later there was a series of all-black paintings. Neither of these developments was unique. The Italian painter Lucio Fontana did a series of all-white canvases in 1946; the Frenchman Yves Klein exhibited his first monochromes in 1950. After these experiments with minimality, Rauschenberg began to move towards 'combine painting', a mode of creation in which a painted surface is combined with various objects which are affixed to that surface. Sometimes the paintings develop into free-standing three-dimensional objects,

Ill. 94
Ill. 95

Ill. 96

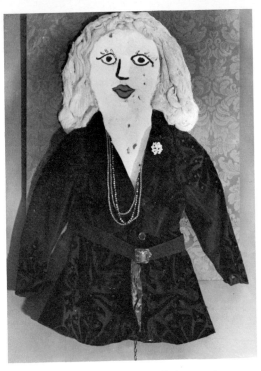

95 ENRICO BAJ *Lady Fabricia Trolopp* 1964

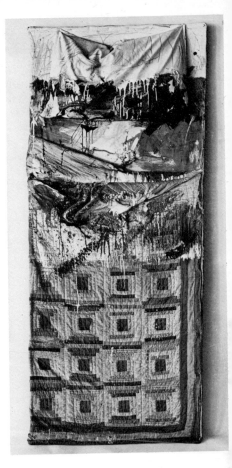

96 ROBERT RAUSCHENBERG *Bed* 1955

such as the famous stuffed goat which has appeared in so many exhibitions of contemporary American art. One painting makes use of a functioning wireless set, another of a clock. The artist has also used photographic images, which are silk-screened on to the canvas.

The aesthetic philosophy informing this is essentially that of the experimental composer John Cage, whom Rauschenberg met in North Carolina. One of Cage's basic ideas is that of 'unfocusing' the spectator's mind: the artist does not create something separate and closed, but instead does something to make the spectator more open, more aware of himself and his environment. Cage says:

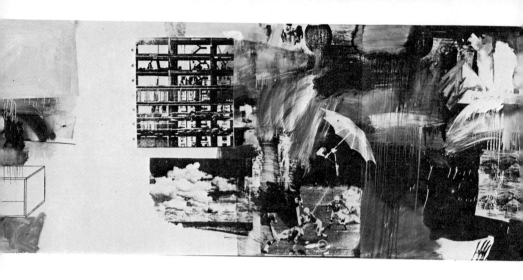

New music; new listening. Not an attempt to understand something that is being said, for, if something were being said, the sounds would be given the shapes of words. Just an attention to the activity of sounds.[2]

Ill. 97   A characteristic painting of Rauschenberg's, such as the enormous *Barge* painted in 1962, is a kind of reverie which the spectators are invited to join; a flux of images which are not necessarily fixed and immutable. Cage remarks on 'the quality of encounter' between Rauschenberg and the materials he uses; one can compare this to the way in which Kurt Schwitters worked. But Rauschenberg is a Schwitters who has passed through the abstract expressionist experience.

So, for that matter, is Jasper Johns, though John's work gives one the impression of greater discipline. Johns is also more of an ironist. One work, entitled *The Critic Smiles*, is a toothbrush cast in sculpmetal, placed upon a plinth of the same material. Unlike Rauschenberg, Johns is chiefly known for his use of

Ill. 92   single, banal images: a set of numbers, a target, a map of the United States, the American flag. The point about these images is largely their lack of point – the spectator looks for a specific

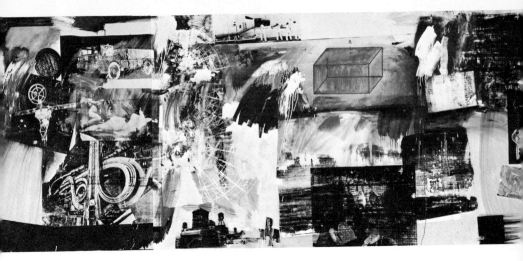

97 ROBERT RAUSCHENBERG *Barge* 1962

meaning, the artist is largely preoccupied with creating a
surface. Where the manipulation of paint is concerned, Johns
is a master technician. The way in which Johns operates
also suggests links with other things besides pop art. Like
Kenneth Noland, he is interested in pictorial inertia, for example.
One of the reasons for choosing banal patterns is the fact that
they no longer generate any energy. He is also interested in the
idea of the painting as an object rather than as a representation.
In some cases, he has used two canvases linked together, with a
pair of wooden balls forced between them, so we see the wall
behind at the point where they join. Other works have attach-
ments: a ruler, a broom, a spoon.

It is clear from this description of the activities of these two
artists that they represent a move away from 'pure' painting.
Even to Johns, for all his virtuosity, painting is no more than
a means of achieving a certain result, which might possibly be
achieved some other way. Rauschenberg was for years
associated with the Merce Cunningham dance company: he
performed with them as well as devising props and scenery, and
clearly this formed as important and central a part of his activity
as painting and making objects.

125

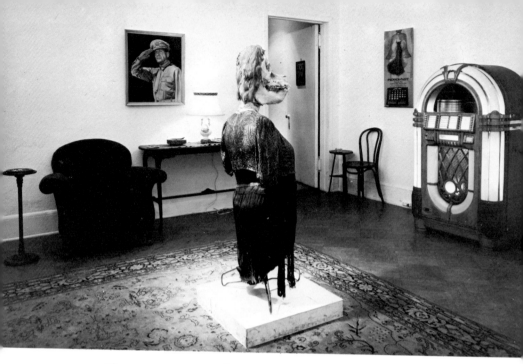

98 EDWARD KIENHOLZ *Roxy's* 1961

One of the directions suggested by a painting like *Barge* is the move towards the tableau, the work of art which surrounds or nearly surrounds the spectator. The bulky and ferocious works *Ill. 98* of Edward Kienholz are an example.

Kienholz also represents one aspect of the tendency which is now often called 'funk', or 'funk art': the liking for the complex, the sick, the tatty, the bizarre, the shoddy, the viscous, the overtly or covertly sexual, as opposed to the impersonal purity of a great deal of contemporary art. Perhaps because if offers this kind of alternative, 'funk' art proved more than a passing fashion. It was responsible for some of the most alarming *Ill. 99* images of the 1960s – things such as Bruce Conner's *Couch* of 1963, which shows an apparently murdered and dismembered corpse lying on a crumbling Victorian sofa, or Paul Thek's *Ill. 100* *Death of a hippie*, or various tableaux by the Englishman, Colin Self. A characteristic one is another corpse, a figure entitled *Nuclear victim*.

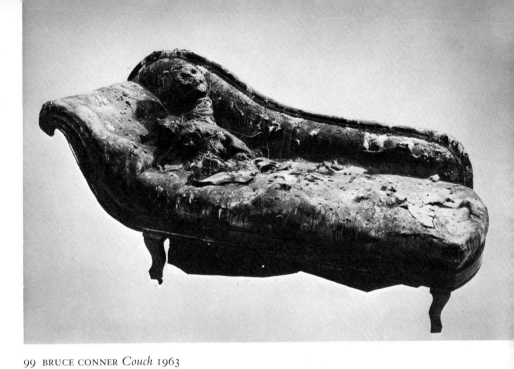

99 BRUCE CONNER *Couch* 1963

100 PAUL THEK *Death of a hippie* 1967

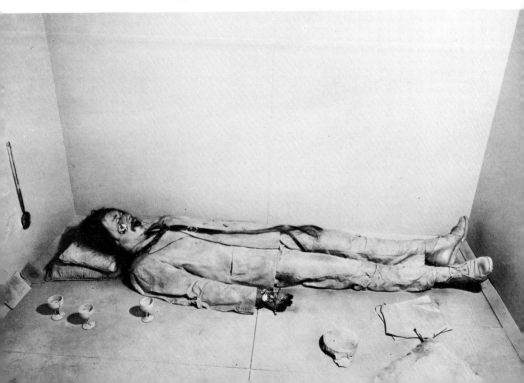

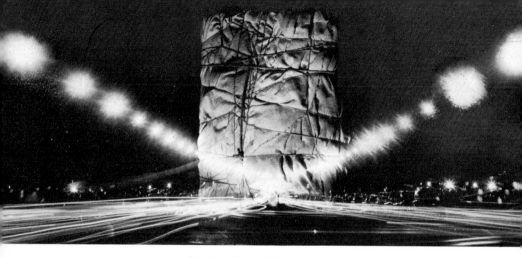

101 CHRISTO *Packaged public building* 1961

In Europe, an equivalent of the American neo-dadaists was supplied by what is sometimes called 'new realism', after the movement founded by the French critic Pierre Restany, in conjunction with Yves Klein and others. Restany claimed that 'the new realism registers the sociological reality without any controversial intention'. What this means one may perhaps

Ill. 93 deduce from the work of Arman, who was one of the adherents of the group. Arman's most characteristic works consist of random accumulations of objects, but objects all of the same sort, encased in clear plastic. These accumulations can exist as panels, or be three-dimensional. For example, Arman has made a plastic torso of a woman, filled with writing rubber gloves.

Ill. 101 Another artist attracted by the systematic is Christo, who is best known for his packages, mysterious lumpish objects which sometimes suggest and sometimes wholly conceal what is wrapped up in them.

The major personality among these European neo-dadaists was undoubtedly Yves Klein. Klein is an example of an artist who was important for what he did – the symbolic value of his actions – rather than for what he made. One sees in him an example of the increasing tendency for the personality of the artist to be his one true and complete creation.

128

102 Yves Klein's painting ceremony

Klein was born in 1928. He was a jazz musician, a Rosicrucian, and a judo expert (he studied judo in Japan and wrote a book about it which is still a standard text). In judo, the opponents are regarded as collaborators, and it is this notion which seems to underlie a great deal of Klein's thinking about art. So does the wish to 'get away from the idea of art'. Klein said:

> The essential of painting is that something, that 'ethereal glue', that intermediary product which the artist secretes with all his creative being and which he has the power to place, to encrust, to impregnate into the pictorial stuff of the painting.[3]

Besides creating the monochromes already mentioned, Klein adopted various unorthodox methods of producing works of art. For example, he used a flame-thrower, or the action of rain on a prepared canvas. (Paintings produced by the action of the

Ill. 103

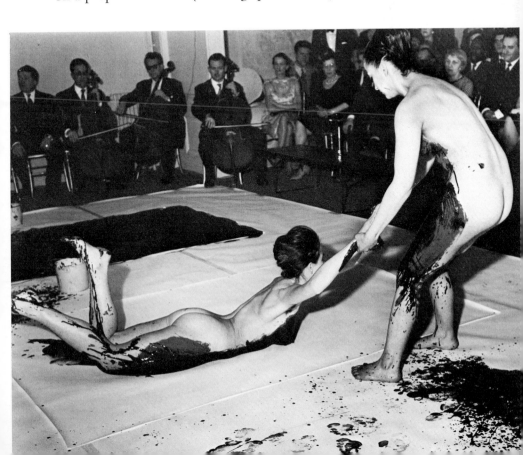

elements he labelled *Cosmogonies*.) At his direction girls smeared with blue paint flung themselves on to canvas spread on the floor. The ceremony was conducted in public while twenty musicians played Klein's *Monotone Symphony*, a single note sustained for ten minutes which alternated with ten minutes silence. The making of these *Imprints* is recorded in the film *Mondo Cane*. On another occasion – in Paris in 1958 – Klein held an exhibition of emptiness: a gallery painted white, with all the furniture removed and a Garde Républicain stationed at the door. Albert Camus came, and wrote the words 'with the void, full powers' in the visitors' book. There were thousands of other visitors to the *vernissage*, so many as to cause a near-riot. Another of Klein's ideas was to offer for sale 'zones of immaterial pictorial sensitivity'. They were paid for in gold-leaf, which the artist immediately threw in the Seine, while the purchaser burned his receipt.

These actions have a certain poetic rightness to them, a quality often absent from the clumsier and more elaborate happenings staged in New York. Klein, at the time of his death in 1962, seemed to stand at the meeting-point of a number of different tendencies. There is the obvious connection with the original dadaists, and also with certain contemporary artists

103 YVES KLEIN *Feu F 45* 1961

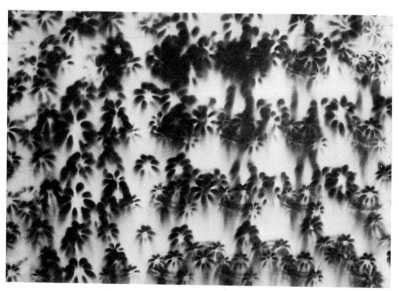

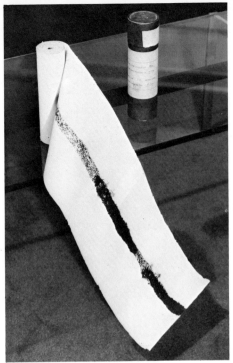

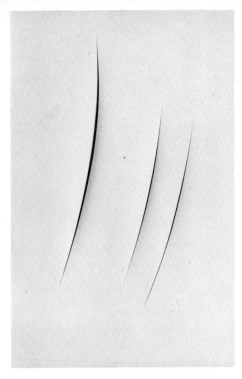

104 PIERO MANZONI
Line 20 metres long 1959

105 LUCIO FONTANA
Spatial Concept 1960

who stand on the fringes of dada, such as Lucio Fontana, whose   *Ill. 105*
own experiments with monochromes developed into the more
familiar slashed canvases. Also reminiscent of Klein's work are
the 'lines' of Piero Manzoni: single, unbroken brushstrokes   *Ill. 104*
which unroll on long strips of paper. All of these, in turn, are
linked in a more general way with the tendency towards
minimality in sculpture. On the other hand, Klein, as much as
Johns and Rauschenberg, is one of the prophets of pop art. His
use of monotony, of the undifferentiated, gives him something
in common with Andy Warhol, for instance.

But only *something* in common. Neo-dada and pop art not
identical, though neo-dada includes pop. The artists I have so
far spoken of in this chapter are not, in my view, genuine
practitioners of pop, though their work has been included in

exhibitions and discussed in books under that label. The factors which created pop art were not universal, but had much to do with the urban culture of Britain and America in the years after the war. Only artists in close touch with that culture caught its special tone and idiom: of all the post-war styles, this is the one which most conspicuously has 'a local habitation and a name'.

After pop scored its initial success, it did, very naturally, exercise an influence elsewhere. Many of the artists connected with Pierre Restany's 'new realism' toyed with it. There are, *Ill. 106* for instance, Michelangelo Pistoletto's photographic figures fastened to mirror backgrounds in which the spectator sees himself reflected, thus completing the composition; and Martial *Ill. 107* Raysse's skilful parodies of painters such as Prud'hon. In a version of Prud'hon's *Cupid and Psyche* entitled *Tableau simple et doux*, Cupid holds a neon heart in his fingers. Another

106 MICHELANGELO PISTOLETTO
Seated figure 1962 (with Pistoletto)

107 MARTIAL RAYSSE
Tableau simple et doux 1965

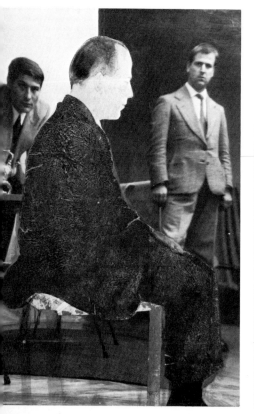

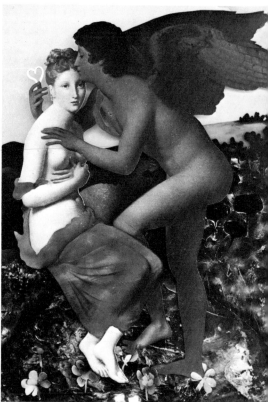

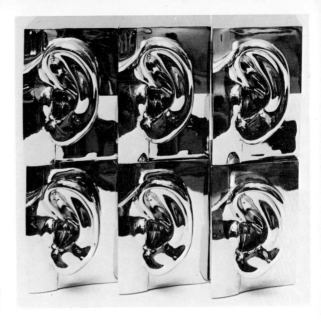

108 TOMIO MIKI *Ears*
(*detail*) 1968

Frenchman Alain Jacquet uses photographic images in a way which is reminiscent of both Warhol and Lichtenstein. The Japanese have been almost equally eager to catch up with pop. Tomio Miki has made almost as much a speciality of ears in cast *Ill. 108* aluminium as Warhol has of endlessly repeated images of Marilyn Monroe. In examining these works, however, one is aware that the involvement with the urban environment is not as immediate as it seems to be in the case of the leading British and American pop artists.

It now seems to be generally agreed that pop art, in its narrowest definition, began in England, and that it grew out of a series of discussions which were held at the Institute of Contemporary Arts in London by a group which called itself the Independent Group. It included artists, critics, and architects, among them Eduardo Paolozzi, Alison and Peter Smithson, Richard Hamilton, Peter Reyner Banham, and Lawrence Alloway. The group were fascinated by the new urban popular culture, and particularly by its manifestations in America. Partly this was a delayed effect of the war, when America, to those in England, had seemed an Eldorado of all good things,

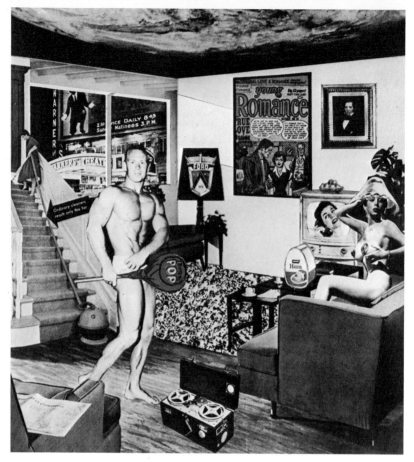

109 RICHARD HAMILTON *Just What is it that Makes Today's Homes so Different, so Appealing?* 1956

from nylons to new motor-cars. Partly it was a reaction against the solemn romanticism, the atmosphere of high endeavour, which had prevailed in British art during the 1940s.

In 1956 the group was responsible for an exhibition at the Whitechapel Art Gallery which was called 'This Is Tomorrow'. Designed in twelve sections, the show was designed to draw the spectator into a series of environments. In his book on pop art, Mario Amaya points out that the environmental aspect probably owed something to Richard Buckle's exhibition of the Diaghilev

Ballet, which was held in London in 1954, and which seized on the excuse of a theatrical subject to provide a brilliantly theatrical display.[4] From the point of view of the future, however, probably the most significant part of 'This Is Tomorrow' was an entrance display provided by Richard Hamilton – a collage picture entitled *Just What is it that Makes Today's Homes so Different, so Appealing?* In the picture are a muscle-man from a physique magazine and a stripper with sequinned breasts. The muscle-man carries a gigantic lollipop, with the word POP on it in large letters. With this work, many of the conventions of pop art were created, including the use of borrowed imagery.

Ill. 109

Hamilton already knew clearly what he thought a truly modern art should be. The qualities he was looking for were, so he said in 1957, popularity, transience, expendability, wit, sexiness, gimmickry, and glamour.[5] It must be low-cost, mass produced, young, and Big Business. These were the qualities which British pop artists of the 1960s were afterwards to worship. But granted Hamilton's priority, and that of the Independent Group, it is still a little difficult to prove that pop art sprang directly from their activities. Of all the artists who belonged to the group, Hamilton himself is the only one who can be classified as a pop painter. In addition, there is the fact that he has always been a very slow worker, and that, at this period, little of his work was to be seen in England.

There were two other British painters who might be labelled 'transitional', both of them, as it happens, among the most interesting that Britain has produced in recent years. Both were students at the Royal College of Art in the mid 1950s. One is Peter Blake, who would classify himself unhesitatingly as a 'realist'. Blake's work represents a reversion to the tradition of the Pre-Raphaelites in the middle of the twentieth century. Like the Pre-Raphaelites, he is nostalgic, but not for the Middle Ages. What he looks back on is the popular culture of the 1930s and 1940s. Unlike other pop painters, Blake is always concerned to be a little out of date. His house is crammed with memorabilia –

Ill. 111

postcards, seaside souvenirs, toys, knick-knacks of every sort – and out of these is distilled a very personal poetry.

Ills 117, 118 Richard Smith represents an attitude which is almost the opposite to this. As a student, he painted in a figurative style which was influenced by the Euston Road School and the Kitchen Sink painters. He was still at the Royal College at the time of 'This Is Tomorrow', and on him, at least, the show had a demonstrable influence. During 1957–9 he shared a studio with Peter Blake, but in 1959 he left for America, and has divided his time between England and the United States ever since. Smith's earliest characteristic works were based on packaging. He was also influenced by colour photography, the kind of thing to be found in magazines such as *Vogue*.

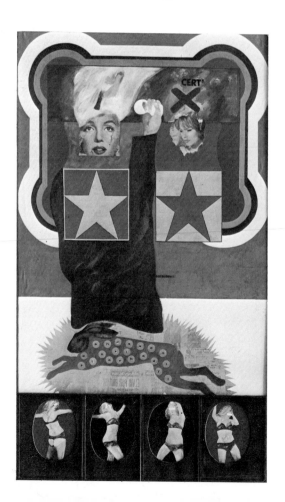

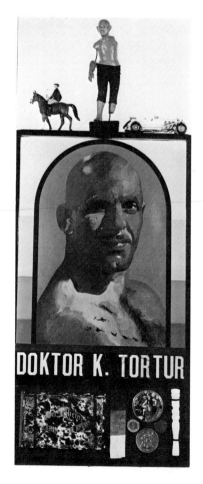

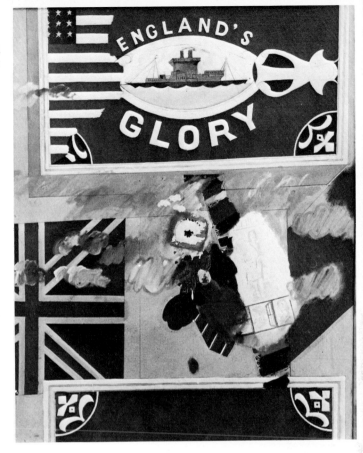

112 DEREK BOSHIER
England's Glory 1961

110 PETER PHILLIPS
*For men only starring
MM and BB* 1961

111 PETER BLAKE
Doktor K. Tortur
1965

His colour sensibility remained unaltered through subsequent changes of style. He himself describes his colour as 'sweet and tender', and speaks of wanting to give 'a general sense of blossoming, ripening, and shimmering', but the work itself has shed any overt association with pop. What Smith has done is to pass through the experience of pop art in order to arrive at a position which approximates to that of the American colour painters. His change to acrylic paint in 1964 was an important step in this process. So was his abandonment of conventional formats in favour of canvases stretched over three-dimensional frames, and his adoption, later, of shapes constructed like kites.

Smith, because he had successfully established himself in New York, meant a lot to his English colleagues, both as an example and as an influence. When he returned to England in 1961, he brought with him on-the-spot information about the activities of artists such as Jasper Johns which had an impact on artists such as Peter Phillips and Derek Boshier. Smith had already absorbed the American indifference to conventional limitations of format, and the American sense of scale, for example.

Ills 110, 112

The key date in British pop was 1961, not so much because of Smith's resumption of contact with British artists, but because of the Young Contemporaries exhibition which was held in that year. This caused perhaps the greatest sensation of any student show held since the war. The reason was the presence of a group of young artists from the Royal College of Art: Phillips, Boshier, Allen Jones, and David Hockney. Exhibiting with them was a slightly older American student, R. B. Kitaj. Kitaj, like Smith, had a first-hand knowledge of American techniques, and he fostered the new obsession with popular imagery among his fellow students.

Ill. 121

One of the weaknesses of British pop art was its easy and rapid success. England, so far as the visual arts were concerned, was at last moving out of its phase of insularity (in literature, insularity was to last much longer). The hedonism of the late 1950s had taken root, and the new artists seemed to offer precisely the gay, impudent, pleasure-centred art which fitted the mood of the times. But modern artists of any talent were still thin on the ground, and the young lions of pop did not meet with much competition.

It soon became clear that the artists who were grouped together after their spectacular début at the Young Contemporaries were temperamentally very different. Phillips was the most genuinely interested in popular imagery, but used it in a rigid and boringly dogmatic way. Boshier came under the influence of Richard Smith and veered away from figurative imagery in the direction of op art. More capricious and personal than either of these two were Hockney and Jones.

138

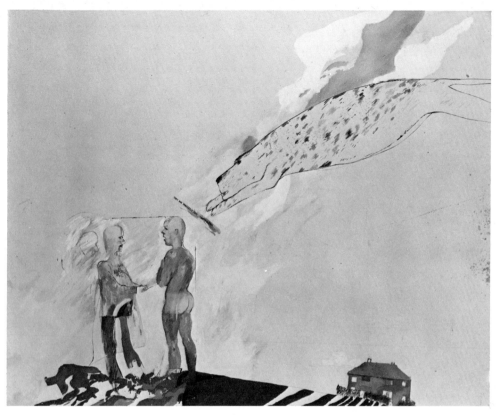

113 DAVID HOCKNEY *Picture emphasizing stillness* 1962–3 (inscription: THEY ARE PERFECTLY SAFE, THIS IS A STILL)

Hockney is an artist who has had an interesting if slightly erratic development. He began as the *Wunderkind* of British art. His life-style was instantly famous; his dyed blond hair, owlish glasses, and gold lamé jacket created – or contributed to – a persona which appealed even to people who were not vitally interested in painting. In this sense, he forms part of the general development of British culture which was symbolized by the sudden and enormous fame of the Beatles. But it was also clear that Hockney was precociously gifted. In his early work, he adopted a cartooning, *faux-naïf* style which owed a lot to children's drawings. Often these early pictures have a delightful deadpan irony.

Ill. 113

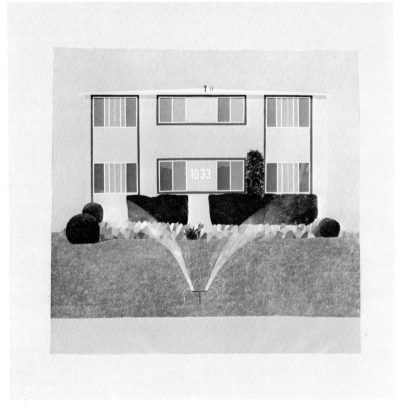

114 DAVID HOCKNEY *A neat lawn* 1967

Some of Hockney's most characteristic work at this time was to be found in his prints. The suite of etchings entitled *The Rake's Progress* chronicles his reactions to the dream-world of America, which he visited for the first time in 1961. They reflect profoundly ambiguous attitudes. The comment is often sharp – the *Bedlam scene*, for instance, shows a group of automata governed by the pocket transistor radios which have become part of their anatomy – but the overall tone of the series is one of avid enjoyment. Hockney has spent a great deal of his time in America ever since, and particularly likes southern California.

Soon, the precarious poise of these early works was threatened. Hockney's painting became increasingly dry, increasingly preoccupied with the wish to be realistic. Some middle-period *Ill. 114* paintings of the Californian landscape have, it is true, become classics – American critics have compared them to Edward Hopper. Others are disconcertingly dull. Eventually Hockney found realism confining, and more recently he has made a series of paraphrases of classic modern art, paying especial attention to Picasso. At the same time he has become increasingly pre-occupied with photography, which in his case seems a diversion from painting.

Allen Jones, like Hockney, is an artist whose early work was captivating because it radiated an air of enjoyment not unspiced with satirical humour. The most 'painterly' of all the British pop painters, he seems to have learned a great deal from Matisse where colour is concerned. There is also a debt to the orphism of Robert Delaunay. Jones is a less narrative artist than Hockney: he is interested in metamorphoses, transformations, visual ambiguities. A series of *Hermaphrodites* (male/female *Ill. 122* images melting into one another on the same canvas) seem particularly characteristic of his work. Jones has shown a particularly deft and ingenious fancy with shaped canvases: a series of paintings of *Marriage medals*, done in 1963, is made up of tall vertical canvases to which octagonal canvases are attached.

Jones resembles Hockney rather less happily because he too seems to have had trouble in deepening and developing his work. It has had a tendency to grow increasingly harder and more strident; the colour has left the comfortable 'fine art' tradition of the fauves. This shows up the extreme thinness of content. The artist insists that the subject-matter of his work has always been of secondary interest to him, but one becomes more and more aware of its insistent banality, a banality that does not seem to have been adopted with any doctrinaire purpose in mind.

No one could accuse R. B. Kitaj's work of lack of complexity. The term 'pop' has to be stretched rather far to cover his work. Kitaj is a hermetic artist; the best comparison is a literary one,

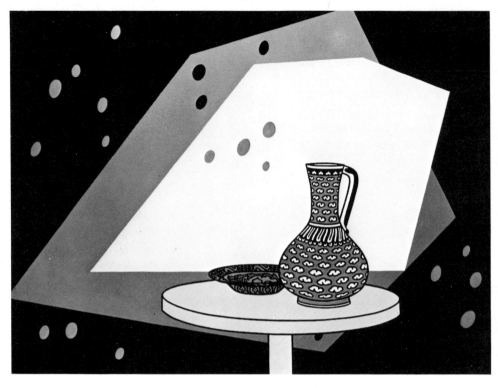

115 PATRICK CAULFIELD *Still-life with red and white pot* 1966

in that his paintings are often rather like the *Cantos* of Ezra
Pound. In them, one finds dense patterns of eclectic imagery.
Often the painter requires that the spectator should try and
match his own experience. The catalogue of one of Kitaj's
infrequent exhibitions tends to pile footnote on footnote,
in the endeavour to explain the complexity of his source
material. These sources are more likely to be *The Journal of the
Warburg Institute* than a favourite comic strip. One's approach
Ill. 121 to Kitaj's work must be intellectual. He is a dedicated and
increasingly excellent draughtsman, and a rather dry colourist.
Because his painting is so nearly a form of literature, it often
seems that his prints are more successful than his paintings, and
a good deal of his recent production has been graphics, mostly

142

silk-screen prints which use this flexible medium with great ingenuity.

There are one or two other artists in Britain who have also been associated by critics with the pop movement, though they stand a little apart from the rest. One is Anthony Donald- *Ill. 116* son, who uses pop imagery – nude or near-nude girls – as components in pictures which are closer to 'hard edge' abstract painting than they are to pop itself. This is because the girls are usually no more than silhouettes, and the silhouettes take their place among the other shapes in the composition. When the girls are omitted, as in some more recent paintings by Donaldson, the effect is still much the same. Another is Patrick Caulfield, who is a little younger than the other members of the   *Ill. 115* 'pop generation'. He did not leave the Royal College of Art until 1963. Caulfield is better described as a cliché painter than

116 ANTHONY DONALDSON *Take away no. 2* 1963

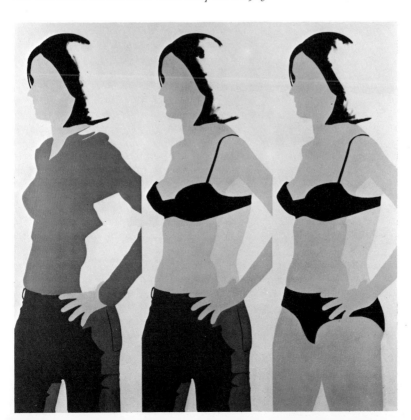

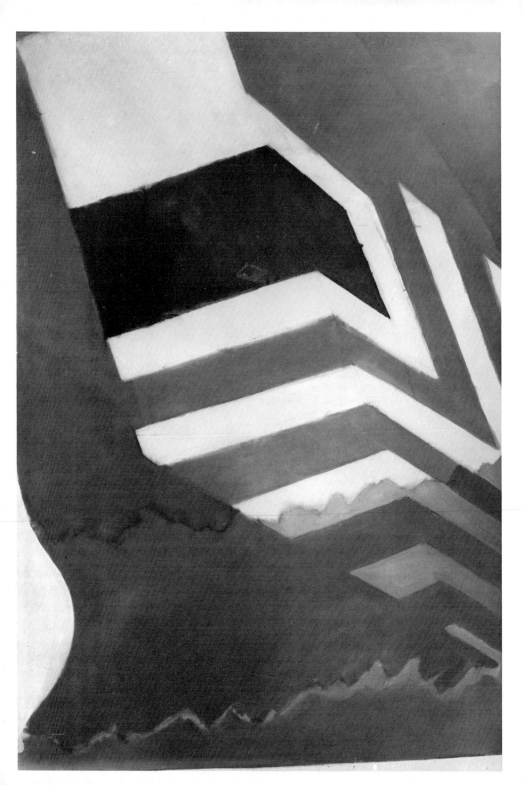

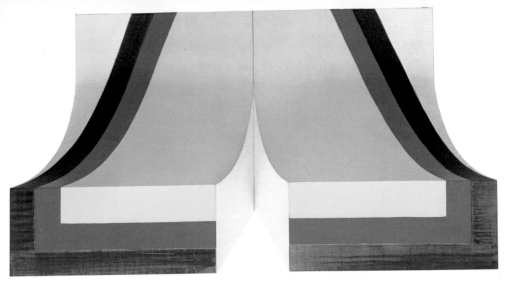

118 RICHARD SMITH *Tailspan* 1965

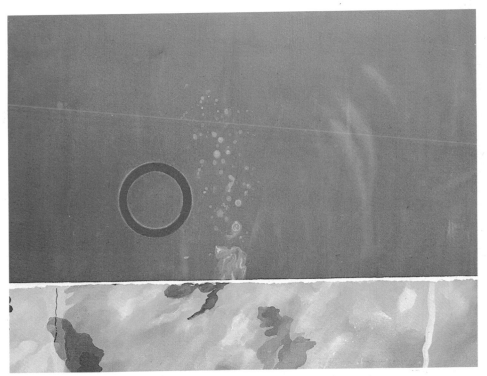

119 DAVID HOCKNEY *Rubber ring floating in a swimming pool* 1971

◀ 117 RICHARD SMITH *Soft Pack* 1963

as a pop painter. His characteristic subject is the department store reproduction, the kind of image that commonly appears in cheap prints, on plastic trays, or in the kits which invite the amateur to 'paint by numbers'. Every shape he uses, every object he depicts, is described by a hard unvaried line, which looks as if it has been printed rather than painted. The colour is equally without modulation. Caulfield is intent on exploring the relationship between fine art and mass culture, and particularly the debased ways of seeing which mass culture seems to encourage. He is thus not fully committed to the pop ethos, but is, rather, a pitiless critic of it.

Before moving on to discuss the American pop artists, who are in some ways very different from their British counterparts, I must say something about a group of Australian artists who have a much greater relevance to the genesis of pop art than is generally admitted. The success of contemporary Australian art in London in the years after the war was one of the phenomena of art-dealing. The spearhead of this success was Sidney Nolan, and the pictures which created his reputation were a series devoted to the career of the Australian outlaw Ned Kelly. The earliest *Ned Kelly* paintings date from the 1940s, and thus antedate pop by some years. In them, Nolan, who had been an abstract painter, established a new, *faux-naïf* style as a vehicle for a fairly sophisticated Australian nationalism.

The status of Australian painting as a kind of pre-pop is interesting in an American as well as in an English context, because it is clear that there is a goodish dose of nationalism in American pop art, or, rather, it is clear that nationalism contributed to its sudden and overwhelming success. Americans found in it a truthful reflection of the society which surrounded them, and they also saw an assertion of the uniqueness of the American vision. It is not too much to claim that pop led to the construction or reconstruction of American art-history, so as to make a larger place for artists such as Hopper, and even (further back) for painters like Frederick Edwin Church.

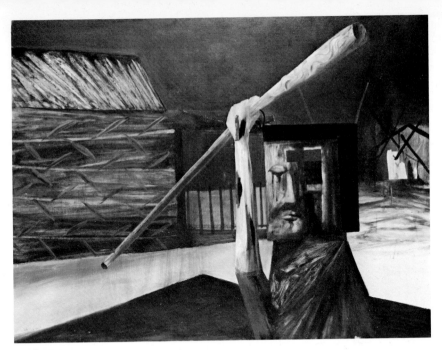

120 SIDNEY NOLAN *Glenrowan* 1956–7

The American pop artists were discovered and promoted by collectors and dealers. The critics and theorists lagged a long way behind these enthusiasts. Indeed, the American art establishment considered, and to some extent still seems to consider, the triumph of pop art as a rejection of itself and of the direction it had chosen to encourage. A leading advocate of abstract expressionism, Harold Rosenberg, had this to say about the new style:

Certainly, Pop Art earned the right to be called a movement through the number of its adherents, its imaginative pressure, the quantity of talk it generated. Yet if Abstract Expressionism had too much staying power, Pop was likely to have too little. Its congenital superficiality, while having the advantage of permitting the artist an almost limitless range of familiar subjects to exploit (anything from doilies to dining-club

147

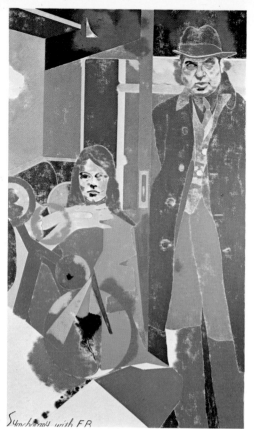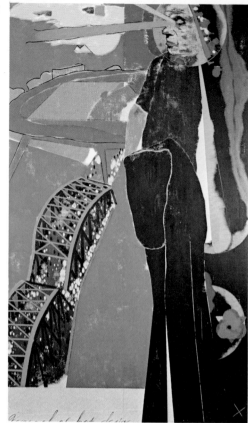

121 R. B. KITAJ *Synchromy with F.B. – General of Hot Desire* (diptych) 1968–9

cards), resulted in a qualitative monotony that could cause interest in still another gag of this kind to vanish overnight. ... Abstract Expressionism still excels in quality, significance and capacity to bring out new work; adding the production of its veterans to that of some of its younger artists it continues to be the front runner in the 'What next?' steeplechase.[6]

In effect, pop art challenged abstract expressionism – or seemed to challenge it – in three different ways. It was figurative, where abstract expressionism was mostly abstract; it was 'newer' than abstract expressionism; and it was 'more American'.

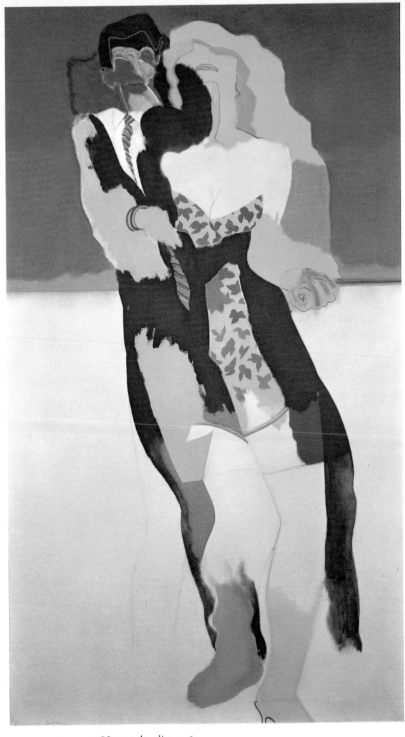

122 ALLEN JONES *Hermaphrodite* 1963

The principal American pop artists – Dine, Oldenburg, Rosenquist, Lichtenstein, and Warhol – differed fairly widely from one another. Jim Dine and Claes Oldenburg were the closest to the neo-dadaists whom I have already discussed. Dine, in particular, has two qualities which link him very closely to Rauschenberg and Johns: he is essentially a combine or assemblage painter, and his subject is the different varieties of reality. In a characteristic work by Dine, a 'ready-made' object or objects – an article of dress, a wash-basin, a shower, some tools – is fastened to canvas, and an environment is created for it with freely brushed paint. Often, whatever is presented is carefully labelled with its name.

Ill. 124

Oldenburg, too, experimented with effects of displacement. His objects hover between the realms of sculpture and painting. These objects range from such things as giant hamburgers to squashy models of wash-basins and egg-beaters. Often these things are made of vinyl stuffed with kapok. Oldenburg said:

Ill. 123

> I use naïve imitation. This is not because I have no imagina-
> tion or because I wish to say something about the everyday

123 CLAES OLDENBURG *Study for Giant Chocolate* 1966

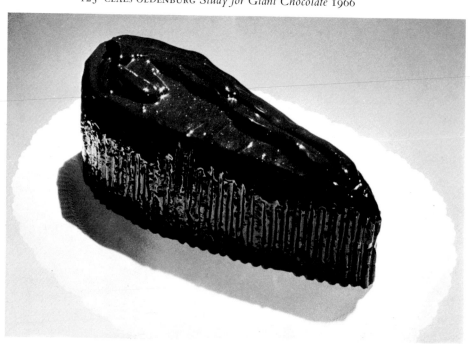

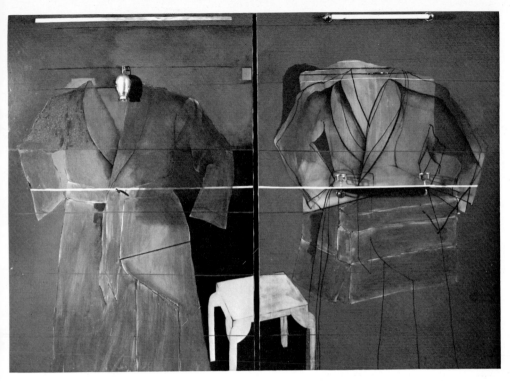

124 JIM DINE *Double red self-portrait (The Green Lines)* 1964

world. I imitate 1. objects and 2. created objects, for example, signs, objects made without the intention of making 'art' and which naïvely contain a functional contemporary magic. I try to carry these even further through my own naïveté, which is not artificial. Further, i.e. charge them more intensely, elaborate their reference. I do not try to make 'art' of them. This must be understood. I imitate these because I want people to get accustomed to recognizing the power of objects, a didactic aim.[7]

Therefore he, too, is interested in reality, with an element of totemism added.

James Rosenquist and Roy Lichtenstein differ from Dine and Oldenburg because to a large extent they accept the limitations of the flat surface, and because they are formalists. At the

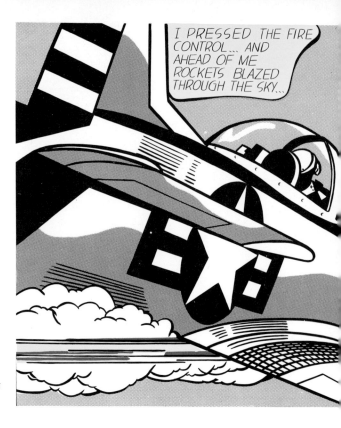

125 ROY LICHTENSTEIN
Whaam! 1963

moment, it seems to be Lichtenstein who has been elevated to a status above the others. He is not as hostile to the word 'art' as Oldenburg is. He has said, for example, that 'organized perception is what art is all about'. He adds that the act of looking at a painting 'has nothing to do with any external form the painting takes, it has to do with a way of building a unified pattern of seeing'.

Ills 125,   Lichtenstein's earliest work was based on comic strips; even
127   the dots which are part of the process of cheap colour printing are meticulously reproduced. The artist once said to an interviewer:

> I think my work is different from comic strips – but I wouldn't call it transformation. . . . What I do is form,

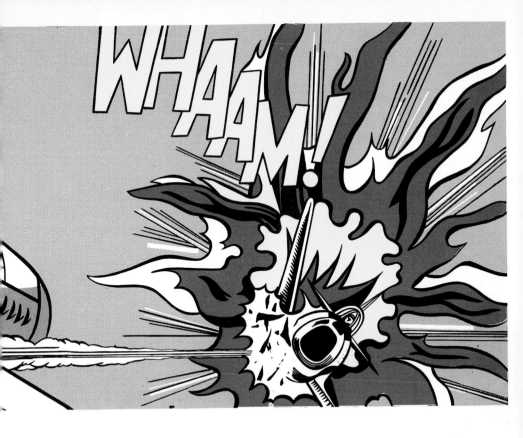

whereas the comic strip is not formed in the sense I'm using the word; the comics have shapes, but there has been no effort to make them intensely unified. The purpose is different, one intends to depict and I intend to unify. And my work is actually different from comic strips in that every mark is really in a different place, however slight the difference seems to some.[8]

That is, the imagery is in part a strategy, a means of binding together the picture surface. Another aim can be seen most clearly in the series of *Brushstrokes*: meticulous, frozen versions (in comic-strip technique) of the marks which an abstract expressionist artist might have made with one sweep of the brush. The series is an experiment in 'removal': a word which

Ill. 126

crops up fairly often in Lichtenstein's discourse. It is also an attempt to make the audience question its own values.

This raises the question of the values put forward by the pop artists themselves. One of the most characteristic and disturbing aspects of pop art is the fact that, though figurative, it often seems unable to make use of the image observed at first hand. To be viable, its images must have been processed in some way. Rosenquist declared: 'I treat the billboard image as it is. I paint it as a reproduction of other things. I try to get as far away from it *Ill. 131* as possible.'[9] His bits and pieces of billboard imagery were jumbled together in such a way as to produce an effect which *Ill. 129* was abstract. Similarly, the nudes of Tom Wesselmann are

126 ROY LICHTENSTEIN *Yellow and red brushstrokes* 1966

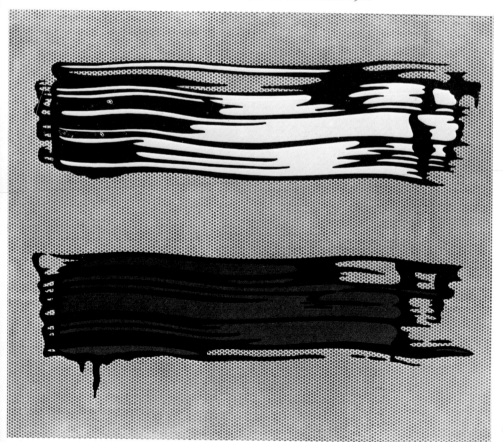

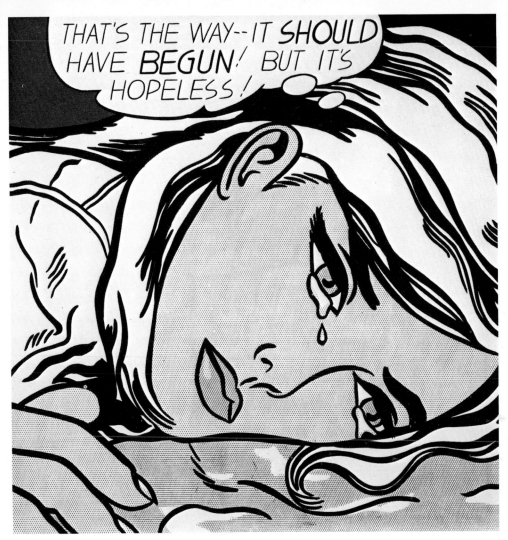

127 ROY LICHTENSTEIN *Hopeless* 1963

transformed into arbitrary, flat silhouettes from which the human presence fades.

There is a comparison to be made between Rosenquist and Larry Rivers, an artist who is best defined as 'near-pop'. Rivers is a seductive artist; he paints in a way which delights admirers

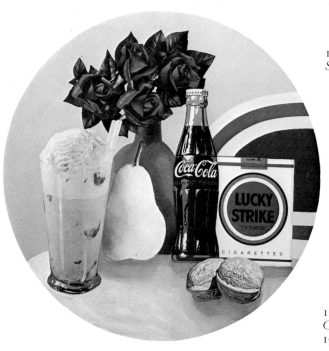

128 TOM WESSELMANN
Still-life no. 34 1963

129 TOM WESSELMANN
Great American Nude no. 44
1963

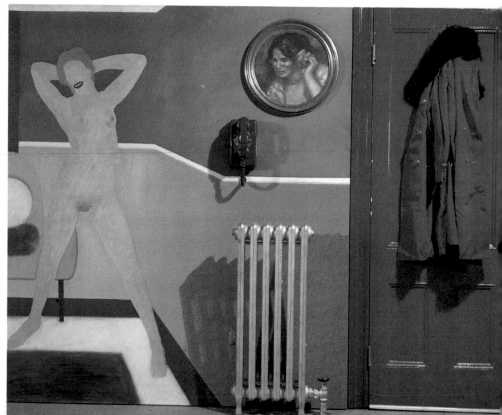

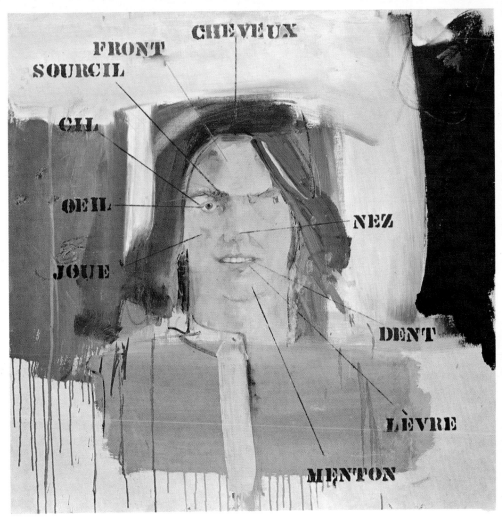

130 LARRY RIVERS *Parts of the face* 1961

of the impressionists, and which, in particular, seems to owe a
good deal to Manet. The imagery he deals with sometimes
recalls pop, because Rivers is interested in subjects such as
packaging, the design of banknotes, and so forth. But he is
concerned always to make painterly variations upon these,
rather than imitations. Rivers is also prepared to paint directly

157

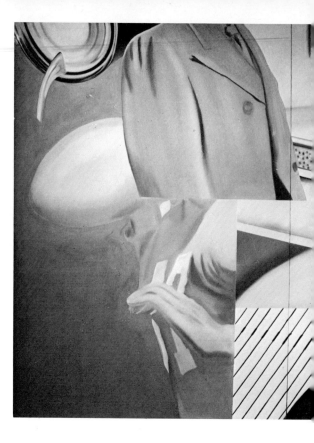

Ill. 130 from nature. He treats some of these pictures as a kind of
vocabulary lesson – a female nude will be carefully labelled with
all the names of the parts of the body, but in French, not in
English. Other paintings are fragmented accounts of a particular
experience, for example a street accident. The outstanding
characteristic of all these paintings is a kind of glancing oblique-
ness, as if the artist were unable to focus on the actual subject for
very long at a time.

George Segal shows much the same helplessness when confronted with an objective reality. His sculptures are made, not
by a process of modelling, but by making life-casts of the
subjects, almost as if the artist didn't trust his own vision of them.

The most controversial, as well as the most famous, of all the
American pop artists is Andy Warhol. Warhol's activities go

158

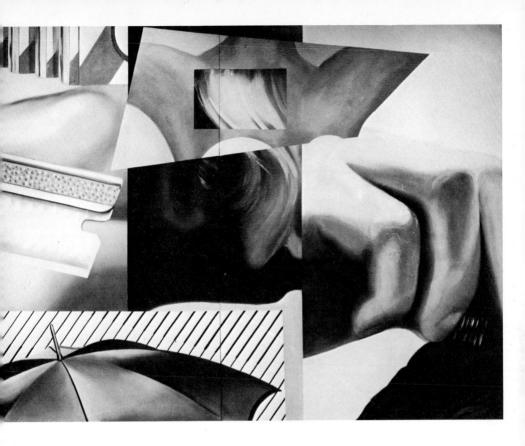

far beyond the conventional boundaries of painting: he has
made numerous films, he has directed a night-club entertainment, the Velvet Underground, and the kind of notoriety
he enjoys is like that accorded to a famous actor or film star.
When the first retrospective of Warhol's work was held, in
Philadelphia in 1965, the crush at the private view was so great
that some of the exhibits had to be removed, for fear of damage.
It was clearly the artist himself, and not his products, whom the
visitors wished to see.

Yet Warhol's attitudes towards the notion of 'personality'
are ambiguous. On the one hand, he labeled the performers in
his films 'super-stars', on the other hand he declared that he
himself wants to be a machine, something which makes, not
paintings, but industrial products. Samuel Adams Green, in his

159

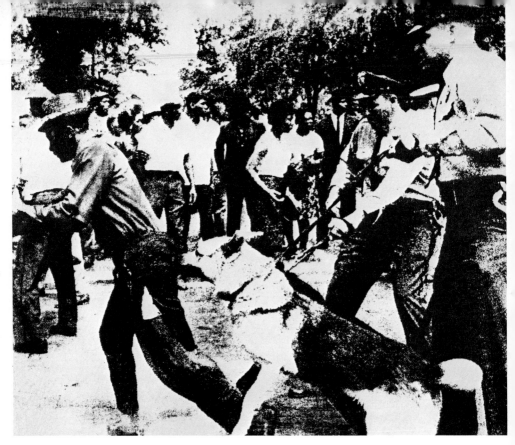

132 ANDY WARHOL *Race riot* 1964

introduction to the catalogue of the Philadelphia exhibition, remarked of Warhol:

Ill. 133

His pictorial language consists of stereotypes. Not until our time has a culture known so many commodities which are absolutely impersonal, machine-made, and untouched by human hands. Warhol's art uses the visual strength and vitality which are the time-tested skills of the world of advertising that cares more for the container than the thing contained. Warhol accepts rather than questions our popular habits and heroes. By accepting their inevitability they are easier to deal with than if they are opposed. . . . We accept

160

the glorified legend in preference to the actuality of our immediate experiences, so much so that the legend becomes commonplace and, finally, devoid of the very qualities which first interested us.[10]

In fact, more than most pop artists, Warhol seems concerned to anaesthetize our reaction to what is put in front of us. Many of his pictures have morbid associations: Mrs Kennedy after the assassination of her husband, Marilyn Monroe after her suicide, 'mug shots' of criminals, automobile accidents, the electric *Ill. 132* chair, gangster funerals, race riots. The images are repeated over and over again in photographic enlargements which are silk-screened on to canvas. The only modification is an overlay of crudely applied synthetic colour. The repetition and the colour are the instruments of a moral and aesthetic blankness which has been deliberately contrived. We are aware of Warhol's narcissism when we look at his pictures, but even this scarcely touches us. Frank O'Hara, the poet and art critic, once remarked that much pop art was essentially a 'put on', a poker-faced attempt to discover exactly how much the audience would swallow. Lichtenstein also said, speaking of the beginnings of pop in America, 'It was hard to get a painting which was despicable enough so no one would hang it – everyone was hanging everything.'[11] Warhol carries this attitude to extremes, so that much of what he does is contemptuously private and aristocratic. This appears in his obsessive concern with boredom, for example. He has made a film of a man sleeping – that and nothing else – which lasts for more than six hours.

With the rise of pop art, both the environment and the Happening took on a new and special importance. There were several reasons for this. One was that pop specialized in the 'given'; this led artists to experiment with the literal reproduction of reality. Edward Kienholz's more ambitious works fall into this category. There was, too, the consuming interest taken by pop artists in the phenomena of popular culture, among them such enfolding experiences as amusement

162

arcades and side-shows in circuses: the 'Tunnel of Love', for
example. Yayoi Kusama's *Endless Love Room* of 1965–6 uses   *Ill. 135*
pure fairground techniques, with a space bewilderingly
enlarged by multiple mirrors.

The classic pop art Happenings, such as Jim Dine's *The Car*   *Ill. 134*
Crash and Claes Oldenburg's *Store Days*, took place in   *Ill. 136*
environments specially constructed by the artists. The
Happening involved the extension of an 'art' sensibility – or,

134 JIM DINE *The Car Crash* 1960

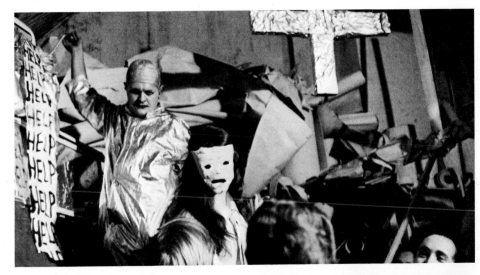

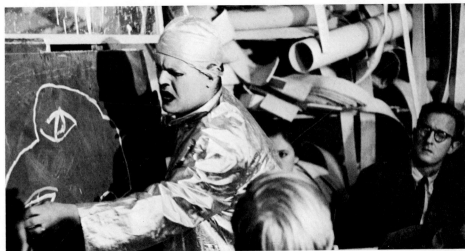

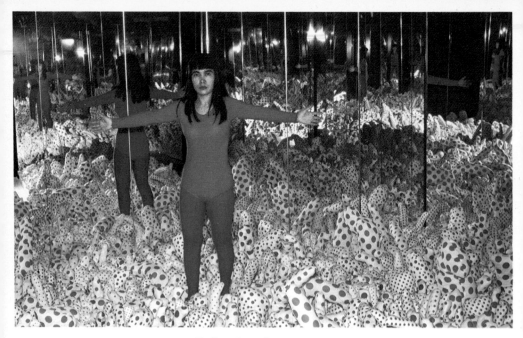

135 YAYOI KUSAMA *Endless Love Room* 1965–6

more precisely, a 'collage-environment' sensibility – into a situation composed also of sounds, time-durations, gestures, sensations, even smells. Its roots remained in the artist's studio and not in the theatre. The spectator was not supplied with a matrix of plot and character; instead, he was bombarded with sensations which he had to order on his own responsibility. *The Car Crash* was a subjective reconstruction of the sensations produced by a traffic accident, and in this is comparable with the very different environmental piece by Beuys illustrated in Chapter One.

Ill. 134

Ill. 7

The events put on by Europeans differed from the American Happenings which preceded them in several ways. They were more abstract, less specific even than their predecessors. Much of their energy went into the exploration of extreme situations. Sometimes, indeed, the artists who took part in them seemed to engage in a desperate search for the unacceptable, for behaviour which would restore them to a position as rebels and enemies of

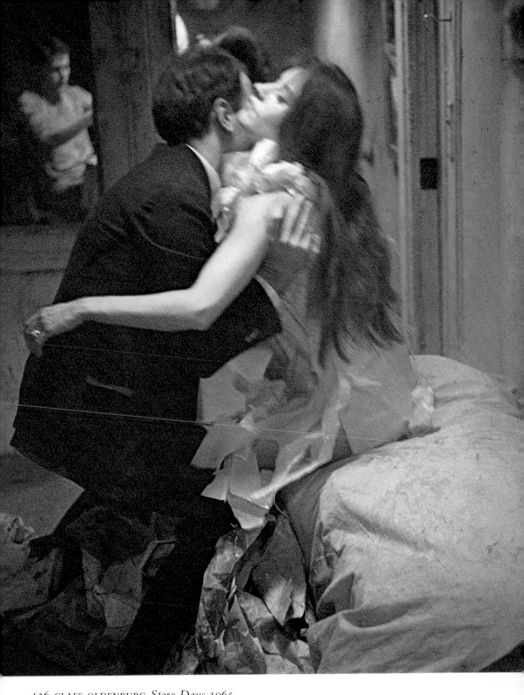

136 CLAES OLDENBURG *Store Days* 1965

society. At the same time there was less disposition to regard this kind of activity as a kind of art-world romp. For one event, the English artist Stuart Brisley spent many hours almost motionless in a bath full of water and animal entrails. Even more extreme was the work done by various members of the Vienna Group in Austria – among them Hermann Nitsch, Otto Muehl, Gunter Brüs and Rudolf Schwarzkogler. Many of their events and actions were unbridled expressions of sado-masochistic fantasy. Nitsch claimed that he took upon himself 'the apparent negative, unsavoury, perverse, obscene, the passion and the hysteria of the act of sacrifice so that YOU are spared the sullying, shaming descent into the extreme.'[11]

Ill. 137

Ill. 138

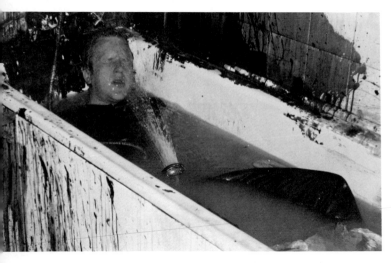

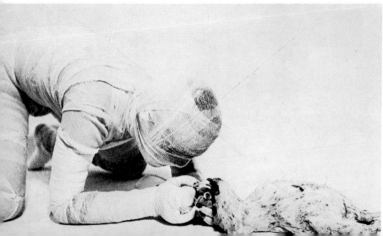

137 STUART BRISLEY *And For Today – Nothing* 1972

138 RUDOLF SCHWARZKOGLER Action, Vienna, May 1965

But not all the work done in Europe was deadly serious. The Englishmen Gilbert and George made their names with a piece called *Singing Sculptures* in which the two participants, with gilded faces, stood on a plinth and mimed to the music–hall song 'Underneath the Arches'. The point was a concern with the idea of style and stylishness. Style was plucked from its context and examined as a separate entity. And, finally, the question of the division, or the lack of it, between the creator and what he creates was brought up. Gilbert and George described themselves as 'living sculptures', and there was more than an implication that everything they did was to be looked upon as art.

Ill. 139

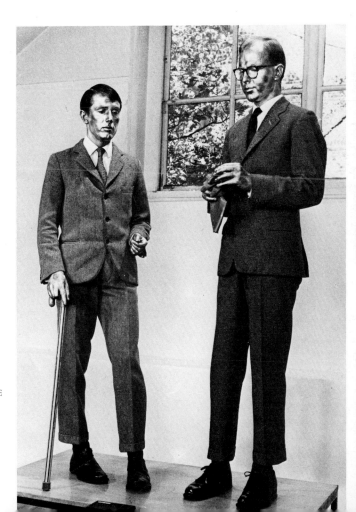

139 GILBERT AND GEORGE
Singing Sculpture 1970

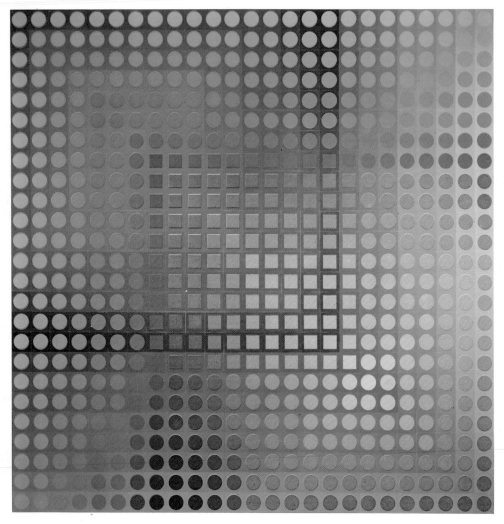

140 VICTOR VASARELY *Arny* 1967–8

CHAPTER SIX

Op and kinetic art

When pop art was succeeded, as a journalistic phenomenon, by 'op art', there was a natural tendency for journalists to seek out as many op artists as possible. Hence the inclusion in this category of artists whose interest in optical effects was in reality very marginal. A more serious distortion was the way in which op art was presented as something which had made a sudden appearance on the scene, rather as pop had done. In fact, optical painting, like 'hard edge' abstraction, had its roots deep in the Bauhaus tradition, and is the consequence of the kind of experiments which the Bauhaus encouraged.

This journalistic overkill, which also had its effect on a related art-form, kinetic art, resulted in these means of artistic expression being abruptly relegated to obscurity after a period of initial success. A few major reputations survived, such as that of the British artist Bridget Riley, but by the end of the 1970s, op and kinetic had come to be regarded as an aesthetic and historical cul-de-sac, though there was still a continuing interest in the application to art of new scientific inventions, such as holography and computer technology.

If post-war optical painting is to be traced back to a single source, that source must unquestionably be Victor Vasarely. *Ills 140, 141* Vasarely was Hungarian by origin, and was born in 1908. He first studied medicine, then went to a conventional art school, and finally, in 1928–9, was a student at the Mühely academy of Alexander Bortnyik, the Budapest Bauhaus. He then settled in France. Characteristically, Vasarely remarked that it was during this period at the Budapest Bauhaus that 'the functional character of plasticity' was revealed to him. He began as a graphic artist, and it was not until 1943 that he turned to painting.

Vasarely is too rich and complex an artist to be thought of simply as an optical painter and nothing else. In fact, his large post-war *œuvre* embodies a whole complex of related ideas. One of the most important of these was the idea of 'work', of art as a practical activity. This made him hostile to the idea of free abstraction, as he noted in 1950:

> The artist has become free. Anyone can assume the title of artist, or even of genius. Any spot of colour, sketch or outline is readily proclaimed a work, in the name of sacrosanct subjective sensitivity. Impulse prevails over know-how. Honest craftsman-like technique is bartered for fanciful and haphazard improvisation.[1]

But Vasarely had been prepared to go further than most of those who condemned free abstraction, by proposing that we regard the artist simply as a man who makes prototypes which can then be reproduced at will: 'the value of the prototype does not consist in the rarity of the object, but the rarity of the quality it represents'. He felt that all the plastic arts form a unity, and that there is no need to split them into fixed categories, such as painting, sculpture, graphics, or even architecture:

> Our time with the encroachment of technics, with its speed, with its new sciences, its theories, its discoveries, its novel materials, imposes its law upon us. Abstract painting, now, new in its conception, different in its approach, still has attachments to the former world, to the old painting, by a common technique and formal presentation that hold it back and cast a shadow of ambiguity over its conquests.[2]

One reads this statement with respect, yet it must be said that Vasarely was in many ways a curiously divided artist, much less inventive formally than he was fertile in new ideas and concepts. His non-kinetic abstract paintings, for instance, owe a great deal to work done some forty years before by Auguste

Herbin. Vasarely specifically acknowledged a debt to Herbin's vocabulary of 'colour-forms' (shapes related to colour, but without naturalistic references, which are used as units in more complex groupings). He claimed that this vocabulary was employed by him in new ways, which free themselves from Herbin's still traditional methods of composition. But the difference is not always as striking as he would have had us suppose.

It is natural, therefore, to focus attention on his exploration of kinetic effects, the source of the most original things he has produced.

Kineticism was important to Vasarely for two reasons: one was personal, the fact that, as he told us, 'the idea of movement has haunted me from my childhood'; and the other was the more general idea that a painting which lives by means of optical effects exists essentially in the eye and mind of the spectator, and not merely on the wall – it completes itself only when looked at.

I have already begun to use the words 'kinetic art' and 'optical art' almost interchangeably. In fact, the former seems to me the better term. Kinetic art can cover a good many categories of object.

There are, first of all, works of art which, though in fact static, appear to move or change. These can be in two or three dimensions. Vasarely, for instance, has concerned himself with paintings, with works composed in separate planes, and with screens and three-dimensional objects. Static works rely for their kineticism on the action of light and on well-known optical phenomena, such as the tendency of the eye to produce after-images when confronted with very brilliant contrasts of black and white, or the juxtaposition of certain hues.

Secondly, there are objects which move at random, without mechanical power, such as the mobiles of Alexander Calder.

Thirdly, there are the works which are mechanically powered, and which use lights, electromagnets, or even water.

The need for precision in works of the first category, and the fact that those of the second and third varieties are actually machines, of however simple a kind, gives kinetic art a mechanistic overtone. It seems to lie on the borders of an art which is actually produced by machines, rather than by men. This, however, is an oversimplification.

Ill. 142   Bridget Riley, for instance, who is probably the most brilliant of all the kinetic artists who have worked in two dimensions, would certainly reject the suggestion that her paintings are not meant to express or to communicate feeling.[3] Her work is often intricately programmed: the forms and their relationship to one another conform to predetermined mathematical series, but the progressions are arrived at instinctively. Miss Riley once worked entirely in black and white, but now,

141 VICTOR VASARELY *Metagalaxy* 1959

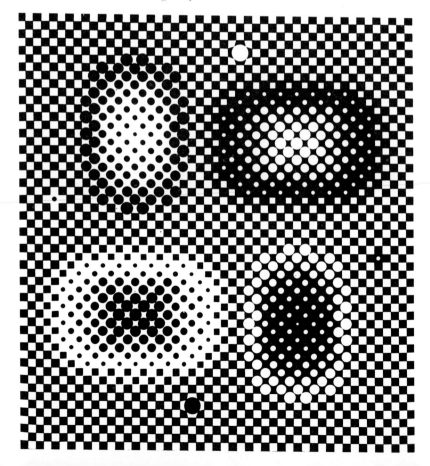

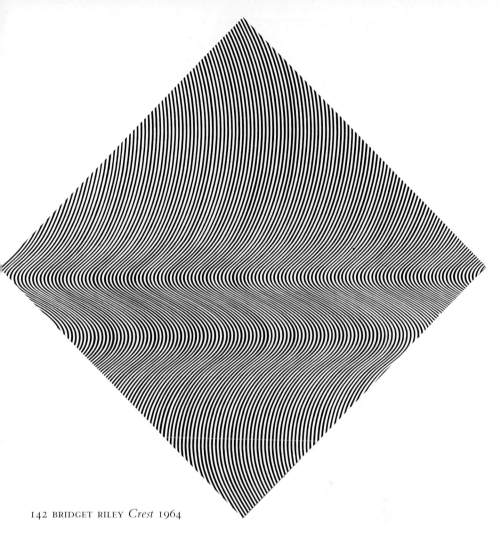

142 BRIDGET RILEY *Crest* 1964

having moved through a phase where muted colours were used, she has created a series of dazzlingly colourful pictures, which explore the way in which one colour can be made, by optical means, to bleed into another; or the way in which the whole picture surface can be made to move from warm to cool through the progression of hues. In contrast to the work of the colour painters, the surface does not remain inert, but ripples with muscular energy.

173

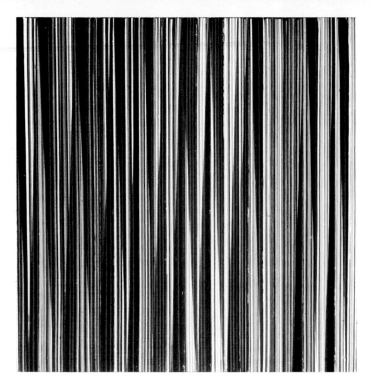

141 CARLOS CRUZ-DIEZ *Physichromie no. 1* 1959

The next stage in optical painting is represented by work which is in very slight relief. Often this extra dimension is used to provide planes of colour which move as the spectator shifts his position in relation to them. The 'physichromes' of the

Ill. 143 Venezuelan Carlos Cruz-Diez are works of this nature, and so
Ill. 145 are some of those of the Israeli artist Yaacov Agam. The principle employed is rather like that to be found in some of the 'trick pictures' made in Victorian times, where one image is suddenly replaced by another, according to the viewpoint one adopts.

A more important artist who sometimes made use of effects of somewhat the same kind is another Venezuelan, J. R. Soto. Soto's original influences were Mondrian and Malevich. In the early 1950s he made paintings which created their effect by repetition of units. The units were so disposed that the rhythm

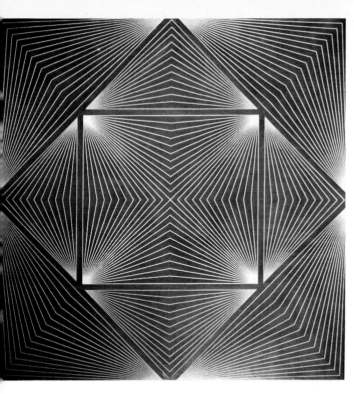

144 RICHARD
ANUSZKIEWICZ
Division of intensity 1964

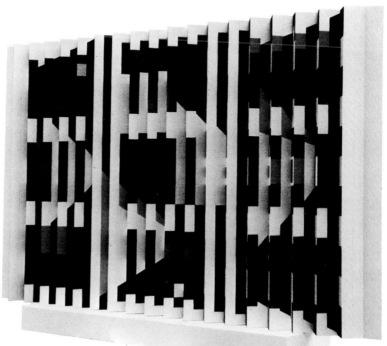

145 YAACOV AGAM *Appearance* 1965–6

which linked them came to seem more important to the eye than any individual part, and the painting was therefore, by implication at any rate, not something complete in itself, but a part taken from an infinitely large fabric which the spectator was asked to imagine. Soto then became interested in effects of superimposition, just as Vasarely did. Two patterns painted on perspex sheets were mounted very slightly apart, and seemed to blend together in a new space which hovered between the front and back planes supplied by the sheets. Later, Soto began a series of experiments with lined screens. These had metal plaques which projected in front of them, or else metal rods or

Ill. 147   wires are freely suspended before this vibrating ground. The vibration tends, from the optical point of view, to swallow up and dissolve the projecting or suspended solids. Each instant, as the spectator moves his eyes, a new wave of optical activity is

146 LUIGI TOMASELLO
Atmosphère
ébromo-plastique
no. 180 1967

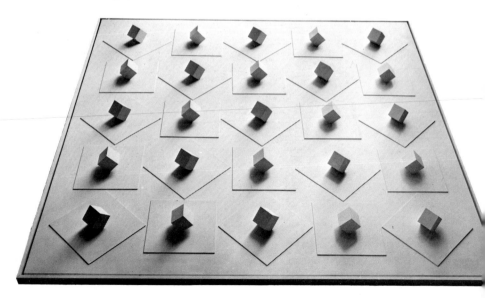

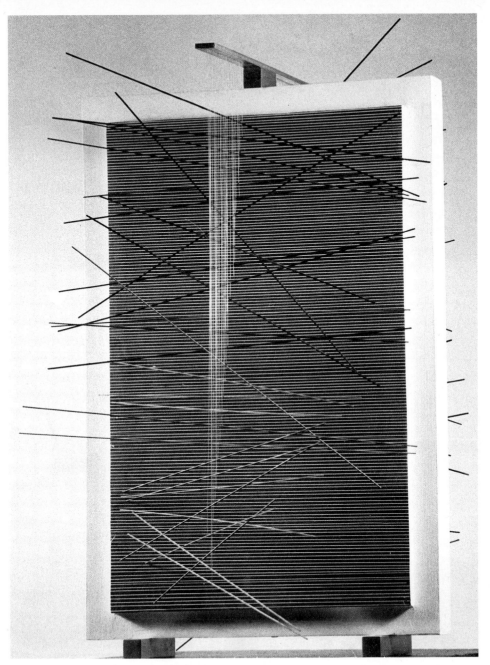

147 JESÚS RAFAEL SOTO *Petite Double Face* 1967

set up. The most intense of all Soto's works are large screens of hanging rods. Hung along the length of a wall, these layers of rods seem to dissolve the whole side of a room, calling into question all the spectator's instinctive reactions to an enclosed space.

Related to Soto's work, but using a slightly different principle, were the reliefs made by the Argentinian, Luigi Tomasello. *Ill. 146* Tomasello attached a series of hollow cubes at an angle to a white surface. The cubes themselves are also white on the outside, but brightly coloured within, and one of the surfaces invisible to the spectator is left open. By reflection, this produces effects of soft, shimmering coloured light on the ground to which the cubes are fastened.

On the borderline of kinetic art, but certainly quite close to Tomasello's work, are the reliefs and sculptures of the Brazilian, *Ill. 148* Sergio de Camargo. Camargo uses small cylindrical units, set at random angles so that the plane at the end of the cylinder is never square to the viewer, to cover the surfaces of his work. The work itself is usually painted white, so that each piece becomes an intricate play of reflections and shadows. Here, too, as in the work of all the South American artists I have just discussed, there seems to be a desire to dissolve everything solid, everything weighty, in favour of an ethereal play of light and colour. Distances, planes, and forms become ambiguous. However physically massive it may be in fact, the work seems weightless and floating.

Weightlessness, as part of the kinetic tradition, might be *Ill. 150* thought to go back to Alexander Calder. Calder was an artist who, while appearing to be lightweight in almost every sense, turned out to have had a powerful influence on the art of his time. Calder first exhibited his mobiles in the 1930s – the original idea came from a delicate and amusing toy circus he had made, but the mobiles themselves, with their brightly painted flanges connected by pivots and wires, seem to have taken a number of ideas from the paintings of Miró, a hypothesis which the Miró-like nature of Calder's drawings con-

178

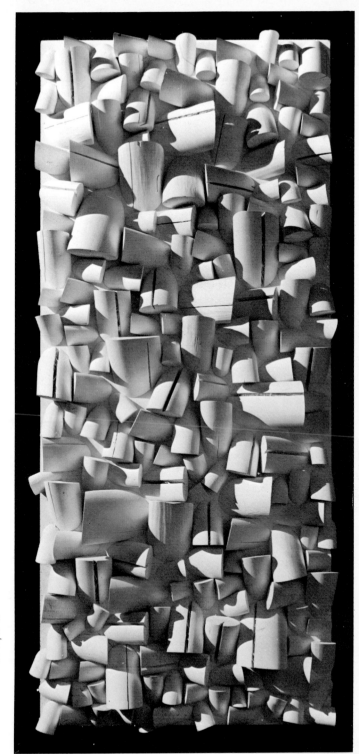

148 SERGIO DE
CAMARGO
*Large split white relief
no. 34/74 1965*

firms. But there was an important difference – the arrangement of shapes in a Calder mobile is of course always provisional, as one flange swings into a new relationship with the others. The possibilities of the object are, of course, governed by such things as the various points of balance, the length of the wires, and the weight of the flanges. The organized capriciousness which this system produces is a quality which is extremely characteristic of post-war kinetic art. Besides making mobiles, Calder also constructed what he called stabiles, some of the largest of which do not incorporate any moving parts at all. They provide an unexpected link between Calder's work and that of sculptors such as David Smith and Anthony Caro, whom I shall discuss in Chapter Eight. Meanwhile Calder, even in the mobiles, remained consistently more inventive than other artists who make sculpture which employs the same principles. One has only to compare Calder's mobiles with the far more *Ill. 149* cumbersome pieces of George Rickey, for instance.

149 GEORGE RICKEY *Summer III* 1962–3

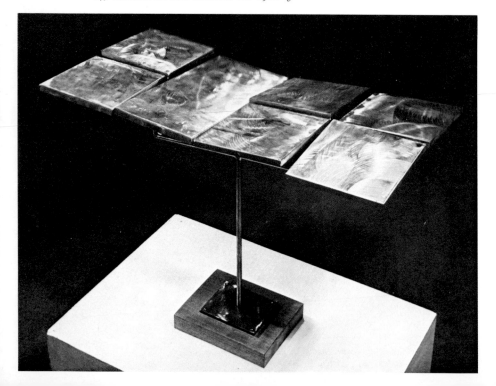

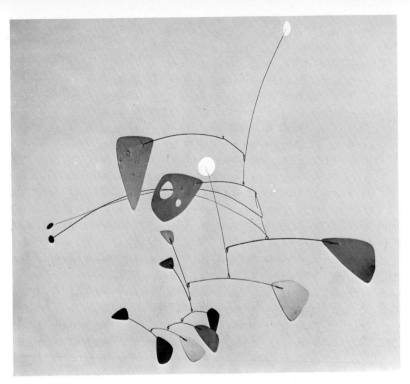

150 ALEXANDER CALDER *Antennae with red and blue dots* 1960

Where most people were concerned, it was the machine-powered objects which seemed the newest and the most fascinating when kinetic art suddenly became fashionable. In fact, works of art powered by machines are not as novel as they seem to be. Even if it is unnecessary to bring such things as the fountains of Versailles into the discussion, mechanically powered sculpture is something which can be traced back at least to the early 1920s. It is both constructivist and dadaist in ancestry. As early as 1920, Naum Gabo made a sculpture which consisted of a single vibrating rod. Duchamp and Man Ray, in the same year, produced the 'rotorelief', a circular glass plate which seemed, as it revolved, to present an illusory design.

Post-war kinetic art tended to reflect this double ancestry. Jean Tinguely's ramshackle mechanisms clearly owed a great deal to the 'mechanical compositions' made by Picabia at the height of the dada period, in 1917–19. Picabia's drawings were elegantly sardonic parodies of conventional blueprints, designs for machines which could never possibly work. One is slyly dedicated 'to the memory of Leonardo da Vinci'.

Tinguely's machines work, but only just. They groan and judder, and one suspects that they often develop both functions and malfunctions which were not anticipated by their author when he originally planned them. In fact, they have been labelled 'pseudomachines', because they move without function. Or sometimes they have functions which imply a satirical *Ill. 151* comment. Tinguely has made machines which produce abstract expressionist drawings, for instance. And perhaps the most famous of all his creations was the self-destructive machine

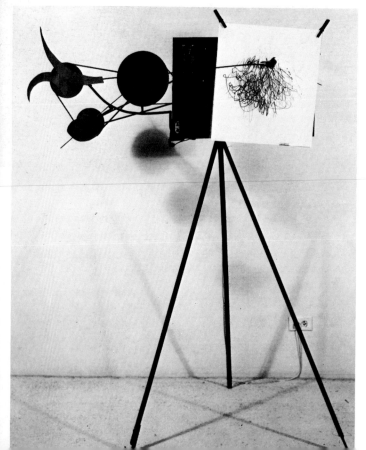

151 JEAN TINGUELY
Metamachine 4
1958–9

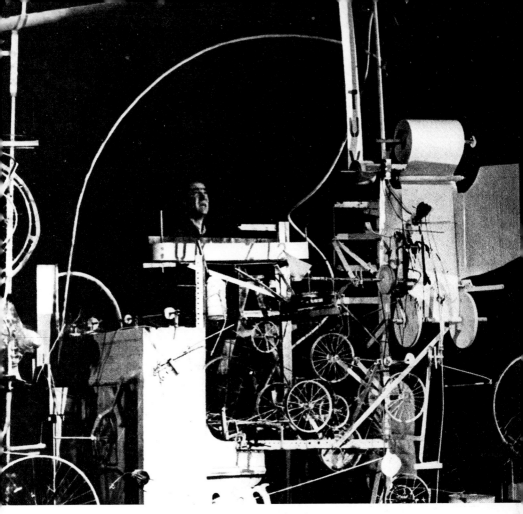

152 JEAN TINGUELY *Homage to New York* 1960

which he made for the sculpture garden of the Museum of Modern Art in New York in March 1960. This created a famous scandal.

Quite different from Tinguely, though often associated with him, is the Greek artist Takis. Where Tinguely mocks the *Ills 153,* clumsiness of machines, and the clumsiness of men in dealing *154*

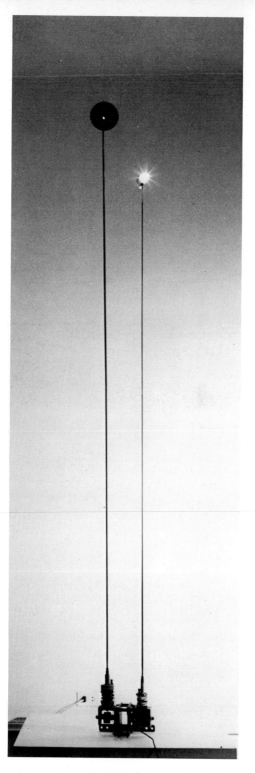

153 TAKIS
Signal 1966

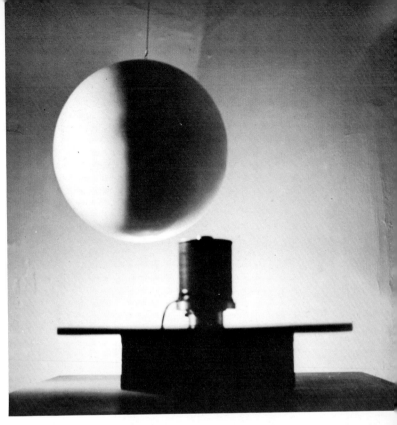

154 TAKIS *Electro magnetic* 1960–7

with them, Takis tries to exploit new technological possibilities. Some of his most interesting works are those which employ the principles of magnetism. In the *Magnetic ballets*, for instance, two magnets are suspended on threads from the ceiling. An electromagnet on a base switches itself on and off in a regular rhythm. When it is on, it attracts the positive pole of one magnet and repels the negative pole of the other. When it is off the two magnets seek each other. Alternatively, Takis will use a magnet to hold a needle suspended, quivering, in the air. What is new about these works is that they do not exist as form, but as an almost immaterial energy. The function of the visible parts is not to be interesting in themselves, but to demonstrate the operations of that energy.

185

Ill. 155

The point is perhaps made clearer if one contrasts the work of Takis with that of the Belgian, Pol Bury. Pol Bury belongs as firmly in the surrealist tradition as Tinguely belongs in the tradition of dada. His machines have their working parts hidden out of view. One critic has remarked on the fact that Bury's work is deliberately mystifying'.[4] His machines stir, stealthily, rather than moving in any very decisive or positive fashion. A set of little balls on a sloping plane click together, move upward with almost imperceptible jerks, instead of rolling down as one might expect. Clusters of needles, or waving feelers, rustle together. Fascinating as all this is, however, the movement is only part of what the work has to say. The slowest ones have a formal presence which strikes us even before we realize that they are in fact moving. The same is not true of any of Takis's inventions when deactivated.

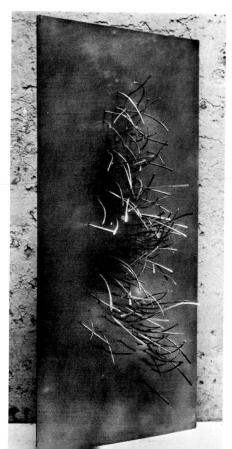

155 POL BURY
The Erectile Entities

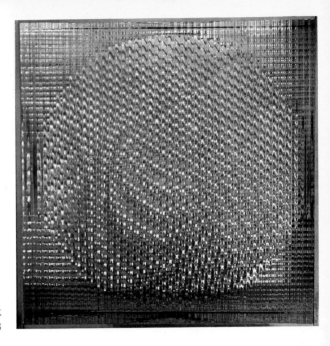

156 HEINZ MACK
Light dynamo 1963

Given this penchant for the immaterial, it seems inevitable
that Takis should have experimented with light. His celebrated
Signals were flashing lights held at the ends of long flexible rods   *Ill. 153*
– another means of expressing the force of the energy which
moves the universe.

In general, light has been the favourite medium of many
kinetic artists. The way in which it is used differs widely from
artist to artist. The German, Heinz Mack, for instance, used a
mechanization of the *moiré* principle. A disc rotating beneath   *Ill. 156*
a transparent, uniformly rippled glass surface makes the surface
itself ambiguous. It is not the motion itself which holds our
attention so much as the slow disturbance of the light rays
which are reflected back at us – these seem drawn into a vortex,
then spilled out again. On the other hand, the American, Frank
Malina, made light boxes, where constantly changing coloured
patterns were projected on to a plexiglass screen. The result was
merely an extension of free abstraction: a picture which never
arrives at its final state, but which is constantly undergoing a
process of metamorphosis.

More imaginative and more radical was the work offered by
artists such as Liliane Lijn and Nicolas Schöffer, though these
two are in sharp contrast to one another. Miss Lijn's *Liquid
reflections* traps drops of liquid under the clear perspex face of a
turntable. On the turntable, moving in counter-motion to its
rotation, is a perspex ball or group of balls. The liquid trapped
in the disc is affected by the movement of these solids, and
breaks up into patterns which are reminiscent of the patterns
which iron filings form under the action of a magnet. One can
observe these patterns closely, as the work is brilliantly lit.

Ill. 157

Schöffer is a baroque artist. His work turns and flashes,
sending out beams of light and flickering reflections. He
combines the movement of a piece of kinetic sculpture with
light projections which extend the movement deep into space.
The whole volume of air that surrounds the sculpture becomes
an ambiguous entity. Schöffer has, on occasion, gone even

Ill. 158

157 LILIANE LIJN *Liquid reflections* 1966–7

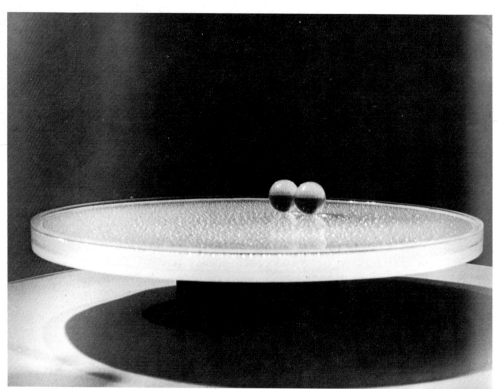

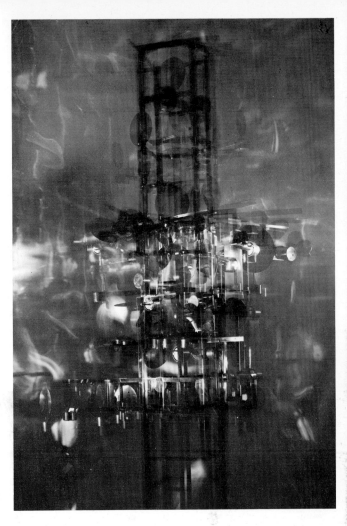

158 NICOLAS
SCHÖFFER
Chronos 8 1968

further than this, by producing work which reacts to the intensity of light, and to sounds. He has also experimented with combinations of light, kinetic movement, and music, notably in the light-and-sound tower which he constructed at Liège in 1961. Work of this kind seemed to translate the experiments of the seventeenth century into contemporary terms – some of Schöffer's enterprises are the equivalent of the masques contrived by Ben Jonson and Inigo Jones for the Stuart court.

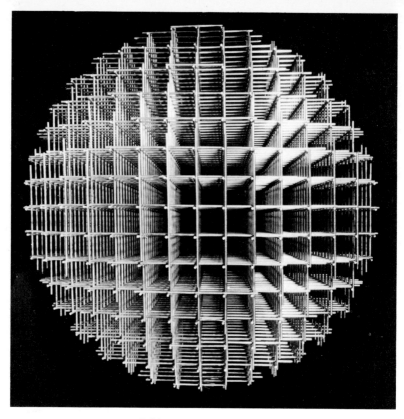

159 FRANÇOIS MORELLET *Sphère-trames* 1962

In fact, kinetic art in its heyday seemed to have two tendencies which both opposed and reinforced one another. One was the tradition of showmanship. Much kinetic art was 'exhibition art'. Its ambitions were environmental. The other was the tradition of scientific or pseudo-scientific research, which was typified by the Groupe de Recherche d'art visuel, founded in Paris in 1959, as a gesture of defiance towards the then triumphant fashion for informal abstraction.

Vasarely's son Yvaral was a member, but the two best-known associates of the group were probably the Argentinian Julio Le Parc, winner of the major prize at the Venice Biennale in 1966, and the Frenchman François Morellet.

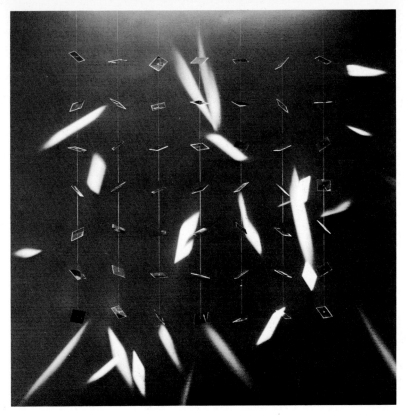

160 JULIO LE PARC *Continuel-mobile, Continuel-lumière* 1963

Le Parc creates devices which belong partly to the laboratory, *Ill. 160*
partly to the funfair. They are experiments with mechanisms,
and also experiments upon the psychology of the spectator.
Mirrors, distorting spectacles, balls which run through
complicated labyrinths – he has made use of all these things. Le
Parc is a minimalist in the sense that nothing he makes is ever
too heavy, or too serious. The spectator is not invited to read a
meaning into what he sees, but merely to react. In this sense Le
Parc is the equivalent of Johns or Cage in America.

Morellet is more severe. His best-known work is the *Sphère-* *Ill. 159*
trames ('Sphere-webs') – a sphere made up of rods laid at right
angles to one another to form a cellular structure which,

191

through its multiple perspectives, has strange effects on light. A related work is a lattice of fluorescent tubes, which seems to dissolve the wall behind it. Morellet, too, is an artist whose work is related to that of the minimalists in America.

The visual and psychological subtlety of kinetic art stood in marked contrast to the simplicity and even crudity of many of the mechanisms used. Some artists, notably Tinguely, even make this mechanical crudity a contributing element in their work. A few others reached a very respectable level of technological complexity by working in conjunction with industrial organizations. Schöffer created the Liège tower in collaboration with the firm of Philips NV. Usually, however, kinetic art aped technology from a distance. The reasons are twofold. Firstly, the limited financial resources available to the artist, or, more exactly, the fact that the kinetic artist was a maker of the 'one-off' in a field geared to volume production. Secondly, there is the fact that most kinetic artists had a very limited scientific background.

Whatever the reasons for this lack of technical sophistication, the claims made by kinetic artists that they were producing 'art for the technological age' must be taken with a pinch of salt. It would, indeed, be fairer to say that the sudden upthrust of kinetic art in the 1950s and early 1960s represented a kind of nostalgia for technology, rather than the presence of technology itself.

There have been one or two other developments in the arts which can be taken in conjunction with kineticism, though they do not add up to precisely the same thing. One is the tendency to compare scientific models, high-magnification photographs, and other by-products of scientific research, with the work of contemporary artists, and to claim that the frequent resemblances to be found there argue for a kinship between the new arts and the new sciences.

The trouble is that the resemblance is more often to the products of the free abstractionists than to those of any artist with an avowed commitment to science. What one sees is not the influence of science upon art, but of artists upon scientists. The most beautiful high-magnification photographs are often almost meaningless from the strictly scientific point of view, and the reason for taking them is aesthetic. Art has taught the photographer to look at his subject in a certain way, has made its appearance meaningful to him. It is one of the most prominent characteristics of the history of photography: the tendency for the man behind the camera to be influenced by whatever style of painting is dominant at the time. Thus, photographs taken by photographers in the Pre-Raphaelite circle tend to look like the paintings of Rossetti or Millais.

A new development in photography has been holography – photographs taken with laser beams which produce fully three-dimensional images behind, or sometimes even in front of, the transparent or reflective surface upon which the image is encoded. A hologram retains full three-dimensionality from *Ill. 161* whatever angle it is viewed. The artists who have experimented

161 STEPHEN BENTON *Crystal beginnings* 1977

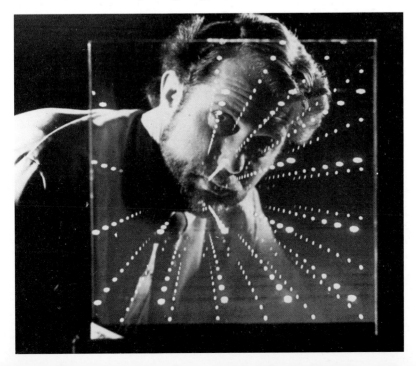

with holography are still trying to discover a viable holographic language. On the whole, abstract designs have so far been more successful aesthetically than figurative images.

Another aspect of the relationship between art and science has been represented by 'computer art' – experiments made to discover what computers could be programmed to produce, and also what they could be persuaded to do if certain random elements were introduced into the programming. The extent to which a computer can actually make art is a matter of dispute. One authority says: 'the computer is used as a tool for the spectator and artist, it does not produce art, but is used to manipulate thoughts and ideas which could be called art'.[5] What it produces at present, certainly in the field of the visual arts as opposed to that of music, tends to be uninteresting.

There is, however, the chance that interest in computers will eventually extend the capabilities of the visual artist, by forcing him to think in new ways. In analyzing ideas so that they can be fed to the machine, the artist is undertaking a more rigorous process of thought than perhaps he is accustomed to. Once programmed, the computer carries out the processes which it has been asked to carry out with unfaltering logic. It can be made to present as many different alternatives as the user desires, and analyses of the finished product can be stored for future use. As a labour-saving tool, the computer opens up a vastly broader range of chance operations, simply because it works both more surely and more rapidly than the artist can hope to do himself. In this sense, the computer can be said to extend the idea of freedom, which is to be found in the work of artists such as Pollock and Louis, into the intellectual as well as the physical sphere. But its full potentialities are unlikely to be realized until the operator can treat it as being as much an extension of his own mind as Pollock treated paint and canvas, rags and brushes as extensions of his own body.

Ills 14, 15, 78, 80

CHAPTER SEVEN

Sculpture: as it was

So far I have said little about sculpture. The reason for this is that sculpture was much slower in responding to the post-war situation. Partly, this was due to the fact that the situation itself seemed to reject what the sculptor had to offer. It was difficult, for example, for any artist to produce a satisfactory three-dimensional equivalent for the work of Jackson Pollock.

In Europe, however, there were a number of dominant figures among the sculptors. The chief of these were the Swiss Alberto Giacometti and the Englishman Henry Moore. It is convenient to speak first of Giacometti, as he stands conspicuously alone. He began as a surrealist, and by force of talent made himself very much a leading figure in the movement during the 1930s. Such works as *The Palace at 4 a.m.* and *Woman with her throat cut* still retain all their original force as works of art. In 1935, however, he felt the urge to work again from the model, and his 'reactionary' activity led to his being excluded from the surrealist group. He made no attempt to exhibit his work again until 1948. *Ill. 162*

The second phase of Giacometti's career really begins in 1940, when he ceased working from the model. The sculptor has left a famous description of what occurred:

> To my terror the sculptures became smaller and smaller. Only when small were they like, and all the same these dimensions revolted me, and tirelessly I began again, only to end up, a few months later, at the same point. A big figure seemed to me to be false and a small one just as intolerable, and then they became so minuscule that often with a final stroke of the knife they disappeared into dust.[1]

Ill. 163   In exploring these attenuated images, Giacometti was acting out, through the medium of sculpture, some of the leading ideas of existentialist doctrine, a fact of which the artist was well aware, since he and Jean-Paul Sartre were close friends. One way of looking at existentialism is to regard it as both a continuation of surrealism and a rejection of it. What it has in common with surrealism is the emphasis which it places upon subjectivity; where it differs is in the fact that it puts stress upon the notion, not only of reality, but of responsibility to reality, however ungraspable this may prove to be.

Yet, though existentialism itself enjoyed an immense intellectual influence, Giacometti was almost the only artist to echo it so precisely in his work. He is almost as isolated as a sculptor as his own figures are in space. Perhaps the artist who comes nearest to him is the Frenchwoman Germaine Richier, the proportions of whose figures often seem to owe something to Giacometti. But there is an important difference. Richier was interested not so much in the problem of reality, and the effort to seize reality, as in the presentation of visual metaphors. In *Ill. 164*   *The Hurricane*, for example, a male figure becomes a threatening

162 ALBERTO GIACOMETTI *Woman with her throat cut* 1932

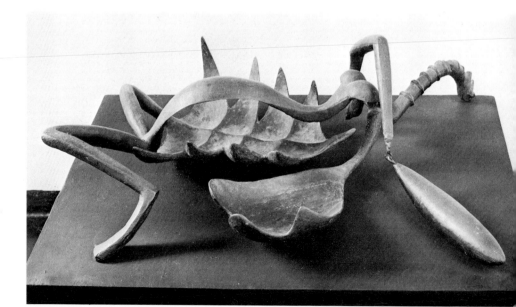

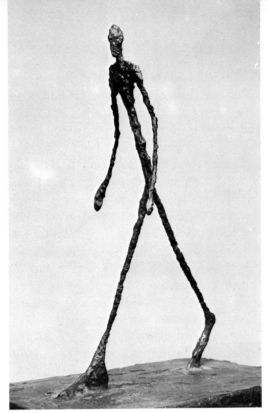

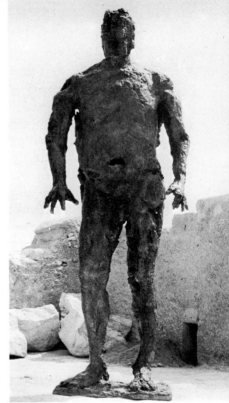

163 ALBERTO GIACOMETTI
Man walking III 1960

164 GERMAINE RICHIER
The Hurricane 1948–9

storm; the form dissolves before our eyes. Essentially, this is a modern variant of baroque allegory.

Giacometti's importance lies, not in his influence over other artists, but in his impact upon the public. In his later work, he created one of the truly recognizable stereotypes of post-war art.

Besides Giacometti, the other major sculptor of the immediately post-war years was Henry Moore. It was surprising that an Englishman should find himself in such a commanding position. Since the end of the Middle Ages, the English sculptural tradition has been a feeble and intermittent one. The last English sculptor to achieve much influence abroad, before Moore's arrival on the scene, was the neoclassicist John Flaxman, and even so it was Flaxman's drawings (his illustrations to the *Iliad* and the *Odyssey*) which won him the respect of his European contemporaries.

Moore has been an important figure in English art ever since the 1930s. During that decade, he was connected with both the major art movements then active in England, surrealism and constructivism. He did not, however, commit himself fully to either of these, but evolved, instead, a personal manner which used elements taken from both, and which also showed the influence of primitive cultures (such as ancient Mexican art) and of the English romantic tradition. The principal themes of Moore's work were soon established: the reclining female figures, the groups of a mother and a child, the more abstract stringed forms. Moore is essentially a biomorphic sculptor, and thus more a surrealist than a constructivist. Two ideas which much influenced him were those of 'truth to materials', and of revealing the full potential of the sculptural form. It was the latter which led him to pierce the forms which he used, to explore the effect of placing one form within another. He also had a keen sense of sculptural metaphor; as the English critic David Sylvester commented:

> Moore's metamorphic forms reveal marvellous and un-suspected likenesses between disparate things, but the revelation is like that of some elemental truth: once recognized, it seems inevitable; it may not lose its mystery, but it does lose its surprise; it seems right and natural, reasonable, not outlandish and questionable.[2]

When the war came, Moore, like a number of other leading British modernists, such as Graham Sutherland, felt the impulse to bring his art closer to the expectations of the mass audience. The result was the creation of works such as the *Northampton Madonna* and the series of 'shelter drawings', a tribute to the stoic endurance of Londoners under the Blitz. The work he did at this period confirmed Moore's stature in the public mind. In 1946, a retrospective exhibition of his work was held at the

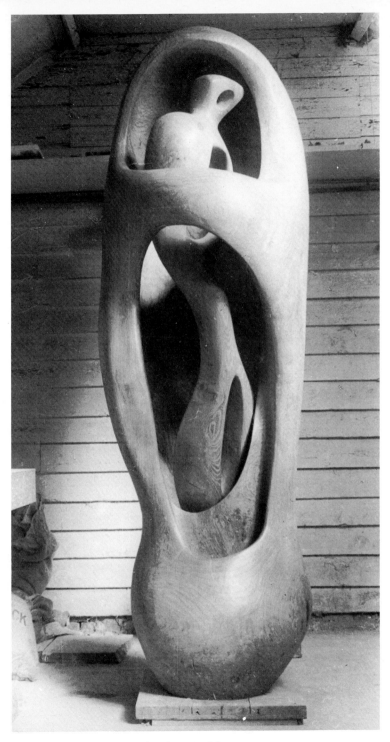

165 HENRY MOORE *Internal and external forms* 1953–4

Museum of Modern Art in New York, the first of over a hundred such retrospectives to be held abroad. The show made a deep impression, and when, in 1948, Moore won the major prize at the Venice Biennale, his international reputation was assured.

Since 1946, Moore has continued to develop the themes which interested him in the 1930s, and some new ones have been added – the sculptures derived from the forms of bones, for example. But in some respects his later career has been a disappointment. He has moved away from materials such as stone and wood, and has made increasing numbers of works in *Ill. 165* bronze, many of them enlarged, with the help of assistants and by traditional methods, from smaller models. It is true that this reflects, not so much a radical break with his previous practice, but the increased scope of the opportunities now being offered to him – the chance to create large-scale public monuments in particular. But too often this later work has seemed flaccid and insensitive compared with what he did earlier.

There is also a sense in which the whole development of post-war sculpture has been a criticism of the things which Moore has always stood for. Naturally, as his work has become more familiar, so it has come to seem less radical. The reclining figures can now be seen to have a clear relationship with the reclining figures of classical art – those of the Parthenon pediments, for instance, and those on Michelangelo's Medici tombs. They are often closer to these predecessors than to anything which has succeeded them. Even Moore's most abstract *Ill. 166* works, such as the big *Locking-piece* of 1963–4, have a deliberately monumental quality – and the sense of the monumental is one of the things which younger sculptors have most reacted against. The American art critic Clement Greenberg caused a mild uproar in the English art world when, in a published interview with me, he criticized what he felt to be Moore's wish to produce 'masterpieces'.[3] The concept of the 'masterpiece' has also played a somewhat controversial role in recent sculpture, because it seems to imply that the spectator is being

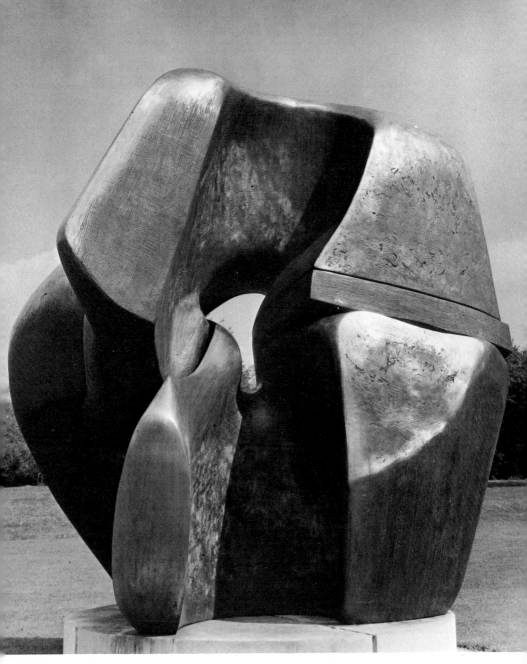

166 HENRY MOORE *Locking-piece* 1963–4

Ills 167, 168

courted in some way, and, in addition, that he is being asked to focus on the personality of the artist and not on the work.

Next to Moore, the most respected British sculptor of the older generation was Barbara Hepworth. Essentially, Hepworth's art sprang from the same intellectual and cultural ethos as Moore's, and she used some of the same formal devices, notably piercing and stringing. But she was a cooler artist, a superb craftsman in wood and stone whose best work has an aloofness and purity which have not been among Moore's aims. More clearly even than Moore, Hepworth belongs to a previous age. One finds the best comparisons for her work among the pioneer modernists, sculptors such as Arp and Brancusi, and few links with sculptors younger than herself. Hepworth provides a striking demonstration of the fact that there were two modernisms rather than one, and that the two often had little to say to one another.

Moore, however, is not as isolated as Hepworth or Giacometti. There is a whole 'middle generation' of sculptors who owe a great deal, both to his influence and to his example.

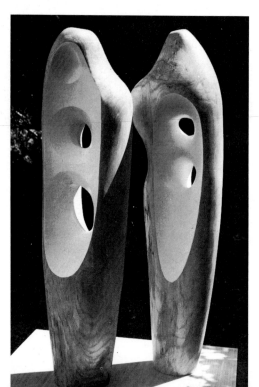

167 BARBARA HEPWORTH
Two figures 1947–8

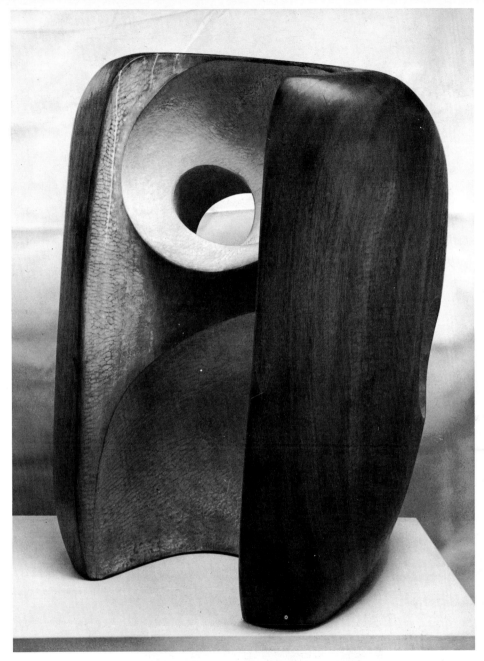

168 BARBARA HEPWORTH *Hollow form (Penwith)* 1955 (Collection The Museum of Modern Art, New York)

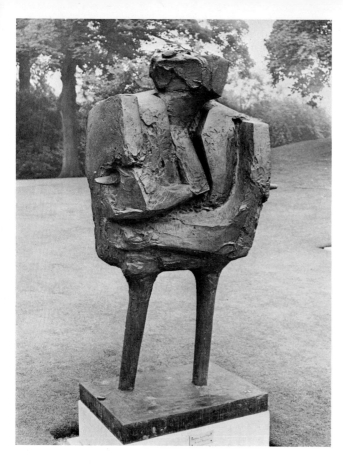

169 BERNARD MEADOWS
Standing armed figure 1962

170 KENNETH ARMITAGE *Figure lying on its side (version 5)* 1958–9

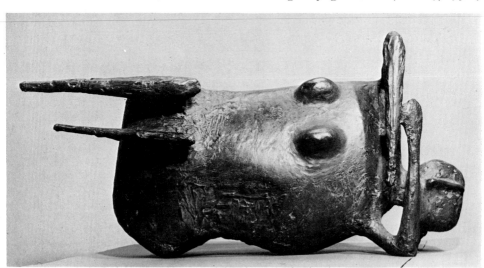

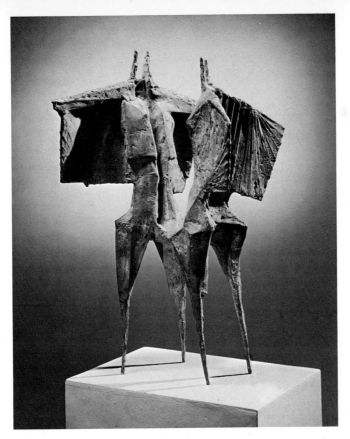

171 LYNN CHADWICK *Winged figures* 1955

Among them are artists such as Kenneth Armitage, Lynn *Ills 169–71,*
Chadwick, Reg Butler, and Bernard Meadows. During the *173*
1950s these sculptors enjoyed a very considerable success.

In varying degrees, their work was figurative. It kept to the
human scale, perhaps for the reason that Reg Butler once gave
to an interviewer, that it was no longer possible to imagine
men with the stature of gods.[4] Certainly Butler's female nudes
are not heroic. They have a keen and rather wry eroticism.
Even Armitage, when eventually he moved away from
figuration to become the most abstract of the group, made a
kind of sculpture which was still to the measure of mankind.

All of these are things which divide a now senior group of sculptors from their younger colleagues. But there is often a vast difference in technique as well, for the artists I have just mentioned are modellers; they work in plaster and then in bronze. Compare their work to that of sculptors such as Anthony Caro or Phillip King, who are scarcely, if at all, younger, and they seem the inhabitants of a different universe.

But British sculptors were not the only ones who, in this immediately post-war period, seemed to be seeking a compromise between modernism and what people had traditionally expected of sculpture. In Italy, for instance, there were a number of sculptors who strove to come to terms with the Italian past, among them Marino Marini, Emilio Greco, and Giacomo Manzù. Marini's bronze horsemen and Greco's

172 MARINO MARINI *Horse and rider* 1947

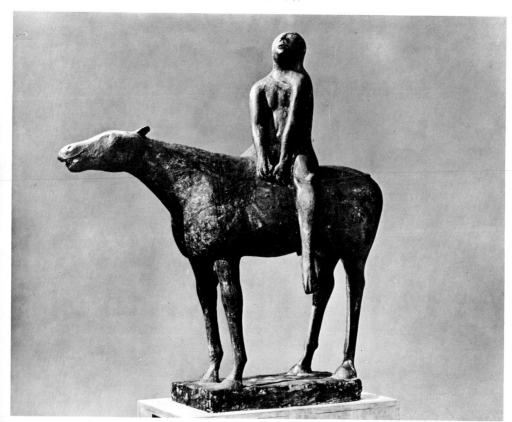

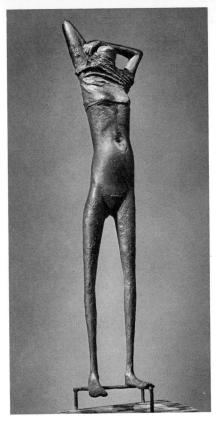 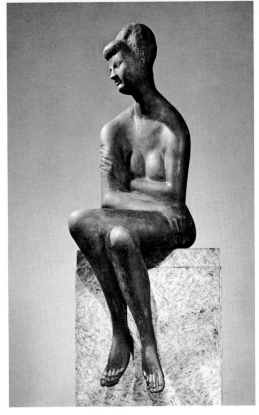

173 REG BUTLER *Girl* 1953–4   174 EMILIO GRECO *Seated figure* 1951

female nudes are seductive images which seem, ultimately, to
fail because of their superficiality. In Marini's horsemen, for
instance, one catches echoes both of Etruscan art (as with
Giacometti) and of the lively polo-players modelled by Chinese
potters in the T'ang dynasty. Greco, too, seems to allude to
Etruscan sculpture, especially that of the later period. Indeed,
for all their apparent simplicity and straightforwardness, these
are two very sophisticated artists, and they require from their
audience the kind of response which summons up memories of
the art of earlier ages. Perhaps for this reason, disillusionment
follows swiftly upon the heels of pleasure when one looks at

Ill. 172

Ill. 174

their work. For what is being alluded to, or hinted at, is more powerful than the sculpture which is the object of contemplation.

Of these three sculptors, Giacomo Manzù is in many ways *Ill. 175* the most interesting. In works such as his *Fruit and vegetables on a chair*, a poker-faced reproduction of reality, he seems to anticipate some of the ideas of pop art; and in the bronze doors which he designed for St Peter's in Rome, he attempts the traditional role of the sculptor who subordinates his work to a religious or commemorative purpose. In ways, the panels for these doors are an impressive feat. The technique of very low relief, which derives from Donatello, is handled with extreme *Ill. 176* sensitivity and skill. The imagery, with its fierce condemnation of cruelty and injustice, exerts a genuine popular appeal. Manzù comes closer, in these panels, to being a genuine 'populist' than does his compatriot Renato Guttuso. And when the sculptor chooses, in one of the panels, to show the death of *Ill. 177* Pope John XXIII, we are convinced that he has been genuinely moved by a contemporary event, and has tried to communicate his emotion.

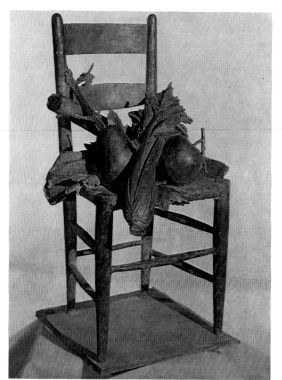

175 GIACOMO MANZÙ
Fruit and vegetables on a chair 1960

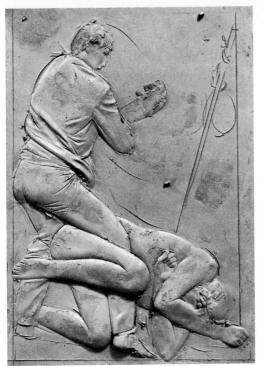 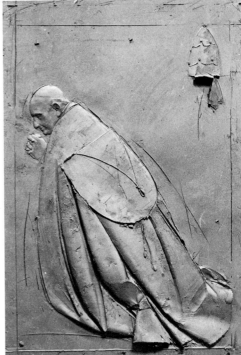

176 GIACOMO MANZÙ *The Death of Abel* 1964   177 MANZÙ *The Death of Pope John* 1964

The trouble is that the very virtuosity of the workmanship emphasizes the lack of true inventiveness. These illustrations – sacred strip cartoons, one might almost call them – are an anthology of other men's ideas. Not only Donatello but Bernini, not only Bernini but Medardo Rosso has been laid under contribution. The hints and borrowings have not been fully assimilated, as Picasso, for example, has usually been able to assimilate his countless borrowings. The great ghosts of Italian art haunt Manzù's work and will not be exorcized.

A less ambitious, and more forward-looking tendency in Italian sculpture is represented by the work of Arnaldo Pomodoro. Pomodoro began his career as a stage designer, and *Ill. 180* then began to make jewellery. His first exhibition of sculpture was not held until 1955.

209

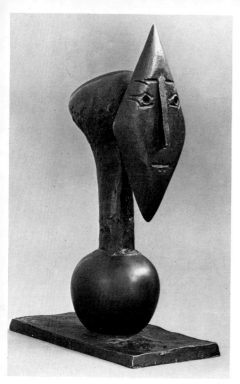

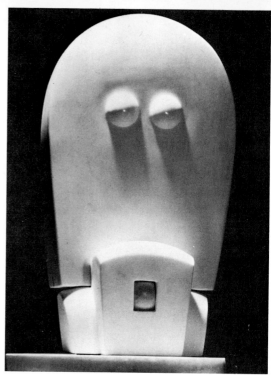

178 PABLO PICASSO
Head of a woman 1951

179 ANDREA CASCELLA
The White Bride 1962

His work, though often executed on a very large scale, has something of the jeweller about it still. Smoothly polished metal surfaces split open to reveal roughened interiors full of complex forms. Pomodoro is a brilliantly skilful craftsman in metal, whose work always reveals a keen eye for the nature and possibilities of his material. But, like Antonio Tapiés, he seems essentially a maker of luxury objects, which titillate the senses without offering any kind of intellectual challenge.

Much the same criticism might be made of Andrea Cascella's finely finished work in marble, though Cascella straddles two worlds. In one sense he resembles Barbara Hepworth: he is a carver who gives us beautiful materials, beautifully used. But

Ill. 179

210

his interest in the constructive aspect – the way in which the sculptures are made in separate parts, which lock intricately together – hints at the concerns of an apparently quite different kind of art, exemplified in the metal constructions of Chillida, which are discussed in the next chapter.

Though, as I noted at the beginning of this chapter, American sculpture found it difficult to respond to the challenge of abstract expressionism, there were a number of sculptors in the United States who strove to learn from the new style. The most important of these is David Smith, whose work eventually moved so far outside the original abstract expressionist orbit that it will be more useful to discuss it later. Among the others

180 ARNALDO POMODORO *Sphere no. 1* 1963 (Collection The Museum of Modern Art, New York)

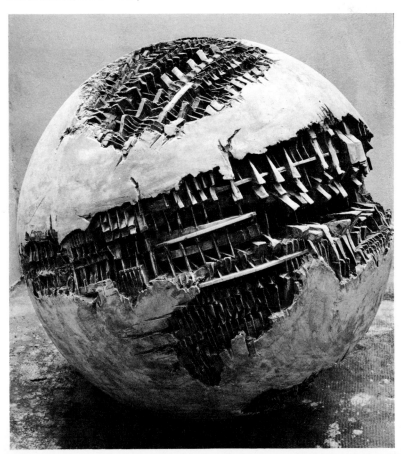

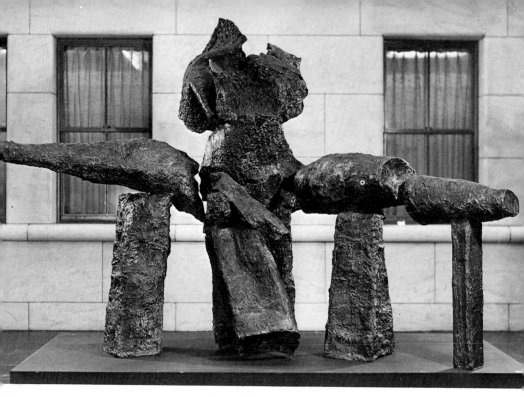

181 REUBEN NAKIAN *The Goddess of the Golden Thighs* 1964–5

Ill. 185
Ill. 183

Ill. 182

Ills 181, 186

who were touched by abstract expressionist concepts were Ibram Lassaw, Herbert Ferber, Theodore Roszak, and Reuben Nakian. Lassaw's open, rather calligraphic work in metal is like the strokes of abstract expressionist brushwork, transferred to a different medium. Ferber experimented with direct welding, perhaps because this seemed to provide an equivalent for the spontaneity with which an artist like Pollock used paint. It is perhaps significant that there is something of a time-lag between the establishment of the new style in painting and its impact in sculpture (this was also true of the sculpture which cubism inspired). Nakian, for instance, who is perhaps the freest and most direct of all the artists I have just listed, embarked on his most abstract expressionist phase only at the beginning of the 1960s. The forms he then used also seem to owe something

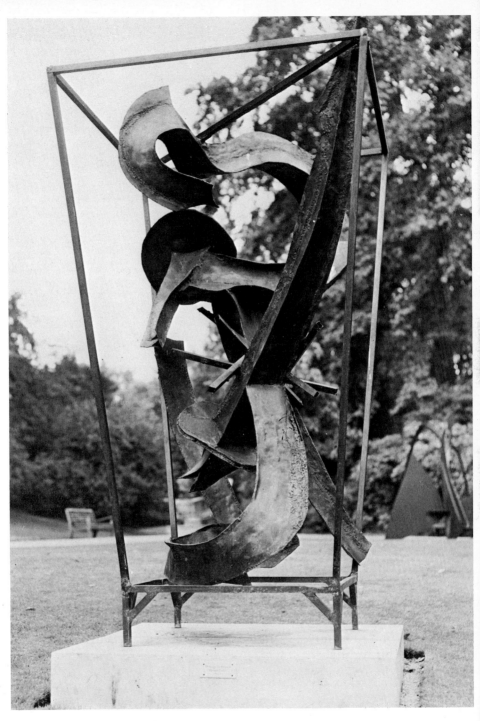

182 HERBERT FERBER *Homage to Piranesi* 1962–3

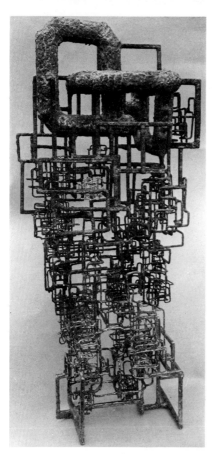

183 IBRAM LASSAW
Space densities 1967

184 ALEXANDER CALDER
The Red Crab 1962

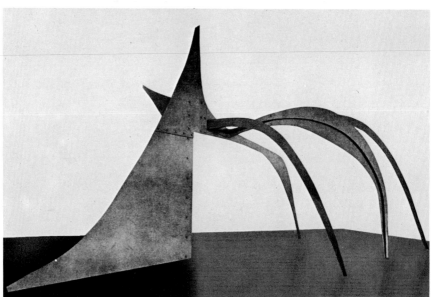

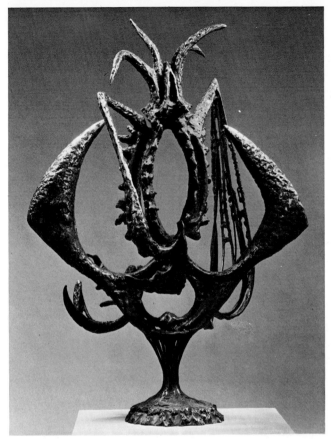

185 THEODORE ROSZAK *Invocation I* 1947

to the billowing veils of paint with which Morris Louis had
been experimenting.

There is a very marked break, however, between the sculpture which I have been discussing in this chapter, and that which
I shall deal with in the next. One is tempted to describe them as
two different art forms, so radical is the difference in attitudes
and techniques. The work I have described is work by artists
who have been content with the traditional categories: they
have tried to participate in the modernist revolution, but they
have also had a bond with the great sculptors of the past. What

215

they make – the imagery – might seem strange to a man of the Renaissance. But he would find their techniques familiar: the casting of metal, the carving of wood and stone. What is more, the man of the Renaissance would agree, very largely, with these successors on the subject of how a work of sculpture *functions*. A monumental piece by Henry Moore, and one by Giovanni da Bologna, are things which belong to the same intellectual ordering. Many of the objects I shall now describe spring from wholly different premises, which Giovanni da Bologna would not have understood.

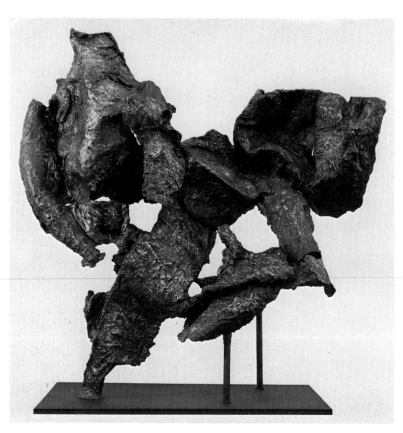

186 REUBEN NAKIAN *Olympia* 1960–2

The new sculpture

Pinpointing how the new sculpture began is a difficult matter. Certain developments and certain ideas seem important in the light of hindsight, but one cannot say that they led inevitably to the break. Some of these developments belong to the early part of the post-war period, others took place earlier. Calder's mobiles, and the welded metal sculptures of Julio González, are important progenitors. The webs of glittering wires created by the American sculptor Richard Lippold in the 1940s foreshadow a more recent feeling for a seemingly weightless sculpture which engulfs and embraces space. The texturing of tiny cog-wheels and small machine-parts which the British sculptor Eduardo Paolozzi applied to the surface of his early bronzes predicts the much bolder use of ready-made components which was to come into fashion some years later. And of course the whole concept of the 'ready-made' was the brainchild of Marcel Duchamp. From this there eventually flowed the idea that sculpture could take almost any form.

Ill. 188

Ill. 187

Ill. 189

It was the new interest in assemblage, following on the heels of abstract expressionism, which brought with it the first stirrings of the new sculpture. An extremely personal example was set by Jean Dubuffet. His work in three dimensions includes figures made of clinker, sponge, charcoal, and vine-shoots. The irrepressible Yves Klein made three-dimensional works from blue-dyed sponges at the end of long stalks. What creations like these seemed to indicate was the desire to question the role of the role of the more traditional sculptor, imagining forms and then imposing them on the surrounding universe.

One consequence of this interest was an apparent revival of the surrealist 'object', an extension into three dimensions of the collage. Rauschenberg's stuffed goat, already described, had

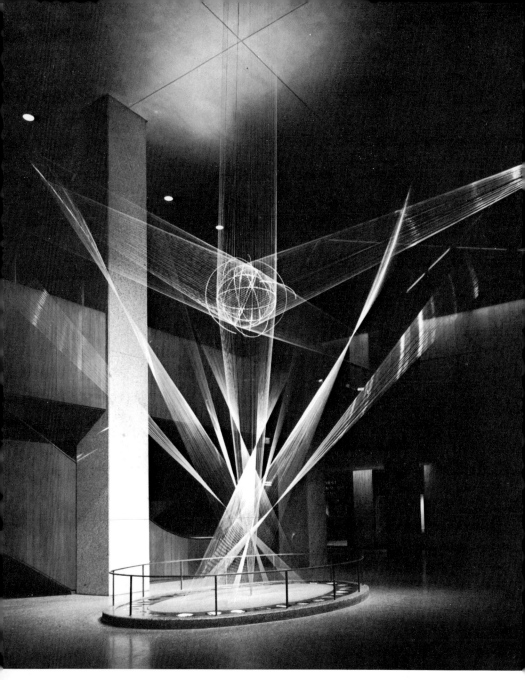

187 RICHARD LIPPOLD *Flight* 1962

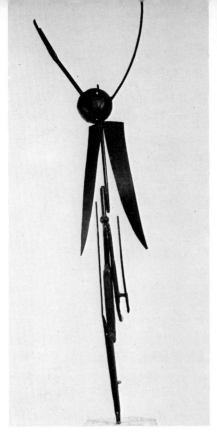 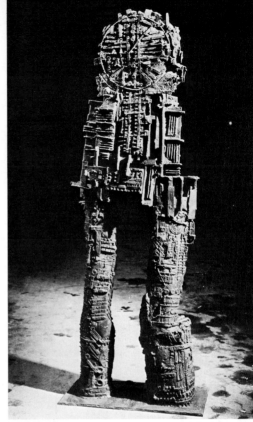

188 JULIO GONZÁLEZ *The Angel* 1933   189 EDUARDO PAOLOZZI *Japanese War God* 1958

already been anticipated by such things as Miró's *Poetic object* of 1936, which is crowned by a stuffed parrot; by Brauner's *Wolf-table* of 1939, which features the head and tail of a stuffed wolf; and even by Meret Oppenheim's celebrated fur teacup. But it was the more strictly sculptural uses of the collage idea which were to have large consequences for the future.

For instance, the American sculptor Louise Nevelson began by using smooth abstract shapes, in a way that was almost comparable to Hepworth. Then she moved towards assemblage: the fitting together of ready-made wooden shapes, such as the splats and backs of chairs, knobs and banisters from

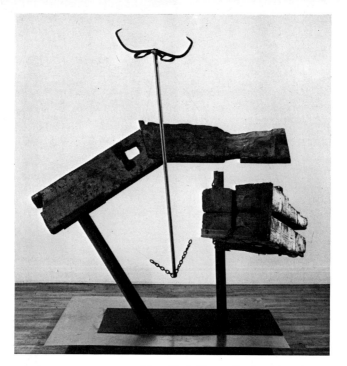

190 MARK DI SUVERO *New York Dawn (for Lorca)* 1965

demolished houses, scrolls and bits of moulding. These fragments are associated within compartments and boxes, and the
boxes themselves are often assembled to form large screens or
Ill. 191   walls. The fact that these intricate sculptures are painted a
uniform colour – white, black, or gold – stresses what would in
any case be clear. Nevelson uses her wide range of wooden
shapes as a grammar of form, and it is the relationship between
them which interests her, rather than each shape in isolation.
The triumph of relationship over form is one of the themes of
the new sculpture.

But despite Nevelson's work, and that of certain other
Ill. 190   artists, such as Mark di Suvero, it was metal, not wood, which
was the favoured material of the first wave of the new sculptors.
One reason for this was the 'junk ethos' which had much to do
with the popularity of assemblage techniques among painters

220

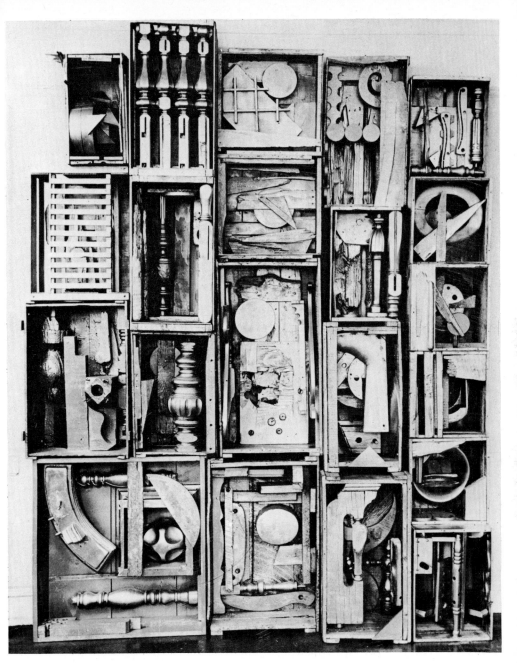

191 LOUISE NEVELSON *Royal Tide V* 1960

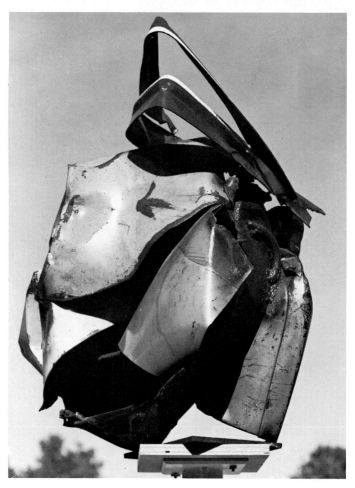

192 JOHN CHAMBERLAIN *Untitled* 1960

and sculptors alike. Junk, in a technological society, is apt to be
Ill. 192 the fragments of wrecked machines. John Chamberlain's
sculptures made from parts of wrecked automobiles, and
Ill. 193 Richard Stankiewicz's, created from scrap steel parts welded
together, were comments on consumer culture. The artists I
have just mentioned are American, but Europeans worked on
the same lines, notably César, who arrived at his *Compressions*

dirigées, objects made with the help of the giant machines which Ill. 194 are used for baling old automobiles and other metal scrap into packages of convenient size.

More important than any of these, however, was David Smith, who occupies almost the same position in the history of post-war sculpture as Pollock does in that of post-war painting. Indeed, there are reasons for regarding Smith as the more important figure. Pollock's work was an assertion of the rights of the individual: the interior world of dream was opposed to the exterior world of fact; the paintings themselves were a rejection of the mechanistic. But it is one of the distinctive things about Smith's work that it could only be the product

193 RICHARD STANKIEWICZ
Kabuki Dancer 1956

194 CÉSAR
Dauphine 1961

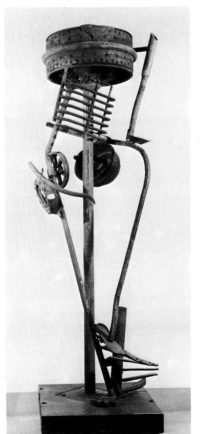

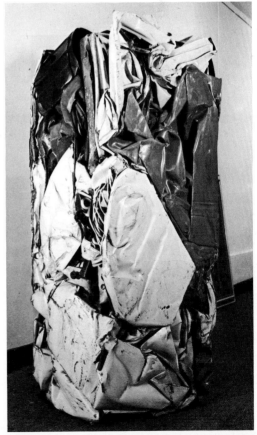

of a highly developed technological civilization. He was a Mid-Westerner, and not only worked in an automobile plant as a young man, but returned to heavy industry during the Second World War. These facts are as crucial to an understanding of his work as the knowledge that he was influenced by Picasso and Julio González.

Smith was born in 1906, and it was in the mid 1920s that he moved to New York and turned painter: among his early associates were Arshile Gorky and Willem de Kooning. When he abandoned painting for sculpture (this happened in the early 1930s) Smith did not think of this as marking a sharp break in his career, or a radical change of interest. As he said later, 'I never recognized any separation except one element of dimension.' At this period, his mind ranged freely over what European artists were doing, though he knew their work for the most part only from reproductions in books and art magazines. He noted: 'While my technical liberation came from Picasso's friend and countryman González, my aesthetics were more influenced by Kandinsky, Mondrian and cubism.'[1]

Even at this period, Smith was doing some important and original work. There are sculptures made in the 1930s from steel and ready-made or 'found' steel parts, which come remarkably close to what Stankiewicz was to produce at a much later epoch. Already, industrial techniques provided Smith with a personal language. Frank O'Hara said of him:

> From the start, Smith took the cue from the Spaniards to lead him toward the full utilization of his factory-skills as an American metal-worker, especially in the aesthetic use of steel glorifying rather than disguising its practicality and durability as a material for heavy industry.[2]

When the war ended, Smith was already a respected artist in mid-career. The Museum of Modern Art had acquired a sculpture by him in 1943. In 1944, he was able to return full time to sculpture, and in January 1946 there was a large-scale retrospective of his work in two New York art galleries. It was

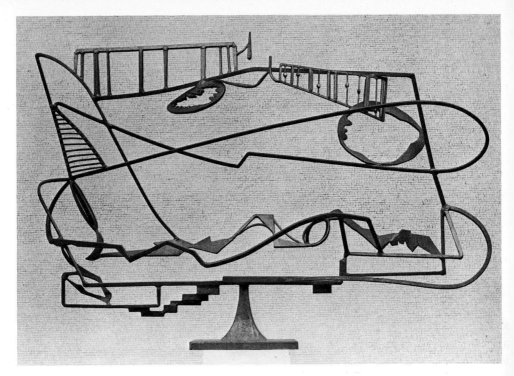

195 DAVID SMITH *Hudson River landscape* 1951

the succeeding years which established him as a key figure, however. First, he went through a linear phase, where the sculptures were like drawings in metal. It is significant that some of the work of this phase is concerned with ideas about landscape: a piece like the well-known *Hudson River landscape* of *Ill. 195* 1951 is almost 'anti-sculptural', both in aims and in effect. The openness of this work, and of others like it, was a portent for the future.

Later in the 1950s, Smith's work became even more unconventional, and larger and larger in scale. Smith was a prodigious worker, and the techniques he adopted enabled him to work very rapidly and freely. In 1962, for example, he was invited by the organizers of the Spoleto Festival to spend a month in Italy, and was offered an old factory as a workshop.

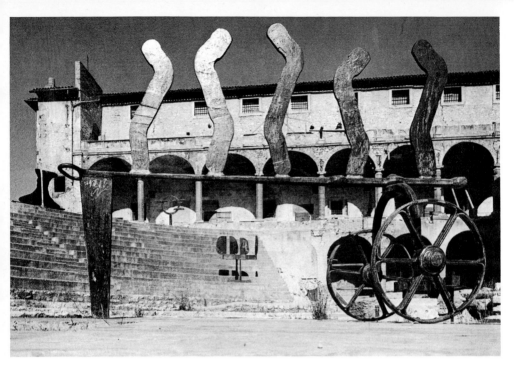

196 DAVID SMITH *Voltri VII* 1962

Ill. 196   He made twenty-six sculptures in thirty days, many of them
gigantic. In fact, the series rather than the individual piece had
now become Smith's chosen means of expression: a single idea
would be put through a great many permutations, until the
artist felt that it had been taken far enough.

These ideas were themselves highly original. In the early
series, *Agricola* and *Tank totem*, Smith is still interested in the
figurative, and, more specifically, in the human figure. Later
he moved towards a more abstract style, in the series he labelled
Ill. 197   *Zig* and *Cubi*. The *Cubi* series, in particular, has an unstable,
dynamic quality which seems very typical of Smith's work.

Smith was a revolutionary artist in a number of ways. The
first, and perhaps the most important, of these is the fact that,
though he worked on a monumental scale, especially towards
the end of his life (he was killed in a car crash in 1965), he is not

226

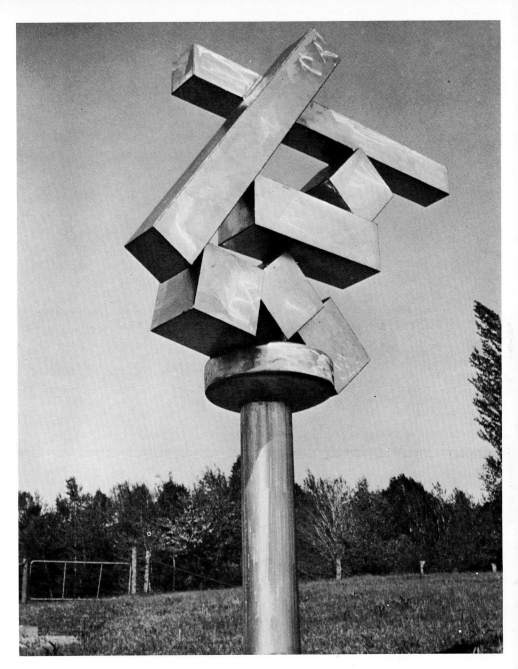

197 DAVID SMITH *Cubi XVIII* 1964

a monumental sculptor in the strict sense. There often seems to be a deliberate avoidance of the massive; there is a lack of sculptural density which can seem disconcerting. No image which Smith produced remains in the mind in the way that Moore's or Brancusi's images do. The shapes are ready-made and their arrangement seems provisional. One sculpture, seen in isolation, is usually much less effective than several from the same series, viewed together or in sequence. The fact that Smith sometimes painted his work, or at other times gave it a rough polish, the raw glitter of metal which is only part of the way through some process of manufacture, reinforces these re-actions. Like the post-painterly abstractionists, Smith tended to eschew associations; in this he is very different from a sculptor such as Moore, who seems to want to summon up the powers of nature – rocks, water, and wind – to help him in his task. All of these procedures and preferences were to be influential upon younger men.

The only other sculptor to enjoy anything like David Smith's prestige in the 1960s and early 1970s was an Englishman, Anthony Caro. Caro, too, made use of ready-made steel parts – I-beams, sheet-steel, pieces of coarse metal mesh – which are assembled in sprawling compositions. He said, in an interview with Andrew Forge in 1966:

Ills 198, 209

> I would really rather make my sculpture out of 'stuff' – out of something really anonymous, just sheets maybe, which you cut a bit off. . . . Much of the sculpture that I'm doing is about extent, and might even get to be about fluidity or something of this sort, and I think one has to hold it from becoming just amorphous.[3]

In fact, Caro was widely recognized as David Smith's heir – paradoxical because he is not only English, but was once (like so many British sculptors) one of Henry Moore's assistants.

But it would be wrong to suggest that Smith and Caro had exactly the same sculptural preoccupations. To take the most obvious difference first: Caro's work usually has a horizontal

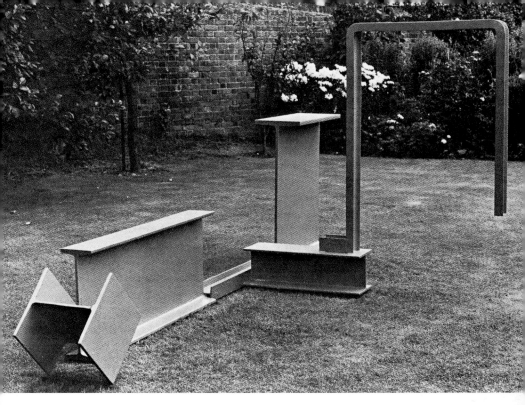

198 ANTHONY CARO *Homage to David Smith* 1966

emphasis, as opposed to the verticality of most of Smith's late sculpture. Caro's sculptures could be described as being both space-devouring and ground-devouring. The base had been abolished, and each piece took possession of a certain territory, and modified the spectator's reactions to the space in which it is put. Smith, like Moore, preferred to have his work shown in the open air; Caro, on the contrary, seemed to like an enclosed space, which the piece can occupy and activate. Most of his earlier sculptures are painted a unifying colour, which often seems chosen for its ambiguity, its quality of making us feel uncertain whether the object we are looking at is heavy or light. A number of his small sculptures, often made to balance on the edge of a table, with some of the mass below the level of the

229

table-top, have a shiny chromium finish which captures the surrounding space in a series of distorted reflections.

It has been customary, especially among American critics, to suggest that this is entirely an abstract, gestural art. Certainly, in Caro's hands, rigid materials acquired a surprising suppleness. But the English eye is apt to find his work at least remotely figurative, whether or not this is intentional. From some angles Caro's sprawling sculptures can seem like Moore's giantesses stripped to their skeletons.

This affinity with Moore, in spite of an apparently firm renunciation of everything Moore stands for, is not the least of the reasons why Caro occupies a pivotal position in mid-1960s sculpture. It is right to mention the work of other artists: that of David Smith, and the sculpture of men who derive more or *Ill. 199* less directly from Smith such as the German Erich Hauser;

199 ERICH HAUSER *Space column 7/68* 1968

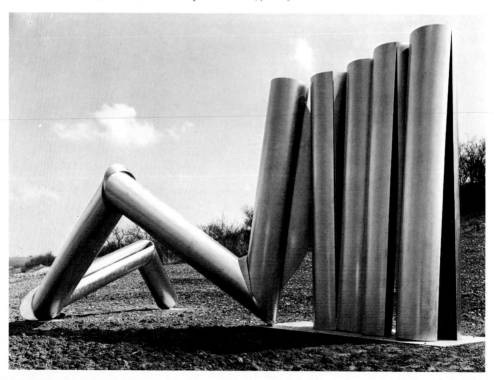

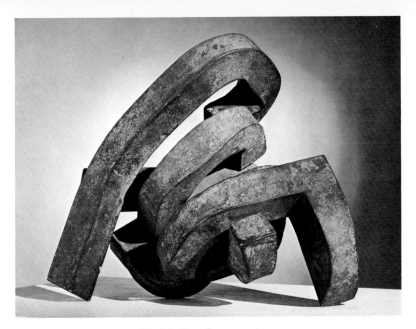

200 EDUARDO CHILLIDA *Modulation of space* 1963

Calder's stabiles, which anticipate Caro's rejection of the customary base or plinth; the wrought iron sculptures of the Spaniard Eduardo Chillida which both cleave to the tradition *Ill. 200* of González and parallel some of Caro's experiments. Caro does not stand completely alone even in the English tradition. The 'screw mobiles' of Kenneth Martin, for instance, where the *Ill. 202* parts can often be assembled in almost any order on a central armature, provide a more extreme example of the industrial approach; while much of the contemporary work of Eduardo Paolozzi belongs to the same category as Caro's, though with *Ill. 201* an influence from pop art which Caro never seems to have felt. But none of these artists stands precisely upon the cusp, and looks both forward and back, as Caro seems to do.

When it comes to giving explanations of this, Chillida and Paolozzi provide the best comparisons. On the whole, European sculpture did not progress in the direction taken by British

231

and American art during the late 1960s. The difference is like that between American post-painterly abstraction and the op art of Vasarely and his followers. Those European artists who work in three dimensions – or at least those of them who are in the vanguard of experiment – have mostly turned towards kinetic art, and have been discussed under that heading in an earlier chapter. Chillida, however, belongs to the Spanish tradition of craftsmanship in wrought iron just as Smith and Caro, in their various ways, belong to the Anglo-American tradition of heavy

201 EDUARDO PAOLOZZI
Etsso 1967

202 KENNETH MARTIN
Rotary rings 1967

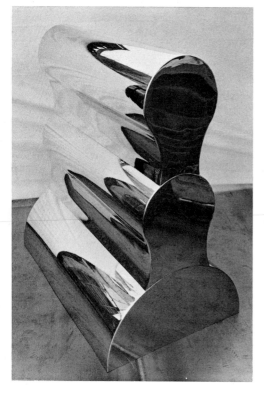

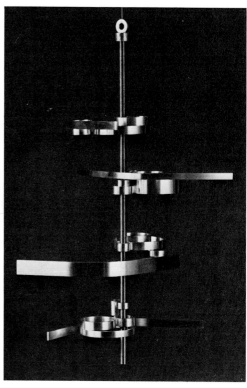

industry. However similar Chillida's ideas are to those of his American and British contemporaries, we are conscious, when we look at his work, that he belongs to a tradition of the 'hand-made' object, which they are rejecting. His intellectual affinities are with them; his sensibility is closer to that of Spanish painters such as Tapiés.

Paolozzi presents an even more interesting case. He is an artist who has gone through a remarkable number of stylistic transformations, but the guiding thread in his work seems always to have been an interest in machines, or, to put it more accurately, in the mechanistic. I have already spoken of his early figurative sculptures, textured with cog-wheels and other *Ill. 189* small machine-parts. In later work, he has made use of ready-made metal parts and sections, but in a different spirit from Caro and David Smith. Paolozzi, unlike Smith or Caro, has mostly tended to assemble these shapes into pseudomachines, or at least into objects which look as if they have some kind of mechanical function, even though there are no moving parts. Paolozzi has also made a series of sculptures which look as if they derive, not directly from machinery, but from the machine-influenced decoration and architecture of the Jazz Age. Characteristic are boxy chromium-plated objects, the horizontal *Ill. 201* planes flat, the vertical ones crimped and rippled like the mouldings in a 1930s movie-palace. These look like the remote cousins of things found in amusement arcades. The point of the contrast between Caro and Paolozzi is that Caro is neutral in the attitudes he adopts towards his materials. To him they are, as he says, just 'stuff'; the technological side of his activity is not romanticized, but exists in its own right.

The work of Smith and Caro marks a moment of transition in a general sense as well as in a particular one. After the war, painting was the dominant art. It was in painting that the major experiments were tried. But in the past two decades, and particularly in American and in British art, there has been a change of attitude. It has been work in three dimensions which has come to seem a natural vehicle of *avant-garde* expression. It is

233

true, as I have noted, that at the same time, the boundaries between sculpture and painting began to dissolve. Despite this, it is apparent that the emphasis has shifted towards the three-dimensional object, something which governs our reactions to the environment in which we move.

One of the best examples of this is the work of the British *Ills 203,* sculptor Phillip King. When King's sculpture was exhibited at *210* the Venice Biennale in 1968, Bryan Robertson summed up its effect as follows:

> The enigmatic character of King's work springs from a built-in, subliminal effect of paradox. Each sculpture is so very much more remarkable than its bare, factual existence as a physical object in space. An essential *logos*, or personal system of clear rules, is so charged by imagination that wholly unexpected conclusions are revealed: each sculpture will shift suddenly into a different identity whilst its structure is examined. The disclosure has the impact of a dramatic event. It is as if two plus two were made to yield five, incontrovertibly and with splendid finality.[4]

Ill. 210 His *Span* is made up of a double box, two leaning slabs, and two square columns, the capitals and bases of which are truncated pyramids. These are placed so that the spectator is free to move between them; he does not merely walk *round* the sculpture, he walks *in* it.

At first King did not work in metal, like Caro, but in brightly coloured fibreglass. The colour was often used to emphasise the movement of the shapes, to impart something dynamic to otherwise static forms. The shift from metal to fibreglass and other kinds of plastic is something which King had in common with younger sculptors, and the implications were interesting. Plastic is man-made; any character can be given to it; it can be tinted any colour. This makes it something quite different from the wood and stone of the days of 'truth to materials'. It also carries none of the industrial overtones of sheet-steel and I-beams. In fact, if it has any implications at all, they are those of a

234

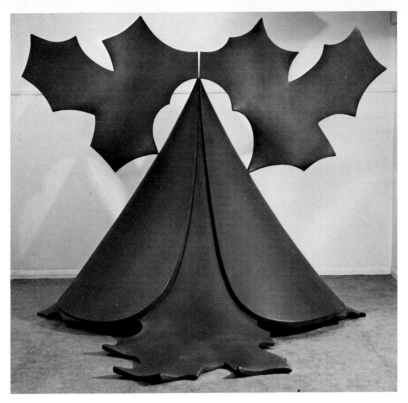

203 PHILLIP KING *Genghis Khan* 1963

culture where everything is disposable, a culture aligned towards exhibitions and events rather than permanent objects.

In Britain, most of these sculptors were introduced to the public through the medium of the second 'New Generation' show at the Whitechapel Art Gallery in 1965. Among the sculptors represented in this exhibition, besides King himself, were David Annesley, Tim Scott, and William Tucker. The *Ills 204–6* exhibition had an immense impact. The favoured material, besides various forms of plastic, was brightly painted sheet metal, but the material itself was never stressed; it was simply the vehicle for the formal idea. It was clear that the young artists concerned had learned a good deal from the American

235

colour painters, and from the sculptural experiments of men who were primarily painters, such as Barnett Newman and Ellsworth Kelly. There was a lack of bulk and volume about most of the pieces which reflected these influences. The sculptures sprawled and twisted. They made play with repeated forms. Tucker, in particular, experimented with a principle of extension which also appears in some of Frank Stella's linked canvases, and, earlier still, in the various versions of Brancusi's *Endless column*. It was noticeable then, and has remained noticeable, how much of the new work not only shunned a base but seemed to hug the floor. A great deal of this sculpture is well below eye-level. Some of the most extreme experiments in this direction were made by David Hall, a sculptor who, though not included in the 'New Generation' exhibition, had much in common with those who were.

Ill. 206

204 DAVID ANNESLEY *Orinoco* 1965

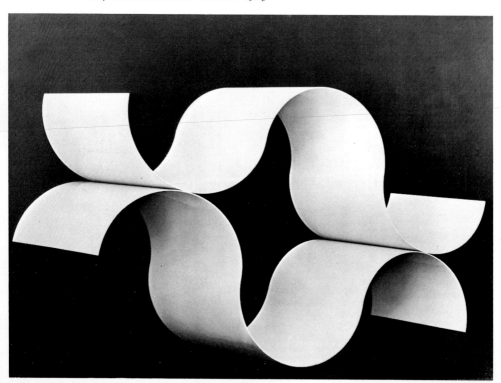

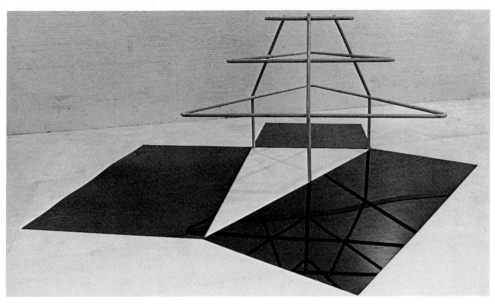

205 TIM SCOTT *Trireme* 1968

206 WILLIAM TUCKER *Memphis* 1965–6

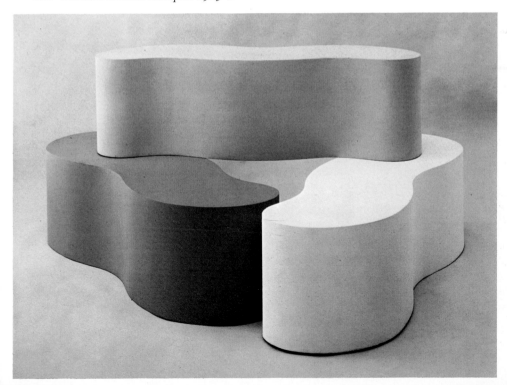

Ill. 208   Hall, for example, made sculptures of metal plates, which
float horizontally at ankle height, suggesting the existence of
another floor surface hovering just above the true one. The
shapes suggest perspectives that conflict with the true perspectives of the room. The whole work acts as a mechanism for
bending and distorting space, and has little physical presence
of its own. One notices, not the piece itself, but its alteration of
the area which it occupies.

British sculpture of the 'new generation' remained a
tightly coherent movement, or school, of a rather insular kind.
Though these sculptors are usually spoken of as being related
to developments in America, they have had their most clearly
marked impact on certain German artists, notably Kaspar
Ill. 213   Thomas Lenk, whose recent work closely parallels theirs, while
what he did earlier was in a totally different style, influenced by
surrealism.

American sculpture, post-David Smith, makes a less coherent
impression than British sculpture, post-Caro. One artist stands
out as having played an important role: the ex-architect Tony

207 TONY SMITH *Playground* 1962

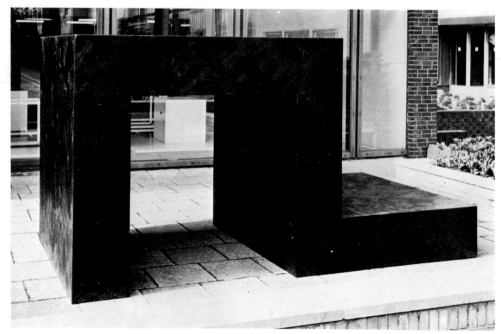

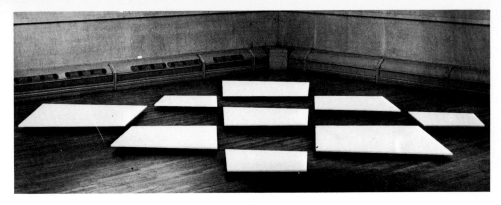

208 DAVID HALL *Nine* 1967

Smith. Smith's career is an example of the suddenness with which even a mature artist could burst upon the current scene. The first single piece of his to be shown was exhibited in 1963. By 1967, he enjoyed a major reputation.

Tony Smith was born in 1912, six years later than David *Ill. 207* Smith, and served his architectural apprenticeship as clerk of the works on several of the houses built by Frank Lloyd Wright. For twenty years, from 1940 to 1960, he had an architectural practice of his own. He gave up architecture because he felt that buildings were too impermanent, and too vulnerable to alterations which would wreck the creator's intention.

His sculptures have been described as 'minimal art', or as examples of the 'single-unit Gestalt', but this is to oversimplify matters. The artist himself spoke of some of them as

> part of a continuous space grid. In the latter, voids are made up of the same components as the masses. In this light, they may be seen as interruptions in an otherwise unbroken flow of space. If you think of space as solid, they are voids in that space. While I hope they have form and presence, I don't think of them as being objects among other objects; I think of them as being isolated in their own environments.[5]

Much of Smith's work seems to reflect his experience of architecture. He said of one piece, called *Playground*: 'I like

239

shapes of this kind; they remind me of the plans of ancient buildings made with mudbrick walls.' Characteristically, the sculptures consist of rectangular boxes fitted together; sometimes this is varied by using tetrahedrons. Smith described one as having come from the accidental conjunction of three Alka-Seltzer boxes; another, called *Black Box*, was suggested by a box for index cards which the artist saw on a friend's desk. Seen one night, the shape became an obsession, so Smith telephoned his friend the next morning and asked for the dimensions.

> I asked him to take his ruler and measure the box. He was so out of it that he didn't even enquire about why I wanted to know the size. I multiplied the dimensions by five, made a drawing, took it to the Industrial Welding Co. in Newark, and asked them to make it up.[6]

Obviously, art of this kind marked a radical break from the sculptural preoccupations of the past. In a way, it could be said to stem from dada, and in particular from the cult of the 'found object'. It could also be said to have something to do with John Cage's notion of unfocusing the spectator's mind. But neither of these goes so far as to imply a concentration on the deliberately inexpressive, and that is what the new American sculpture more and more tended to do.

Minimal art was not simply a question of the activity of one artist, but of a whole school of artists, among them Carl André, Dan Flavin, Robert Morris, Sol Lewitt, and John McCracken. One of the most articulate of these artists is Donald Judd, who spoke of his practice thus:

> Three dimensions are real space. That gets rid of the problem of illusionism and of literal space, space in and around marks and colours – which is riddance of one of the most salient and most objectionable relics of European art. The several limits of painting are no longer present. A work can be as powerful as it can be thought to be. Actual space is intrinsically more powerful and specific than paint on a flat surface.[7]

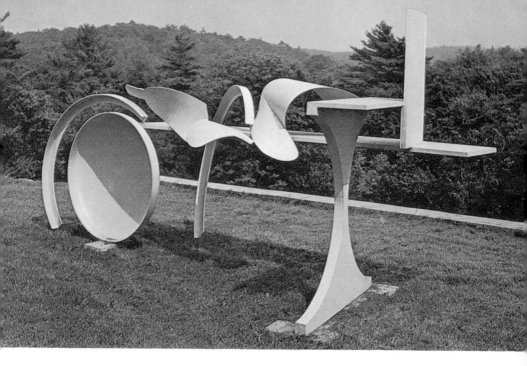

209 ANTHONY CARO *Sun-feast* 1969–70

210 PHILLIP KING *Span* 1967

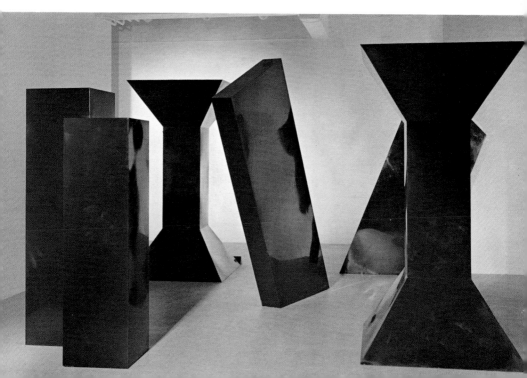

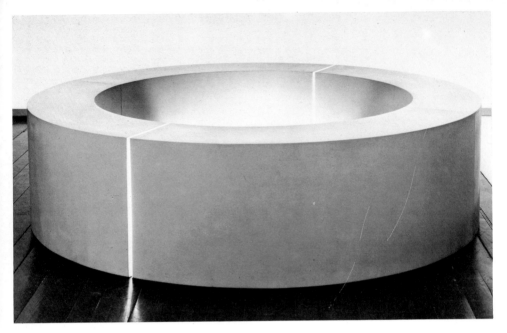

211 ROBERT MORRIS *Untitled (circular light piece)* 1966

His interpretation of this credo is less liberal than the words
themselves might lead one to suppose: a string of galvanized
iron boxes strung out at regular intervals across the wall.

Judd's colleague, Robert Morris, defended minimality in
equally emphatic terms:

> Simplicity of shape does not necessarily equate with simplicity
> of experience. Unitary forms do not reduce relationships.
> They order them. If the predominant, hieratic nature of the
> unitary form functions as a constant, all those particularizing
> relations of scale, proportion, etc., are not thereby cancelled.
> Rather they are bound more cohesively and indivisibly
> together. The magnification of this single most important
> sculptural value, shape, together with greater unification and
> integration of every other essential sculptural value, makes,
> on the one hand, the multipart, inflected formats of past

Ill. 212

242

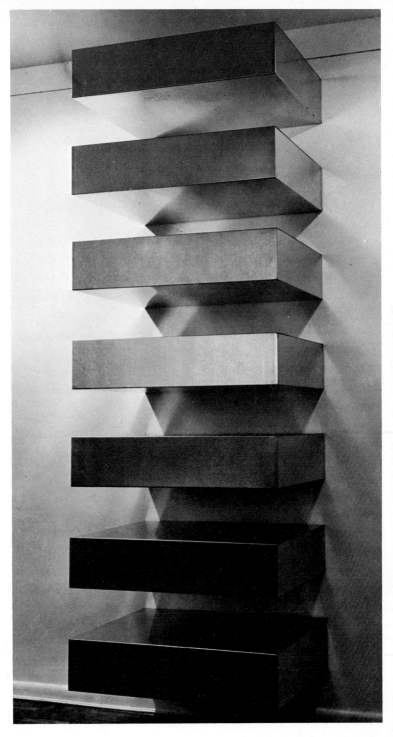

212 DONALD JUDD
Untitled 1965

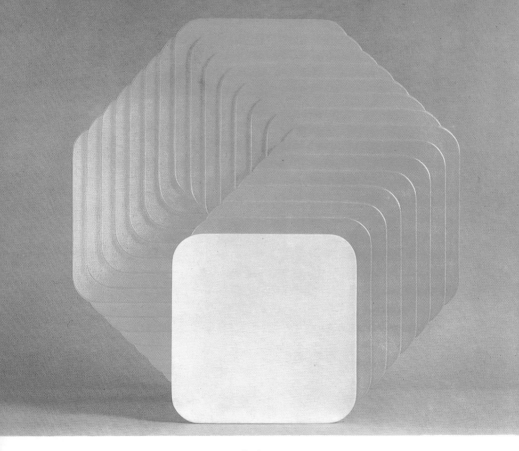

213 KASPAR THOMAS LENK *Schichtung 22a* 1966

sculpture extraneous, and on the other, establishes both a new limit and a new freedom for sculpture.[8]

These justifications are in some ways beside the point, because it became increasingly clear that the minimal artist did not really wish to express himself, or express some meaning, in the old sense. There is, it is true, a sense of *ordering*, which often takes the form proposed by Tony Smith: the artist provides a partial image of a complete order throughout all the space which can be imagined, and leaves the spectator to fill the rest in.

244

214 JOHN MCCRACKEN *There's No Reason Not To* 1967

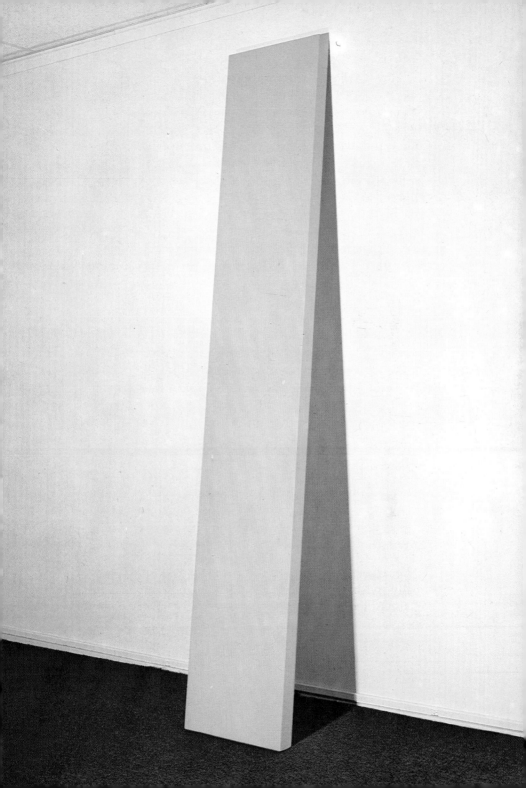

This is exactly what happens, for instance, in much of the work of Sol Lewitt. In April 1968 Lewitt had an exhibition in New York which consisted of a single sculpture, descriptively entitled *46 Three-part variations on three different kinds of cubes.* The cubes were boxes of standard size. Some were closed, some open on one side only, some open on two facing sides. These were piled together in groups of three. The cubes were regularly aligned in their stacks, and the stacks regularly aligned with one another. Each of the eight rows set out the possible solutions in a fixed order of permutation, beginning with a row which established all the possible permutations when each stack contained just one of each of the three kinds of cubes.

Ill. 215 Some minimal art is less dour – and less naïve. Dan Flavin's work, for instance, makes use of straight lengths of fluorescent tubing, and is the point at which minimal art meets kinetic art. Flavin regards not only light, but space, as his material. 'I knew', he says, 'that the actual space of a room could be broken down and played with by planting illusions of real light [electric light] at crucial junctures in the room's composition.'[9]

Flavin, therefore, is aiming at a kind of dematerialization of art, and much the same might be said about the Californian Ill. 216 artist Larry Bell, who made use of plates of coated glass which are placed at right angles. These both reflect the spectator and allow him to see what lies beyond. The art object is not the cube itself, but fleeting effects of reflection and transparency.

Ill. 214 John McCracken, another Californian, also seemed concerned that the play of light should be regarded as part of the effect of the work. He made long plywood and fibreglass boards, which lean casually against a wall. These boards are lacquered in gleaming colours. The artist said: 'I think of colour as being the structural material I use to build the forms I am interested in.'[10]

Colour, light, transparency – these were the materials of much of the new sculpture in America. There was also a tension between extremes of formality and formlessness. Robert Morris said:

246

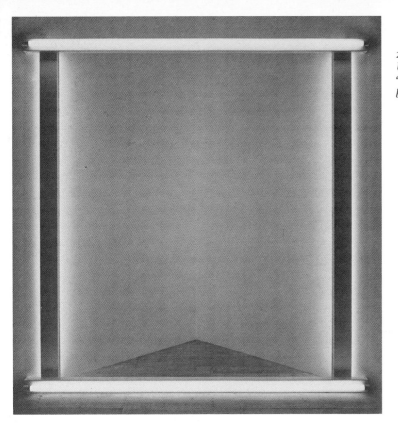

215 DAN FLAVIN
*Untitled (to the
'innovator' wheeling
beachblow)* 1968

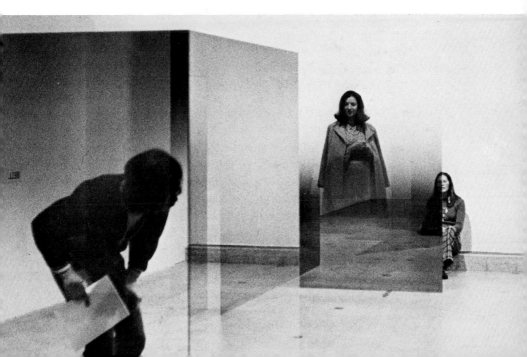

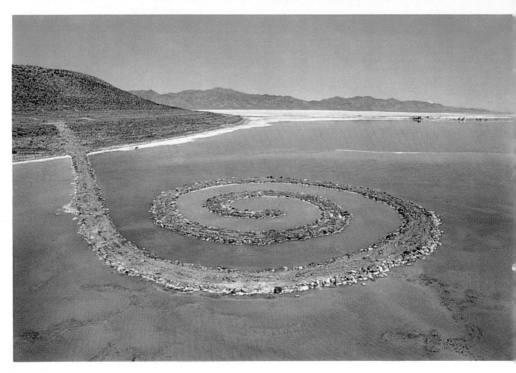

217 ROBERT SMITHSON *Spiral Jetty* 1970

> In recent object-type art the invention of new forms is not
> an issue. A morphology of geometric, predominantly
> rectangular forms has been acceptable as a given premise. . . .
> Because of the flexibility as well as the passive, unemphasized
> object-type shape it is a useful means.[11]

He proceeded to try to prove his point by showing works, still
minimal in intent, which consisted of loosely piled pieces of
grey felt. These, as he pointed out, co-opted both Pollock and
Oldenburg as forerunners of his own tradition.

Since Morris showed these deliberately soft, formless works,
minimal artists have gone still further in the direction of anti-
art. Specimens of rock and earth gathered in a particular
place and piled in boxes have been shown in New York
galleries as 'sculpture', and so have photographs of diggings

made by the artists: trenches in the desert, piles of sand on the beach, gigantic earth-sculptures, meant to be viewed from the air. The concept of the 'art object' is thus discarded in favour of that of the 'art idea'.

Ills 217, 218

218 RICHARD LONG *A line in Ireland* 1974

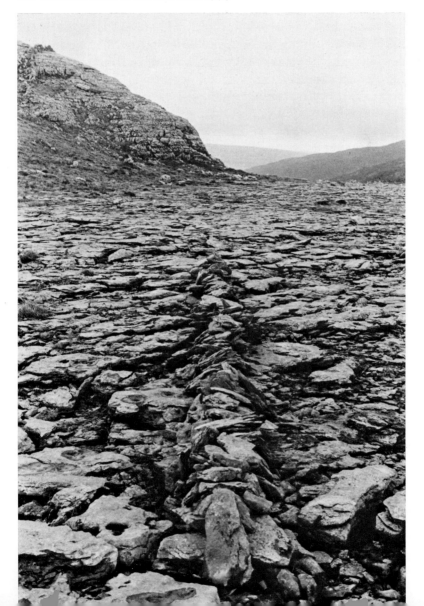

CHAPTER NINE

Super realism

It might seem that pop art's successor 'super realism' is in direct contradiction to what has just been said about the replacement of the 'art object' by the 'art idea'. On the face of it, we are here confronted with a reaction towards the most conservative kind of representational painting and sculpture. Even more than pop art, super realism's reputation was made by an alliance between dealers and collectors, in the teeth of hostile critical response. Yet one can also see that art of this kind owes much of its character to its dependence upon conceptual thinking. The painter, at least, does not approach reality directly, but tries to reproduce what a camera would see.

The transition from pop to what is recognizably super realism, at least where painting is concerned, appears in the work of the English-born but American-domiciled Malcolm Morley. In common with many pop artists, from Lichtenstein to David Hockney, Morley was fascinated, not so much by what the painting showed, as by the method used to show it – in other words, by the convention of representation. The main difference between his work and that of, say, Lichtenstein, that he allowed himself much less freedom to manoeuvre.

Morley began by painting pictures which were based on the kind of illustration one would find in a travel brochure – an ocean liner upon an improbably blue sea, for example. But there was no aping of the distortions imposed by cheap processes of colour reproduction. Rather, the artist seemed to want to get the effect of a good-quality four-colour separation. The pictures were painted area by area, and often upside down, so that the artist did not see how close he had managed to come to his model until the task of copying it was completed. An

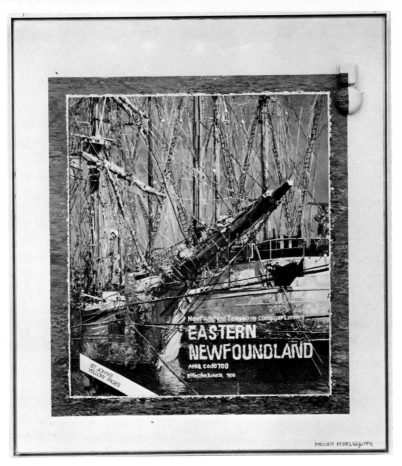

219 MALCOLM MORLEY *St John's Yellow Pages* 1971

apparently realistic painting was therefore produced in an intensely abstract way.

Even so, Morley seems to have found that the perfection of finish worked against the alienation effect intended; and in later paintings, such as *St John's Yellow Pages*, he was careful to introduce devices which make it plain that the painting is in fact a reproduction of a reproduction.

Painters who are more thoroughly identified with the super realist movement, such as Richard Estes and Ralph Goings,

Ill. 219

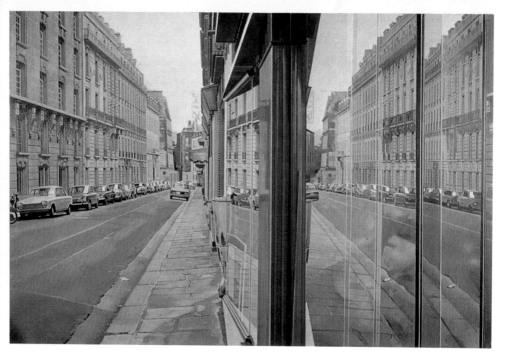

220 RICHARD ESTES *Paris street-scene* 1973

Ill. 220 have tempered this strictness of approach. The fascination of Estes's work lies in the extreme precision with which it seems to reproduce appearances. The New York street scenes which form the subject-matter of nearly all his paintings and prints are depicted with a meticulous care which recalls the Dutch masters of the seventeenth century. Indeed, the likeness between some of his pictures and paintings such as Vermeer's *View of Delft* and the church interiors of Saenredam seems to suggest that Estes departs from super realist principles in the degree of covert organization which he imposes on his compositions. The more one looks at his work, the more clearly one sees that it depends on carefully plotted geometric structures of a kind that the camera can seldom discover for itself.

Goings differs from Estes in several important respects, despite an apparently identical smoothness of finish. It is clear

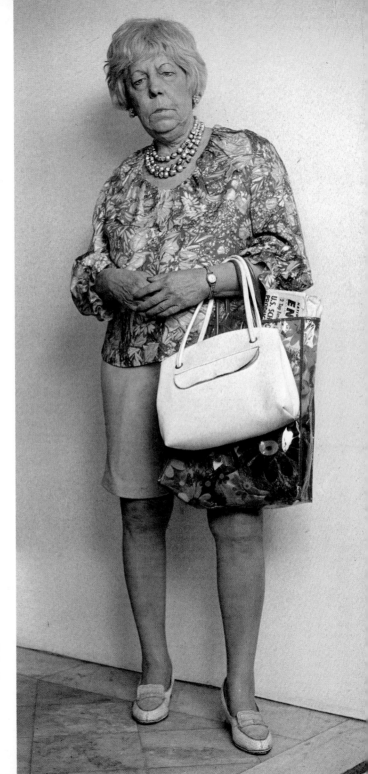

221 DUANE HANSON
Florida shopper
1973

enough, for instance, that in his work, as also in that of an artist such as Robert Bechtle, the subject-matter does count for something. The aggressive banality seems designed to make a comment on the quality of the life which is lived in these

Ill. 223 desolate surroundings. But this is secondary to his desire to create a dialogue with the monocular vision of the camera. The neutrality of finish (the result of using an air-brush) is meant to match the neutrality of a good colour-slide.

Super realist sculpture, unlike super realist painting, involves no act of translation from three dimensions into two. The sculpture is therefore even more literal in its representation of reality. Or so it might seem when we first look at these mostly

Ill. 221 life-size figures. If we look at the work of Duane Hanson, for example, we are struck by its extraordinary quality of lifelike-ness. For a moment it seems as if the person represented stands living and breathing before us. Certainly every care is taken to give us this feeling: the figure not only wears real clothes, but is equipped with carefully selected accessories. The face

222 GEORGE SEGAL *Girl on red wicker couch* 1973

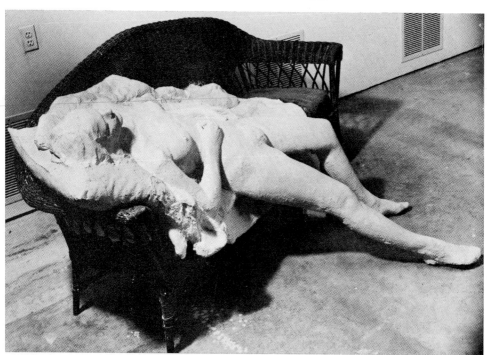

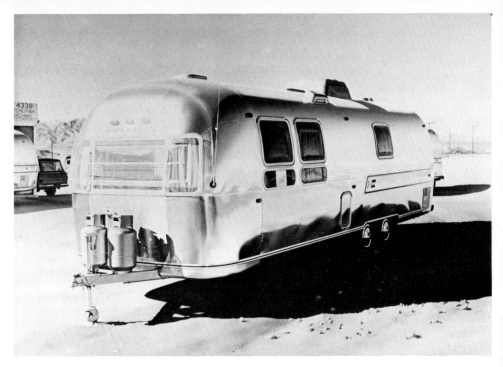

223 RALPH GOINGS *Airstream* 1970

and other flesh-areas are painted to imitate life. Yet Hanson's
work has a quality which is not to be found in the fairground
waxworks that try to trick us in the same way. There is an
element of subtle intensification – one might almost call it
caricature – which makes these figures more memorable than
their models.

Hanson's technique, and that of other super realist sculptors
such as John de Andrea, has its roots in procedures which were
first used (at least in the period under review) by the pop
sculptor George Segal. Hanson and de Andrea, like Segal, base
their work on the use of life-casts. In their hands these serve as
the equivalent of the camera-lens in super realist painting, a
way of reproducing reality more exactly than the eye itself
can see it. This is a method which is also employed by the
British sculptor John Davies. It is interesting to note what

Ill. 222

255

very different results these artists get. In Segal's case, the rough, white surface of the figures serves to distance them into the realm of what is recognizably 'art'. Hanson and de Andrea, on the other hand, seem to want to thrust their work into direct competition with the living figures we see moving around us. Davies, in his *Head of William Jeffrey*, adopts a compromise solution. The power of the head reminds us of certain Roman Republican portrait busts, which were also based on life-masks. The 'device' that surrounds it (a blue wire cage with pendant pearls) serves to put it firmly in a different domain from the one we ourselves inhabit.

Ills 221, 227

Ill. 225

To help us to grasp the character of super realist art, and the different aims of the painters and sculptors, comparison between the head by Davies and the portrait illustrated by Chuck Close is useful. Close is perhaps the 'purest' of all the painters who have been classified as belonging to this school. The artist said categorically: 'My main objective is to translate photographic information into paint information.' He said, too, that he wanted to bring about a different mode of seeing:

Ill. 224

> My large scale forces the viewer to focus on one area at a time. In that way he is made aware of the blurred areas that are seen with peripheral vision. Normally we never take those peripheral areas into account. . . . In my work the blurred areas don't come into focus, but they are too large to be ignored.[1]

Sculpture, which cannot control our actual method of seeing in this way, is naturally forced to seek other ways of making its effect. Davies, for example, by his use of 'devices' of various kinds, seems to try to externalize the inner psychological strangeness of the characters he depicts. Duane Hanson uses tricks which are derived from the stage. His figures, like certain actors, have expressions and poses which pinpoint the essence of the character. A flow of motion has been stopped at its most expressive point. Even John de Andrea, at first sight the blandest and most non-committal of super realist sculptors, has ways

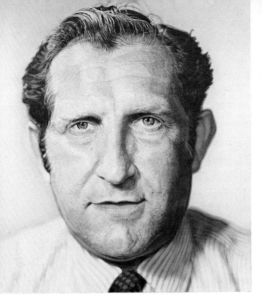

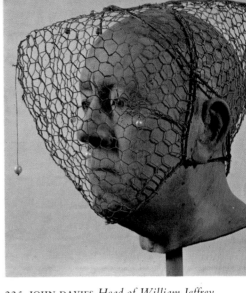

224 CHUCK CLOSE *Nat* 1972   225 JOHN DAVIES *Head of William Jeffrey*

of eliciting a particular planned reaction to what he puts before us.

We can better understand the character of a de Andrea nude by comparing it with a similar nude by Reg Butler. There are a number of superficial resemblances. Butler, though the figure is made of bronze, paints it flesh-colour, and gives it 'real' hair and 'real' eyes. We are keenly conscious, none the less, that this is a personal vision of female sexuality, expressed by means of deliberate adjustments of what is objectively seen. De Andrea, on the other hand, while apparently content with literal reproduction, has chosen and posed a model to project her personality, and even her social class. This girl has the confidence of someone who has never been hungry. The more one looks at super realist art, the more one is impressed by the element of social comment which emerges from its apparent neutrality.

Ill. 226

This is an art which, in one sense, seems to appeal to entirely trivial responses – to the shock of delight at seeing something exactly imitated, no matter what that thing is – yet at a deeper level speaks to its audience because it expresses, without rhetoric, the nullity and despair to be found in large areas of urban society. Although we see this particularly clearly in the sculpture of Duane Hanson, who so often seems to concentrate exclusively on the ugliness of his fellow Americans, we can detect it, too, in the apparently fresh and innocent co-eds of de Andrea, whose milk-fed mindlessness and complacency is tellingly portrayed, despite the physical beauty the sculptor depicts. In more than one sense, super realism is the representative art of the Western democracies in the later twentieth century.

226 REG BUTLER *Girl on a long base* 1968–72

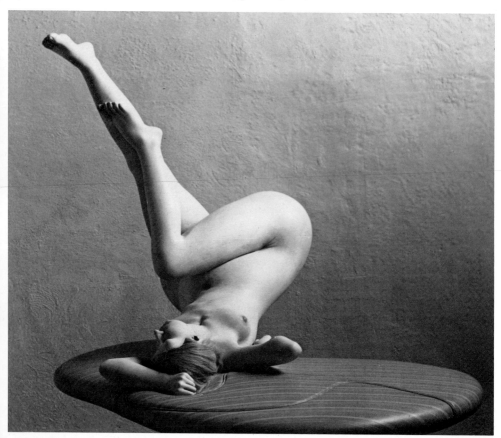

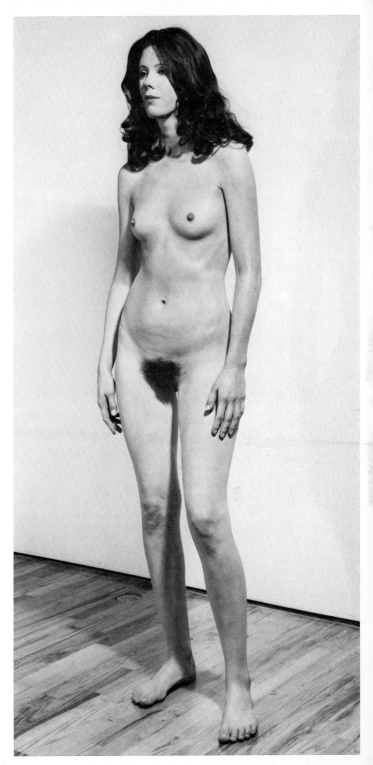

227 JOHN DE ANDREA
Freckled woman
1974

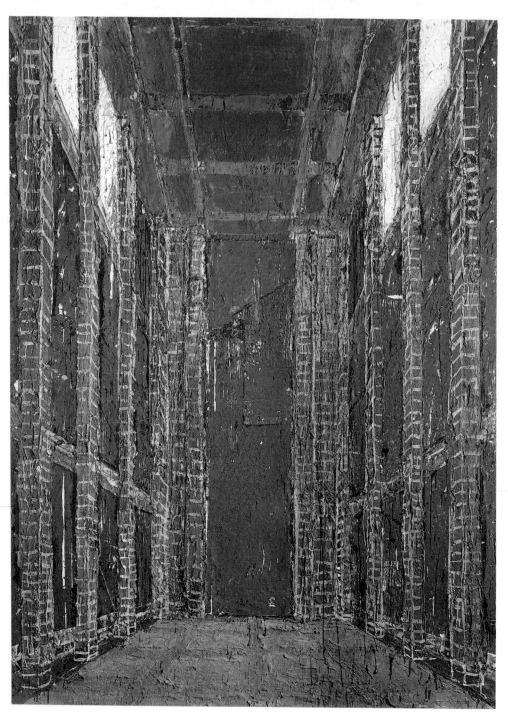

228 ANSELM KIEFER *Untitled* 1978

CHAPTER TEN

Multiple choices: conceptual art to neo-expressionism

Contemporary artists are free to approach the making of art in
radically different ways. Virtually all the styles discussed in the
preceding chapters, from abstract expressionism to traditional
figuration, have distinguished exponents in the younger as well
as the older generation. Innovation continues, but since pop,
there has been no consensus about what an *avant-garde* artwork
should look like, or even what it should try to do. At one
extreme, with the emphasis on pure intellect, is the 'conceptual
art' of the 1960s and 1970s. At the other is the emotional
clamour of neo-expressionism.

    Conceptual art was essentially an art of intellectual patterns,
embodied by any means the artist saw fit. Joseph Kosuth's *One*   *Ill. 229*
and three chairs of 1965 is a good example. It consists of a wooden
folding chair, a photograph of a chair, and the photographic
enlargement of the dictionary definition of a chair. The artist
asks his audience in which of the three the identity of the object
is to be found – in the thing itself, the representation, or the
verbal description; and, if it can really be discovered in all of
them?

    Conceptual art developed during the 1960s alongside the
environments, Happenings and performances of pop art, and,
despite its claim to be purely an art of ideas, often manifested
itself in elaborately environmental form. This was the case with
Giulio Paolini's *Apotheosis of Homer*, which used taped sound   *Ill. 230*
and a series of thirty-two photographs on music-stands
scattered round the available space. Sometimes, indeed, space
and spatial relationships become the basic subject-matter of the
conceptual artist – this approach is exemplified by Daniel
Buren's severe *On two levels with two colours*, where a simple

Ill. 231　vertically striped band is run at floor level throughout the available space provided by two linked galleries, one of which was a step up from the other. Both are left completely empty.

　　Sometimes, paradoxically, conceptual art became totally physical – an idea is expressed in the most literal sense through

Ill. 232　flesh and blood. Dennis Oppenheim's *Reading Position* of 1970 consists of two photographs which record the effects of sunburn on the artist's own torso – part of it sheltered by an open book, and part left exposed. This kind of expression is often classified as body art or performance art. To create his piece Oppenheim had to do something at least mildly painful. Masochism is a frequent characteristic of body art. In the work of Stuart Brisley, for example, it takes on the aspect of a ritual ordeal.

230 GIULIO PAOLINO *Apotheosis of Homer* 1970–1

231 DANIEL BUREN *On two levels with two colours* 1976

229 JOSEPH KOSUTH *One and three chairs* 1965

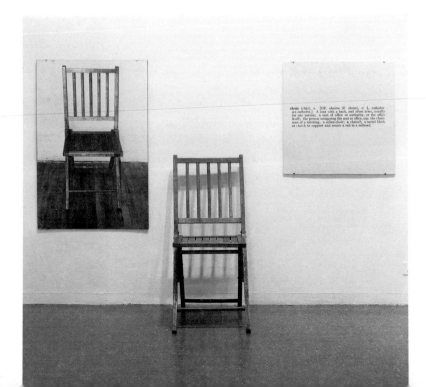

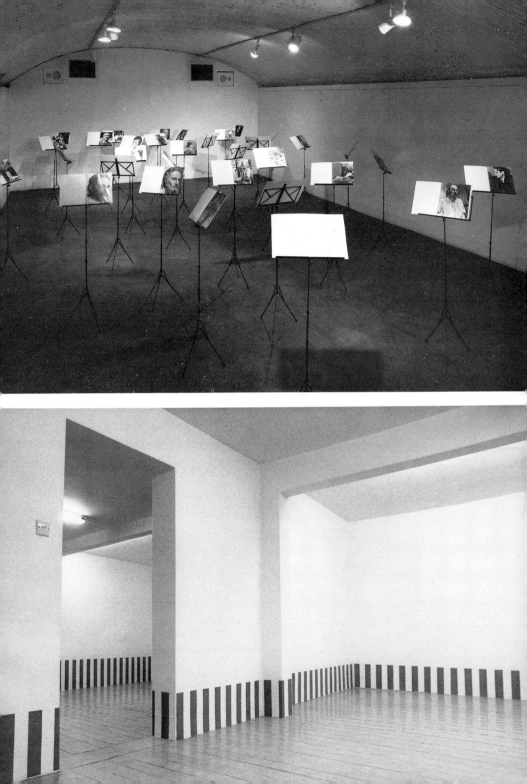

Jon Borofsky's *Hammering Man at 2,772,489 (JB27 sculp)* shifts the emphasis from object to idea in a different manner. Here the structure is deliberately flimsy and ephemeral, produced to suit a particular space and a particular occasion. It is conceptual in that it is using fairly minimal means of embodiment to put across a comment on the nature of traditional monumental sculpture. The artist presents the viewer with a giant caricature of the traditional concerns of the artist, and the setting – an old-fashioned art gallery – adds force to the satire.

232 DENNIS OPPENHEIM *Reading position* 1970

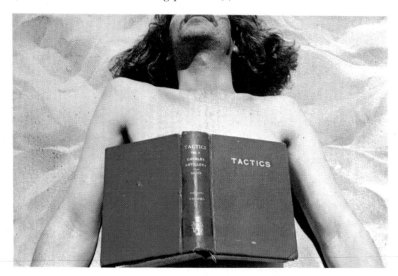

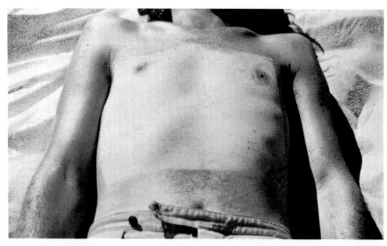

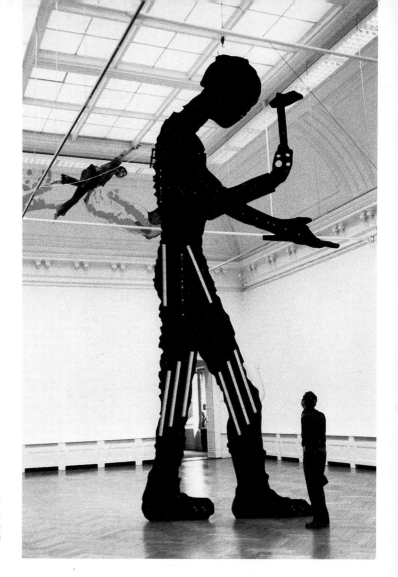

233 JON
BOROFSKY
Hammering Man
at 2722, 489 (JB
27 sculp) 1981

Parody has become a very important element in the art of the
1970s and 1980s. Brad Davis, who belongs to a group who have
been labelled the 'Pattern Painters' because much of their work
seems to derive from designs for fabric and wallpaper rather
than from 'fine art', presents the spectator with a romantic
landscape, but deliberately puts it between quotation marks, as

Ill. 234

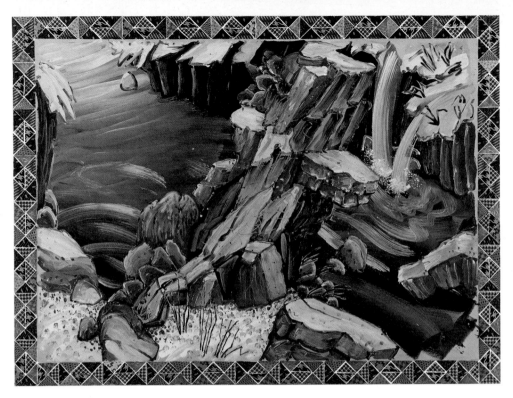

234 BRAD DAVIS *Evening shore* 1983

Ill. 236   the patterned border makes plain. Nancy Graves' *Triped* (the work of one of the most energetic and versatile of contemporary American artists) mocks the open forms typical of David Smith at the period when he produced *Hudson River*

Ill. 195   *Landscape* by transmuting them into toytown vegetation – a giant springbean consorts with an eroded leaf. Jokiness is a staple ingredient in contemporary ceramic sculpture, especially the sculpture associated with a large group of Californian artists. It is nowhere better exemplified than in Robert Arneson's long

Ill. 235   series of self-mocking self-portraits. These two pieces, so very different in style, and united only by a sense of irony, typify the huge stylistic variety to be found in contemporary American and European sculpture.

266

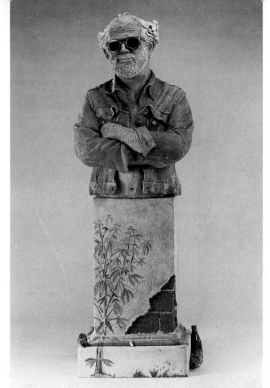

235 ROBERT ARNESON
Californian artist 1982

236 NANCY GRAVES *Triped*
1983

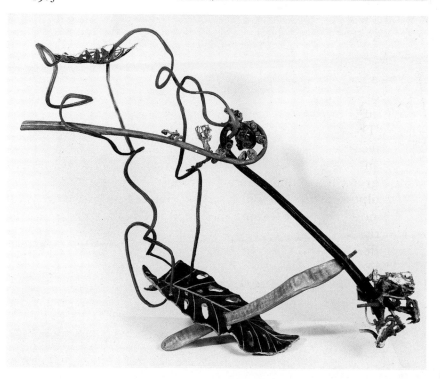

The impulse towards parody had already started to take on a sardonic tinge in the early seventies, with the work of a brash group of Chicago-based painters who called themselves The Hairy Who. One of the most individual artists in this group was *Ill. 137* Ed Paschke, and, despite a marked difference of texture, it is not hard to discern an affinity between his work and the late *Ill. 238* paintings of Philip Guston. In both, the cartoon style shades into something bleak and sardonic.

Guston is regarded as one of the progenitors of the international art movement variously known as 'Bad Painting' (because of its deliberate stylistic crudity), 'the Wild Ones', or

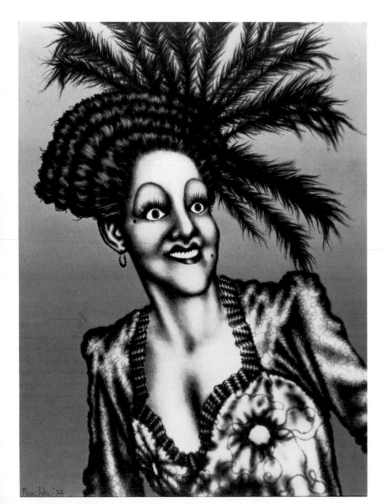

237 ED PASCHKE
Minnie 1974

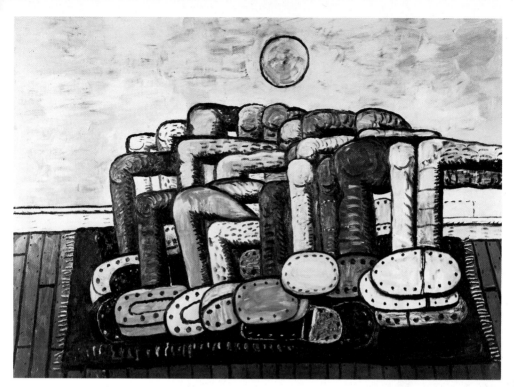

238 PHILIP GUSTON *The rug* 1979

the 'Transavantgarde' – this last name suggesting the notion that the artists concerned have outstripped the old Modern Movement and conventional ideas about avant-gardism. In America, the leading figure in the group is Julian Schnabel, famous for huge canvases where paint is applied to broken pieces of crockery glued to the surface. This has the effect of breaking up the imagery and making it difficult to construe – not only for the spectator but for the artist himself as he creates it. It is thus a quasi-mechanical means of freeing the creative unconsciousness.

Ill. 239

Despite Schnabel's celebrity, however, the movement's real centre of gravity lies in Europe, not in the United States. It includes a number of Italian and West German painters. In the work of the Italians associated with the group – Sandro Chia,

Ills 240–1

Ill. 242
Mimmo Paladino and Francesco Clemente – the affection for parody remains strong. Chia, perhaps the most striking of the three, draws heavily on work by artists favoured by Mussolini's regime during the 1920s and 1930s – on the later work of Carrà, Sironi and Giorgio de Chirico.

The German members of the group show a more anguished and serious pre-occupation with their country's past. Anselm *Ill. 228* Kiefer, one of the most gifted, has based many paintings on the architectural projects designed for Hitler by Albert Speer. But there is also a dialogue with the history of modernism, and their work is full of echoes of early twentieth-century art. A number of members of the group – which includes, in addition to Kiefer, artists such as Georg Baselitz, Rainer Fetting, Markus Lupertz and A. R. Penck – sustain a kind of love-hate

239 JULIAN SCHNABEL *Humanity asleep* 1982

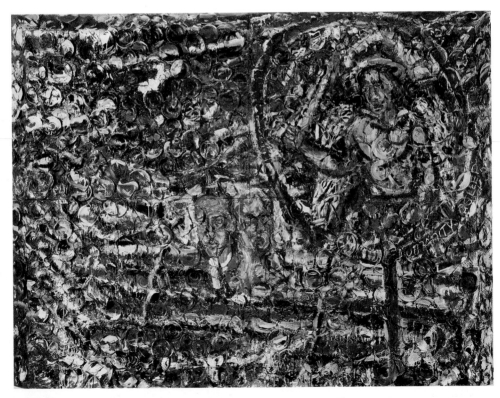

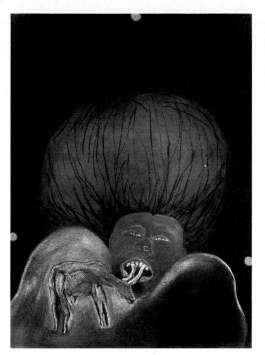

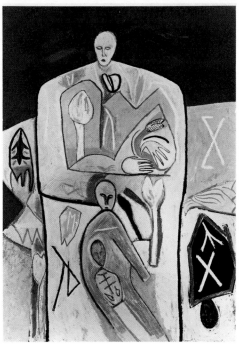

240 FRANCESCO CLEMENTE
Toothache 1981

241 MIMMO PALADINO
It's always evening 1982

relationship with the German Expressionism of the years before
the First World War. Fetting's *Dancers III* – a typical work – *Ill. 245*
seems like an attempt to rework Matisse's famous *The Dance* of
1909–10 in terms of the work of Kirchner or Erich Heckel. But
there are other elements as well. One is a search for the rawest
kind of primitivism, and another is an exploration of the idea of
awkwardness. Baselitz took to painting his images upside
down, with paint trickles to show that he had not simply
reversed the canvas after it was completed. A. R. Penck *Ill. 244*
explored pictographs and graffiti, in a way which sometimes
recalled the work of Picasso and Miró, and sometimes that of
Dubuffet (an earlier apostle of awkwardness). The welcome
the painters receive showed how eager the art-market was
for a return to conventional formats, if not to conventional
ideas.

271

242 SANDRO CHIA
Crocodile tears 1982

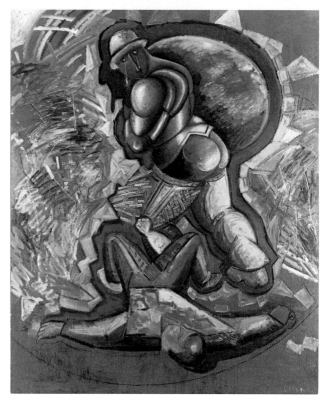

243 GEORG BASELITZ
Model for a sculpture
1981

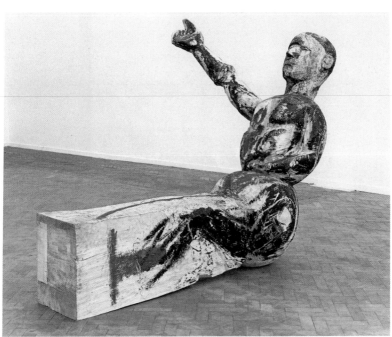

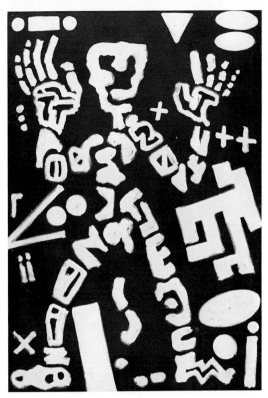

244 A. R. PENCK
T3 (R)

245 RAINER FETTING
Dancers III 1982

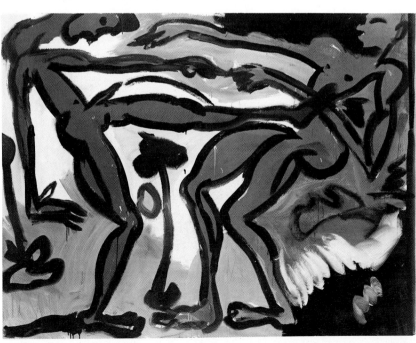

Not many women have been involved with the Bad Painting movement, and this is mildly surprising, as the 1970s and 1980s saw a tremendous rise to prominence of women artists, especially in England and the United States. One gifted American, rather on the fringe of the Bad Painting movement, is Susan Rothenberg. Her almost monochromatic canvases have *Ill. 246* the force of emblems – a *Beggar* is reduced to a long skinny arm holding out a bowl. It was a sign of women's liberation, as far as the art-world was concerned, that women became almost more prominent as sculptors than as painters. Many undertook physically ambitious projects – for example Alice Aycock, with *Ill. 247* mysterious sculptures often using mechanical or quasi-mechanical elements. Other works by the same artist are mock-architectural, non-functional buildings which act as sculptures.

246 SUSAN ROTHENBERG *Beggar* 1982

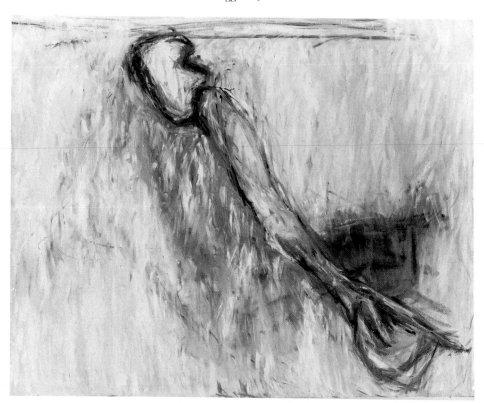

It is not surprising that a great deal of the energy in women's art should take specifically feminist form. The most ambitious feminist artwork of the 1970s was undoubtedly Judy Chicago's *The Dinner Party*. This environmental piece was designed as homage to 33 women whom the artist considered to be major figures in western history, 'plus 999 others'. There were 33 place settings at a triangular table, each with a special plate, goblet and runner, thus making the image of a triple Eucharist. The decorative images on the plates were emblematic of each participant, and many were based on a combination of the vagina and the butterfly. The decoration was done in traditional china-painting technique, because china-painting is a skilled craft hobby which has long been popular with American women.

Ill. 249

247 ALICE AYCOCK *The savage sparkler*

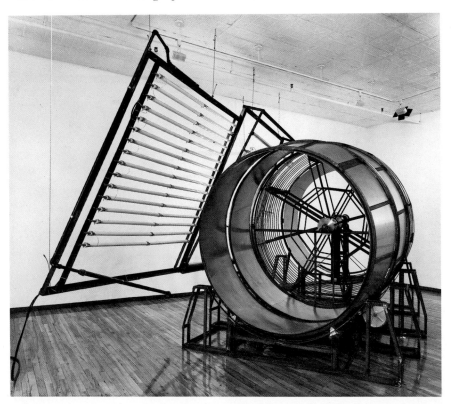

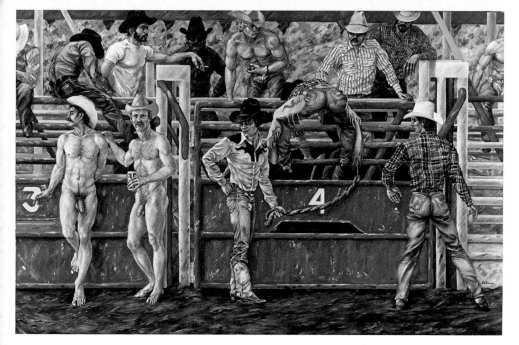

248 DELMAS HOWE *Theseus and Pirithoüs at the chutes* 1981–2

Feminist art was only one of a number of different kinds of art which asserted a special view of reality. Other special interest groups which evolved their own art-forms were ethnic – for example Black and American Hispanic, with wall-paintings addressed to local audiences in poor communities – and gay. Homosexual art gradually emerged from the ghetto of *Ill. 248* pornographic illustration. The 'Gay Rodeo' series by the American painter Delmas Howe combines Western, Greek classical and homosexual themes. On the surface totally different from the symbolic expression of *The Dinner Party*, this is still an art which emphasizes the power of imagery, is less concerned with style than with group identity, and wants its meanings to be generally accessible. Such work defiantly negates the hermetic tradition associated with classic modernism. Perhaps, indeed, it contains the seeds of a new modernism, of a very different kind.

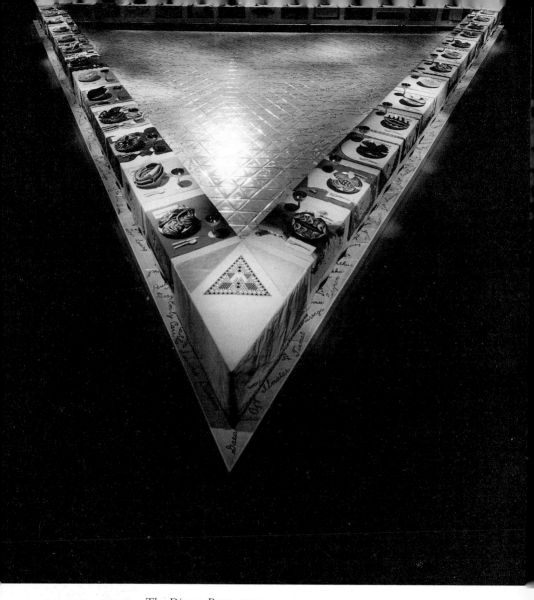

249 JUDY CHICAGO *The Dinner Party* 1979

Text References

Chapter One

1   Hans Richter, *Dada – Art and Anti-Art*, London, Thames and Hudson, and New York, McGraw-Hill, 1966, pp. 207–8.

2   Clement Greenberg, 'Recentness of Sculpture', in *American Sculpture of the Sixties*, catalogue of an exhibition held at the Los Angeles County Museum of Art, 28 April–25 June 1967, and at the Philadelphia Museum of Art, 19 September–29 October 1967, p. 27.

3   Pierre Restany, catalogue of *Superlund* exhibition, Lund, Sweden, 1967.

Chapter Two

1   André Breton, *Manifestes du Surréalisme*, Paris, J.-J. Pauvert, 1962, p. 40.

2   Maurice Nadeau, *The History of Surrealism*, New York, Collier Books, 1967, and London, Jonathan Cape, 1968, p. 202.

3   Barbara Rose, *American Art Since 1900*, New York, and London, 1967, pp. 127 et seq.

4   Harold Rosenberg, 'Arshile Gorky: the Man, the Time, the Idea', *Horizon*, New York, 1962, p. 106.

5   *Arshile Gorky: Paintings, Drawings, Studies*, catalogue of an exhibition held at the Museum of Modern Art, New York, in collaboration with the Washington Gallery of Modern Art, 1962, p. 45.

6   Talcott B. Clapp. 'A painter in a glass house', quoted in *Arshile Gorky: Paintings, Drawings, Studies*, catalogue of an exhibition held at the Museum of Modern Art, New York, in collaboration with the Washington Gallery of Modern Art, 1962, p. 43.

7   Jackson Pollock, 'My Painting', *Possibilities* 1, New York, George Wittenborn, winter 1947–8.

8   André Breton, op. cit., p. 44.

9   Harold Rosenberg, *The Tradition of the New*, London, Thames and Hudson, 1962, p. 31.

10   Ibid., p. 30.

11   Frank O'Hara, *Jackson Pollock*, New York, George Braziller, 1959, p. 116.

12   Patrick Heron, 'The Ascendancy of London', *Studio International*, London, December 1966.

Chapter Three

1   From interviews with Francis Bacon by David Sylvester, recorded and filmed in London for BBC Television, May 1968, in *Francis Bacon: Recent Paintings*, catalogue of an exhibition at the Marlborough New London Gallery, March–April 1967, p. 26.

2   Peter Selz and Jean Dubuffet, *The Work of Jean Dubuffet*, New York, The Museum of Modern Art, 1962, pp. 81–2.

3   Jean Dubuffet, *Prospectus et tous écrits suivants II*, Paris, Gallimard, 1967, p. 74.

Chapter Four

1   Barbara Rose, op. cit., p. 234.

2   Max Kozloff, 'The New American Painting' in Richard Kostelanetz ed., *The New American Arts*, New York, Collier Books, 1967, p. 102.

3   Clement Greenberg, 'Louis and Noland', *Art International*, vol. 4, No. 5, Zurich 1960.

4   Michael Fried, introduction to *Morris Louis 1912–1962*, Boston, Museum of Fine Arts, 1967, p. 21.

5   Michael Fried, catalogue of *Three American Artists*, an exhibition at the Fogg Art Museum, Harvard University, 1965, p. 27.

Chapter Five

1   William C. Seitz, *The Art of Assemblage*, New York, The Museum of Modern Art, 1961, p. 87.

2   John Cage, *Silence*, Middletown, Conn., Wesleyan University Press, 1961, p. 10.

3   Quoted by Pierre Descargues in *Yves Klein*, catalogue of an exhibition at the Jewish Museum, New York, 1967, p. 18.

4   Mario Amaya, *Pop as Art*, London, Studio Vista, 1965, p. 33.

5   Ibid., p. 33.

6   Harold Rosenberg. *The Anxious Object*, London, Thames and Hudson, 1964, pp. 27–8.

7   Quoted by Gene Baro in 'Claes Oldenburg, or the things of this world', *Art International*, New York, November 1966.

8   From replies to questions put by G. R. Swenson, *Art News*, New York, November 1963.

9   Quoted by Mario Amaya, op. cit., p. 95.

10   *Andy Warhol*, catalogue of an exhibition at the Institute of Contemporary Art, University of Pennsylvania, 8 October–21 November 1965.

11   Quoted by Adrian Henry, *Environments and Happenings*, London, Thames and Hudson, 1974, p. 168.

Chapter Six

1   Vasarely in *Vasarely*, Neuchâtel, Editions du Griffon, 1965, pp. 10–12.

2   Ibid., p. 14.

3   Bridget Riley, 'Notes on Some Paintings', *Art and Artists*, III, No. 3, London, June 1968.

4   Guy Brett, *Kinetic Art*, London, Studio Vista, 1968, p. 53.

5   Statement by Johan Severtson in 'Cybernetic Serendipity', a special issue of *Studio International*, London 1968, p. 32.

Chapter Seven

1   Quoted by David Sylvester, catalogue of *Alberto Giacometti, Sculpture, Paintings, Drawings*, an exhibition at the Tate Gallery, London 1965.

2   David Sylvester, catalogue of the retrospective exhibition *Henry Moore* at the Tate Gallery, London 1968, p. 36.

3   In *Studio International*, London January 1968.

4   Statement by Reg Butler on the gramophone record *Five British Sculptors Talk*, London, Caedmon TC 1181.

Chapter Eight

1 Quoted by Frank O'Hara in the catalogue of *David Smith 1906–1965*, an exhibition at the Tate Gallery, London, 1966, p. 7.

2 Ibid, pp. 9–10.

3 'Anthony Caro Interviewed by Andrew Forge', London, *Studio International*, 1968.

4 Bryan Robertson, catalogue of the British Pavilion, Venice Biennale, 1968.

5 Statement in the catalogue of *Tony Smith: Two Exhibitions of Sculpture*, Wadsworth Atheneum, Hartford, Conn., and The Institute of Contemporary Art, University of Pennsylvania, 1966–7.

6 Ibid., note on *Black Box*.

7 Donald Judd, 'Specific Objects', *Contemporary Sculpture*, New York, *The Art Digest (Arts Yearbook 8)*, 1965, p. 79.

8 Robert Morris, 'Notes on Sculpture', *Art-forum*, New York, February 1966, p. 44.

9 Dan Flavin '...In Daylight or Cool White', *Artforum*, New York, December 1965, p. 24.

10 Robert Morris, 'New Talent USA', *Art in America*, New York, July–August 1966, p. 66.

11 Robert Morris, 'Anti-Form', *Artforum*, New York, April 1968, p. 33.

Chapter Nine

1 Interview in *Artforum*, New York, January 1970.

Further Reading

The best sources of information on the development of contemporary art are the files of the following magazines:

In the United States: *Art News*; *Art in America*; *Artforum*; *Arts Magazine*; *Show* (no longer published).

In Great Britain: *Studio International*; *Art and Artists*; *Arts Review*; *Ark* (journal of the Royal College of Art).

In France: *L'Oeil*; *Connaissance des Arts*; *Cimaise*.

In Germany: *Das Kunstwerk*; *Syn*.

In Holland: *Sigma*.

In Italy: *Domus*; *Critics d'Arte*; *L'Arte Moderna*.

In Sweden: *Konstrevy*.

In Switzerland: *Art Internaional*; *Du*.

In Spain: *Goya*.

In Canada: *Arts Canada*.

Another principal source of information consists in the catalogues issued in connection with important exhibitions, notably those at the Museum of Modern Art, New York, and the successive Documenta exhibitions at Kassel. See also:

MICHAEL COMPTON, *New Art at the Tate Gallery*. Exhibition publication, London, Tate Gallery 1983.

Una Generazione postmoderna, catalogue of an exhibition held at the Teatro del Falcone, the Palazzo Bianco and the Palazzo Rosso, Genoa, November 1982–January 1983.

A New Spirit in Painting, catalogue of an exhibition held at the Royal Academy of Arts, London, January–March 1981.

Who Chicago?, catalogue of an exhibition held at the Camden Arts Centre, London, December 1980–March 1981.

Some books of interest (besides those mentioned in the notes) are:

Painting in general

DORE ASHTON, *American Art Since 1945*, London and New York, 1982.

FRANK H. GOODYEAR Jr., *Contemporary American Realism Since 1960*, Boston and Philadelphia, 1981.

WERNER HAFTMANN, *Painting in the 20th Century*, London, 1961, new ed. 1965 (a particularly good source of information for painting in the 1950s).

UDO KULTERMANN, *The New Painting*, London, 1969.

ALDO PELLEGRINI, *New Tendencies in Art*, New York, 1966, and London, 1967 (unreliable critically, covers a wide range of artists).

Sculpture in general

A Dictionary of Modern Sculpture, ed. Robert Maillard, Paris, 1960, and London, 1962 (a source of information for the sculpture of the 1950s).

JACK BURNHAM, *Beyond Modern Sculpture*, London, 1968.

UDO KULTERMANN, *The New Sculpture*, London and New York, 1968.

Pop art

LUCY R.LIPPARD, *Pop Art*, New York and London, 1966.

JOHN RUSSELL and SUZI GABLIK, *Pop Art Redefined*, London and New York, 1969.

CHRISTOPHER FINCH, *Pop Art – Object and Image*, London and New York, 1968.

Kinetic art

FRANK POPPER, *Naissance des arts cinétiques*, Paris, 1967.

STEPHEN BANN, REG GADNEY, FRANK POPPER and PHILIP STEADMAN, *Four Essays on Kinetic Art*, London, 1966.

Later developments

DOUGLAS DAVIS, *Art and the Future*, London, 1973.

ADRIAN HENRI, *Environments and Happenings*, London, 1974. Published in the US as *Total Art*, New York, 1974.

UDO KULTERMANN, *New Realism*, Greenwich, Conn., 1972.

EDWARD LUCIE-SMITH, *Art in the Seventies*, Oxford, 1980.

ALAN SONDHEIM (ed.), *Individuals: Post-Movement Art in America*, New York, 1977.

JOHN A. WALKER, *Art since Pop*, London, 1975.

List of Illustrations

Dimensions are given in centimetres and inches, height preceding width

AGAM, Yaacov (b. 1928)
145 *Appearance* 1965–6. Freestanding metapolymorphic painting, oil on corrugated aluminium painted on both sides 50.2 × 76.2 ($19\frac{3}{4}$ × 30). Collection the Marlborough-Gerson Gallery, New York.

ALBERS, Josef (1888–1976)
69 *Homage to the Square 'Curious'* 1963. Oil on canvas 76.2 × 76.2 (30 × 30). Collection R. Alistair McAlpine, London.

ALECHINSKY, Pierre (b. 1927)
62 *The Green Being Born* 1960. Oil on canvas 184.1 × 205.1 ($72\frac{1}{2}$ × $80\frac{3}{4}$). Musée Royal d'Art Moderne, Brussels.

ANDRÉ, Carl (b. 1935)
4 *144 pieces of aluminium* 1967. Aluminium 111.8 × 365.8 × 365.8 (44 × 144 × 144). Dwan Gallery, New York.

ANNESLEY, David (b. 1936)
204 *Orinoco* 1965. Painted metal 128.9 × 203.2 × 173.9 ($50\frac{3}{4}$ × 80 × $68\frac{1}{2}$). The Tate Gallery, London.

ANUSZKIEWICZ, Richard (b. 1930)
144 *Division of intensity* 1964. Liquitex on canvas 121.9 × 121.9 (48 × 48). Courtesy of the Martha Jackson Gallery, Inc., New York.

APPEL, Karel (b. 1921)
61 *Women and birds* 1958. Oil on canvas 174.6 × 130.2 ($63\frac{3}{4}$ × $51\frac{1}{4}$). Private Collection.

ARMAN (Fernandez Arman, b. 1928)
93 *Clic-Clac Rate* 1960–6. Accumulation of photographic apparatus 60 × 100 ($23\frac{5}{8}$ × $39\frac{3}{8}$). Galleria Schwarz, Milan.

ARMITAGE, Kenneth (b. 1916)
170 *Figure lying on its side (version 5)* 1958–9. Bronze 81.3 (32) long. Collection The British Council, London.

ARNESON, Robert (b.1930)
235 *Californian artist*, 1982. Glazed ceramic 198 × 71 (78 × 28 × 21). Allan Frumkin Gallery, New York.

AUERBACH, Frank (b. 1931)
38 *Head of Helen Gillespie III* 1962–4. Oil on board 74.9 × 61 ($29\frac{1}{2}$ × 24). Courtesy Marlborough Fine Art Ltd, London.

AVEDISIAN, Edward (b. 1936)
86 *At Seven Brothers* 1964. Liquitex on canvas 91.4 × 91.4 (36 × 36). Kasmin Gallery, London.

AYCOCK, Alice (b. 1946)
247 *The savage sparkler*. Mixed media 304.8 × 1,219 × 1,524 (120 × 480 × 600). Plattsburgh College, New York.

BACON, Francis (b. 1910)
41 *Study after Velázquez: Pope Innocent X* 1953. Oil on canvas 152.5 × 118.1 ($60\frac{1}{8}$ × $46\frac{1}{2}$). Collection Carter Burden, New York.

45 *One of three studies for a Crucifixion* 1962. Oil on canvas (centre panel) 198.1 × 144.8 (78 × 57). Courtesy Malborough Fine Art Ltd, London.

BAJ, Enrico (b. 1924)
95 *Lady Fabricia Trolopp* 1964. Collage 100 × 81 ($39\frac{3}{8}$ × $31\frac{7}{8}$). Galleria Schwarz, Milan.

BALTHUS (Balthazar Klossowski de Rola, b. 1908)
44 *The Bedroom* 1954. Oil on canvas 270 × 330 ($106\frac{1}{4}$ × 129 $\frac{7}{8}$). Private Collection.

BASELITZ, Georg (b. 1938)
243 *Model for a sculpture*, 1981. Limewood 199.4 × 199.4 ($78\frac{1}{2}$ × $78\frac{1}{2}$). Whitechapel Art Gallery, London.

BAZAINE, Jean (1904–75)
48 *Shadows on the hill* 1961. Oil on canvas. Galerie Maeght, Paris.

BAZIOTES, William (1912–63)
17 *Congo* 1954. Oil on canvas 181 × 151.8 ($71\frac{1}{4}$ × $59\frac{3}{4}$). Los Angeles County Museum of Art. Gift of Mrs Leonard Sperry.

BELL, Larry (b. 1939)
216 *Untitled* 1971. Coated glass, nine units. Each unit 182.9 × 152.4 × 0.6 (72 × 60 × $\frac{1}{4}$). Tate Gallery, London.

BENTON, Dr Stephen (b. 1941)
161 *Crystal beginnings* 1977. White light transmission holograph together with the inventor. *Photo M. Lutch, MOH Photo Archive.*

BEUYS, Joseph (b. 1921)
2 *Action in 7 Exhibitions* 1972. Tate Gallery, London. *Photo Lucie-Smith.*

7 *Dernier espace avec introspecteur* 1982. Mixed media. Installation, Anthony d'Offay Gallery, London.

BILL, Max (b. 1908)
68 *Concentration to brightness* 1964. Oil on canvas 105.4 × 105.4 ($41\frac{1}{2}$ × $41\frac{1}{2}$).

BLAKE, Peter (b. 1932)
111 *Doktor K. Tortur* 1965. Cryla, collage on hardboard 61 × 25.4 (24 × 10). Robert Fraser Gallery, London.

BOMBERG, David (1890–1957)
37 *Monastery of Ay Chrisostomos, Cyprus* 1948. Oil on canvas 91.4 × 91.4 (36 × 36). Courtesy Marlborough Fine Art Ltd, London.

BOROFSKY, Jon (b. 1942)
233 *Hammering Man at 2,772,489 (JB27 sculp)*, 1981. Aluminium and steel, h. 792.5 (312). Installation, Kunsthalle, Basel. *Photo Paula Cooper Gallery, New York.*

BOSHIER, Derek (b. 1937)
112 *England's Glory* 1961. Oil on canvas 101.6 × 127.6 (40 × $50\frac{1}{4}$). Grabowski Gallery, London.

BRAQUE, Georges (1882–1963)
34 *Studio IX* 1952–6. Oil on canvas 145.4 × 146 ($57\frac{1}{4}$ × $57\frac{1}{2}$). Galerie Maeght, Paris.

BRATBY, John (b. 1928)
33 *Window, self-portrait, Jean and hands* 1957. Oil on board 121.9 × 365.8 (48 × 144). The Tate Gallery, London.

BRISLEY, Stuart (b. 1933)
137 *And For Today – Nothing* 1972. Action, Gallery House, London.

BUFFET, Bernard (b. 1928)
66 *Self-portrait* 1954. Oil on canvas 146.4 × 114 ($57\frac{5}{8}$ × $44\frac{7}{8}$). The Tate Gallery, London.

BUREN, Daniel (b. 1939)
231 *On two levels with two colours*, 1976. Installation, Lisson Gallery, London.

BURRI, Alberto (b. 1915)
56 *Sacco 4* 1954. Burlap, cotton, rinavil glue, silk and paint on cotton canvas 114.3 × 76.2 (45 × 30). Collection Anthony Denney, London.

BURY, Pol (b. 1922)
155 *The Erectile Entities*. Copper. Collection Günther Sachs, Lausanne.

BUTLER, Reg (1913–81)
173 *Girl* 1953–4. Bronze 177.8 × 40.6 × 24.1 (70 × 16 × $9\frac{1}{2}$). The Tate Gallery, London.

226 *Girl on long base* 1968–72. Painted bronze h. 147.3 (58). Courtesy of the artist.

CALDER, Alexander (1898–1976)
150 *Antennae with red and blue dots* 1960. Kinetic metal sculpture. 111 × 128.3 × 128.3 ($43\frac{3}{4}$ × $50\frac{1}{2}$ × $50\frac{1}{2}$) (range). The Tate Gallery, London.

184 *The Red Crab* 1962. Stabile, steel plates 304.8 × 609.6 × 304.8 (120 × 240 × 120). Museum of Fine Arts, Houston, Tex.

CAMARGO, Sergio de (b. 1930)
148 *Large split white relief no. 34/74* 1965. Assembled relief 215.3 × 92.1 × 27.3 ($84\frac{3}{4}$ × $36\frac{1}{4}$ × $10\frac{3}{4}$). The Tate Gallery, London.

CARO, Anthony (b. 1924)
148 *Homage to David Smith* 1966. Painted steel 137.2 × 304.8 × 162.6 (54 × 120 × 64). Collection Mary Swift, Washington DC.

209 *Sun-feast* 1969–70. Painted steel 181.6 × 416.6 × 218.4 ($71\frac{1}{2}$ × 164 × 86). Private Collection.

CASCELLA, Andrea (b. 1920)
179 *The White Bride* 1962. White marble, 3 parts 61 × 36.8 (24 × $14\frac{1}{2}$). Grosvenor Gallery, London.

CAULFIELD, Patrick (b. 1936)
115 *Still-life with red and white pot* 1966. Oil on board 160 × 213.4 (63 × 84). Harry N. Abrams Family Collection, New York.

CÉSAR (César Baldaccini, b. 1921)
194 *Dauphine* 1961. Bronze 160 (63). Galerie Claude Bernard, Paris.

CHADWICK, Lynn (b. 1914)
171 *Winged Figures* 1955. Bronze 55.9 (22). The Tate Gallery, London.

CHAMBERLAIN, John (b. 1927)
192 *Untitled* 1960. Welded metal 50.8 × 40.6 × 30.5 (20 × 16 × 12). Joseph H. Hirshhorn Collection.

CHIA, Sandro (b. 1946)
242 *Crocodile tears*, 1982. Oil on canvas 287 × 234 (113 × 92). Anthony d'Offay Gallery, London.

CHICAGO, Judy (Judy Cohen Gerowitz, b. 1939)
249 *The Dinner Party*, 1979. Mixed media, length of each side 119.4 (47). *Photo Michael Alexander, courtesy Through the Flower Corporation.*

CHILLIDA, Eduardo (b. 1924)
200 *Modulation of space* 1963. Metal 54 × 69.8 × 40 ($21\frac{1}{4}$ × $27\frac{1}{2}$ × $15\frac{3}{4}$). The Tate Gallery, London.

CHRISTO (Christo Jaracheff, b. 1935)
101 *Packaged public building* 1961. Photomontage 33 × 91.1 (13 × $35\frac{7}{8}$). Collection the artist.

CLEMENTE, Francesco (b. 1952)
241 *Toothache*, 1981. Pastel on paper 61 × 45.7 (24 × 18). Anthony d'Offay Gallery, London. *Photo Prudence Cuming Associates.*

CLOSE, Chuck (b. 1940)
224 *Nat* 1972. Watercolour on paper 173 × 167.3 ($68\frac{1}{8}$ × $65\frac{7}{8}$). Ludwig Collection, Neue Galerie, Aachen.

CONNER, Bruce (b. 1933)
99 *Couch* 1963. Assemblage 80 × 671 × 1,831 ($31\frac{1}{2}$ × 264 × 721). Pasadena Art Museum.

CORNEILLE (Cornelis van Beverloo, b. 1922)
63 *Souvenir of Amsterdam* 1956. Oil on canvas 120 × 120 ($47\frac{1}{4}$ × $47\frac{1}{4}$). Private Collection, Paris.

CORNELL, Joseph (1903–73)
94 *Eclipse series c.* 1962. Construction 304.8 × 487.7 × 152.4 (120 × 192 × 60). Collection of Allan Stone, New York.

CRUZ-DIEZ, Carlos (b. 1923)
143 *Physichromie no. 1* 1959. Plastic and wood 49.8 × 49.8 ($19\frac{5}{8}$ × $19\frac{5}{8}$). Collection the artist.

DALI, Salvador (b. 1904)
8 *Christ of St John of the Cross* 1951. Oil on canvas 205.1 × 116.2 ($80\frac{3}{4}$ × $45\frac{3}{4}$). Glasgow Art Gallery and Museum.

DAVIE, Alan (b. 1920)
60 *The Martyrdom of St Catherine* 1956. Oil on canvas 182.9 × 243.9 (72 × 96). Collection Mrs Alan Davie.

DAVIES, John (b. 1946)
225 *Head of William Jeffrey*. Painted polyester resin, fibreglass and inert fillers 30.5 × 20.3 × 39.4 (12 × 8 × $15\frac{1}{2}$). The Tate Gallery, London. *Photo John Webb.*

DAVIS, Brad (b. 1942)
234 *Evening shore*, 1983. Acrylic and polyester on canvas 182.9 × 248.9 (72 × 98). Private Collection, New York. *Photo Holly Solomon Gallery, New York (D. James Deel).*

DE ANDREA, John (b. 1941)
227 *Freckled woman* 1974. Polyester and fibreglass polychromed. Life size. Courtesy of O. K. Harris Gallery, New York.

DENNY, Robyn (b. 1930)
90 *Growing* 1967. Oil on canvas 243.8 × 198.1 (96 × 78). Collection The Peter Stuyvesant Foundation.

DINE, Jim (b. 1935)
124 *Double red self-portrait (The Green Lines)* 1964. Oil and collage on canvas 304.8 × 213.4 (120 × 84). Courtesy Sidney Janis Gallery, New York.

134 *The Car Crash* 1960 (Happening). *Photo Robert McElroy, New York.*

DONALDSON, Anthony (b. 1939)
116 Take Away no. 2 1963. Oil on canvas 152.4 × 152.4 (60 × 60). Collection R. Alistair McAlpine, London.

DUBUFFET, Jean (b. 1901)
65 *Corps de Dame* 1950. Watercolour 31.1 × 23.5 ($12\frac{1}{4}$ × $9\frac{1}{4}$). Collection Peter Cochrane, London.

DUCHAMP, Marcel (1887–1968)
3 *Bottle rack* 1914. Readymade 64.1 ($25\frac{1}{4}$). Now lost.

ERNST, Max (1891–1976)
35 *Cry of the seagull* 1953. Oil on canvas 94.6 × 130.2 ($37\frac{1}{4}$ × $51\frac{1}{4}$). Collection François de Menil, Houston, Tex.

ESTES, Richard (b. 1936)
220 *Paris street-scene* 1972. Oil on canvas 105.1 × 152.1 ($41\frac{3}{8}$ × $59\frac{7}{8}$). Collection Sydney and Frances Lewis.

ESTEVE, Maurice (b. 1904)
47 *Composition 166* 1957. Oil on wood 50.5 × 63.8 ($19\frac{7}{8}$ × $25\frac{1}{8}$). The Tate Gallery, London.

FAUTRIER, Jean (1897–1964)
49 *Hostage* 1945. Oil on canvas 27.3 × 21.6 ($10\frac{3}{4}$ × $8\frac{1}{2}$). Private Collection, London.

FERBER, Herbert (b. 1906)
182 *Homage to Piranesi* 1962–3. Copper 233.7 × 124.5 (92 × 49). Collection the artist.

FETTING, Rainer (b. 1949)
245 *Dancers III*, 1982. Powder paint on cotton 224.8 × 280.7 ($88\frac{1}{2}$ × $110\frac{1}{2}$). Anthony d'Offay Gallery, London.

FLAVIN, Dan (b. 1933)
215 *Untitled (to the 'innovator' wheeling beachblow)* 1968. Fluorescent light (pink, gold and 'daylight') 243.9 × 243.9 (96 × 96). Dwan Gallery, New York.

FONTANA, Lucio (1899–1968)
104 *Spatial Concept* 1960. Oil on canvas 97.1 × 59.7 ($38\frac{1}{4}$ × $23\frac{1}{2}$). McRoberts and Tunnard Gallery, London.

FRANCIS, Sam (b. 1923)
25 *Blue on a point* 1958. Oil on canvas 182.9 × 243.8 (72 × 96). Private Collection.

FRANKENTHALER, Helen (b. 1928)
77 *Mountains and sea* 1952. Oil on canvas 219.4 × 297.8 ($86\frac{3}{8}$ × $117\frac{1}{4}$). Collection the artist.

GIACOMETTI, Alberto (1901–66)
40 *Portrait of Jean Genet* 1959. Oil on canvas 64.8 × 54.6 ($25\frac{1}{2}$ × $21\frac{1}{2}$). Private Collection.

162 *Woman with her throat cut* 1932. Bronze 87.9 ($34\frac{5}{8}$) long. Collection Mr and Mrs Pierre Matisse, New York.

163 *Man walking III* 1960. Bronze. Galerie Maeght, Paris.

GILBERT AND GEORGE (both b. 1942)
139 *Singing Sculpture* November 1970. *Photo courtesy of Nigel Greenwood Inc.*

GOINGS, Ralph (b. 1928)
223 *Airstream* 1970. Oil on canvas 152.1 × 214 ($59\frac{7}{8}$ × $84\frac{1}{4}$). Ludwig Collection, Neue Galerie, Aachen.

GONZÁLEZ, Julio (1876–1942)
188 *The Angel* 1933. Iron 160 (63). Musée National d'Art Moderne, Paris.

GORKY, Arshile (1904–48)
11 *The Betrothal II* 1947. Oil on canvas 128.9 × 96.5 ($50\frac{3}{4}$ × 38). Collection Whitney Museum of American Art, New York.

GOTTLIEB, Adolph (1903–74)
19 *The Frozen Sounds Number 1* 1951. Oil on canvas 91.4 × 121.9 (36 × 48). Collection Whitney Museum of American Art, New York. Gift of Mr and Mrs Samuel Kootz.

GRAVES, Nancy (b. 1940)
236 *Triped*, 1983. Bronze with polychrome patina 88.9 × 114.3 × 68.6 (35 × 45 × 27). M. Knoedler and Co., New York.

GRECO, Emilio (b. 1913)
174 *Seated figure* 1951. Bronze 132.4 ($52\frac{1}{8}$). The Tate Gallery, London.

GUSTON, Philip (1913–80)
24 *The Clock* 1956–7. Oil on canvas 193 × 162.9 (76 × $64\frac{1}{8}$). Collection The Museum of Modern Art, New York. Gift of Mrs Bliss Parkinson.

238 *The rug*, 1979. Oil on canvas 203.2 × 279.4 (80 × 110). Private Collection.

GUTTUSO; Renato (b. 1912)
42 *The Discussion* 1959–60. Tempera, oil and collage on canvas 220 × 248 ($86\frac{5}{8}$ × $97\frac{5}{8}$). The Tate Gallery, London.

HALL, David (b. 1937)
208 *Nine* 1967. Lamin board and polyurethane paint, sprayed pale blue/grey 579.1 × 518.2 × 7.6 (228 × 204 × 3). Collection the artist.

HAMILTON, Richard (b. 1922)
109 *Just What is it that Makes To-day's Homes so Different, so Appealing?* 1956. Collage 26 × 24.8 ($10\frac{1}{4}$ × $9\frac{3}{4}$). Collection E. Janss, Los Angeles.

HANSON, Duane (b. 1928)
221 *Florida shopper* 1973. Mixed media. Life size. Collection Mr and Mrs Charles Saatchi, London. *Photo Courtesy of DM Gallery, London.*

HARTUNG, Hans (b. 1904)
51 *Painting T 54–16* 1954. Oil on canvas 129.9 × 96.8 ($51\frac{1}{8}$ × $38\frac{1}{8}$). Musée National d'Art Moderne, Paris.

HAUSER, Erich (b. 1930)
199 *Space column 7/68* 1968. Steel 328.9 × 860.4 × 250.2 ($129\frac{1}{2}$ × $338\frac{3}{4}$ × $98\frac{1}{2}$). Galerie Müller, Stuttgart.

HELD, Al (b. 1928)
72 *Echo* 1966. Acrylic on canvas 213.4 × 182.9 (84 × 72). André Emmerich Gallery, New York.

HEPWORTH, Barbara (1903–75)
167 *Two figures* 1947–8. Elm, painted white 121.9 (48). Collection of the University Gallery, University of Minnesota.

168 *Hollow form (Penwith)* 1955. Lagos wood 91.4 (36). Collection The Museum of Modern Art, New York.

HERON, Patrick (b. 1920)
26 *Manganese in Deep Violet*: January 1967. Oil on canvas 101.6 × 152.4 (40 × 60). Collection J. Walter Thompson Company, London.

HOCKNEY, David (b. 1937)
113 *Picture emphasizing stillness* 1962–3. Oil on canvas 182.9 × 152.4 (72 × 60). Collection Mark Glazebrook, London.

114 *A neat lawn* 1967. Acrylic on canvas 243.8 × 243.8 (96 × 96). Kasmin Gallery, London.

119 *Rubber ring floating in a swimming pool* 1971. Acrylic on canvas 90.8 × 121.9 ($35\frac{3}{4}$ × 48). Private collection, Japan.

HOFMANN Hans (1880–1966)
16 *Rising Moon* 1964. Oil on canvas 213.4 × 198.1 (84 × 78). André Emmerich Gallery, New York.

HOWE, Delmas (b. 1935)
248 *Theseus and Pirithoüs at the chutes*, 1981–2. Oil on canvas 111.8 × 172.7 (44 × 68). Collection the artist.

HOYLAND, John (b. 1934)
87 *28.5.66* 1966. Acrylic on canvas 198.1 × 365.8 (78 × 144). The Tate Gallery, London.

HUNDERTWASSER (Fritz Stowasser, b. 1928)
64 *The Hokkaido Steamer* 1961. Watercolour on rice-paper, with a chalk ground 47.9 × 66 ($18\frac{7}{8}$ × 26). Collection S. and G. Poppe, Hamburg.

JARAY, Tess (b. 1939)
88 *Garden of Allah* 1966. Oil on canvas 198.1 × 243.8 (72 × 96). Collection the artist.

JOHNS, Jasper (b. 1930)
92 *Numbers in Colour* 1959. Encaustic and collage on canvas 168.9 × 125.7 ($66\frac{1}{2}$ × $49\frac{1}{2}$). Albright-Knox Art Gallery, Buffalo, N.Y. Gift of Seymour H. Knox.

JONES, Allen (b. 1937)
122 *Hermaphrodite* 1963. Oil on canvas 182.9 × 61 (72 × 24). Walker Art Gallery, Liverpool.

JORN, Asger (1914–73)
59 *You never know* 1966. Oil on canvas 64.8 × 81.3 ($25\frac{1}{2}$ × 32). Arthur Tooth & Sons, Ltd, London.

JUDD, Donald (b. 1928)
212 *Untitled* 1965. Galvanized iron and aluminium 88.8 × 358.1 × 76.2 (33 × 141 × 30). Leo Castelli Gallery, New York.

KELLY, Ellsworth (b. 1923)
71 *White – Dark Blue* 1962. Oil on canvas 147.9 × 83.8 ($58\frac{1}{4}$ × 33). Arthur Tooth & Sons, Ltd, London.

KIEFER, Anselm (b. 1945)
228 *Untitled*, 1978. Oil, emulsion, woodcut, shellac, latex and straw on canvas 260.3 × 189.9 ($102\frac{1}{2}$ × $74\frac{3}{4}$). Anthony d'Offay Gallery, London. *Photo Prudence Cuming Associates.*

KIENHOLZ, Edward (b. 1927)
98 *Roxy's* 1962. Mixed media 240 × 540.7 × 669.9 ($94\frac{1}{2}$ × $212\frac{5}{8}$ × $263\frac{3}{4}$). Collection the artist. *Photo Dwan Gallery, New York.*

KING, Phillip (b. 1934)
203 *Genghis Khan* 1963. Purple plastic 213.4 × 365.8 (84 × 144). Collection The Peter Stuyvesant Foundation.

210 *Span* 1967. Metal 243.8 × 472.2 × 533.4 (96 × 186 × 210). National Gallery of Victoria, Melbourne. *Photo Hugh Gordon.*

KITAJ, R. B. (b. 1932)
121 *Synchromy with F.B. – General of Hot Desire* (diptych) 1968–9. Oil on canvas 152.4 × 91.4 (60 × 36) each panel. Courtesy Marlborough Fine Art Ltd, London.

KLEIN, Yves (1928–62)
102 Painting ceremony (the creation of *Imprints*). *Photo Shunk-Kender, Paris.*

103 *Feu F 45* 1961. Oil on paper 79.4 × 102.9 (31¼ × 40½). Private Collection, Paris.

KLINE, Franz (1910–62)
21 *Chief* 1950. Oil on canvas 148.3 × 186.7 (58⅜ × 73½). Collection The Museum of Modern Art, New York. Gift of Mr and Mrs David M. Solinger.

KOONING, Willem de (b. 1904)
23 *Woman and bicycle* 1952–3. Oil on canvas 194.3 × 124.5 (76½ × 49). Collection Whitney Museum of American Art, New York.

KOSSOF, Leon (b. 1926)
39 *Profile of Rachel* 1965. Oil on board 86.4 × 61 (34 × 24). Courtesy Marlborough Fine Art Ltd, London.

KOSUTH, Joseph (b. 1945)
229 *One and three chairs*, 1965. Mixed media. The Museum of Modern Art, New York, Larry Aldrich Foundation Fund.

KUSAMA, Yayoi (b. 1940)
135 *Endless Love Room* 1965–6. Environment.

LASSAW, Ibram (b. 1913)
183 *Space densities* 1967. Steel, brass, phosphor bronze 134.6 × 63.5 × 43.2 (53 × 25 × 17). Wichita Art Museum, Wichita, Kans.

LÉGER, Fernand (1881–1955)
29 *The Constructors* 1950. Oil on canvas 302.3 × 215.9 (119 × 85). Musée Fernand Léger, Biot.

LENK, Kaspar Thomas (b. 1933)
213 *Schichtung 22a* 1966. Coloured wood 109.9 × 109.9 × 40 (43¼ × 43¼ × 15¾). Galerie Müller, Stuttgart.

LE PARC, Julio (b. 1928)
160 *Continuel-mobile, Continuel-lumière* 1963. Assembled relief 160 × 160 × 22.9 (63 × 63 × 9). The Tate Gallery, London.

LEWITT, Sol (b. 1923)
5 *A7* 1967. Painted metal sculpture 34.9 × 34.2 × 34.2 (13¾ × 13½ × 13½). Dwan Gallery, New York.

LICHTENSTEIN, Roy (b. 1923)
125 *Whaam!* 1963. Acrylic on canvas 172.7 × 40.6 (68 × 160). The Tate Gallery, London.

126 *Yellow and red brushstrokes* 1966. Oil on canvas 205.1 × 174 (80¾ × 68½). Collection Philippe Durand-Ruel.

127 *Hopeless* 1963. Oil on canvas 111.8 × 111.8 (44 × 44). Collection Mr and Mrs Michael Sonnabend, Paris–New York.

LIJN, Liliane (b. 1939)
157 *Liquid reflections* 1966–7. Perspex disc filled with water and oil, light source separate 55.9 wide × 20.3 high (22 × 8) including balls. Axiom Gallery, London.

LIPPOLD, Richard (b. 1915)
187 *Flight* 1962. Gold, stainless steel 914 × 2,436 × 1,219 (360 × 960 × 480). Vanderbilt Avenue Lobby of the Pan American Building, New York.

LOHSE, Richard (b. 1902)
70 *Fifteen systematic colour scales merging vertically* 1950–67. Oil on canvas 120.6 × 120.6 (47¼ × 47¼). Kunsthaus, Zurich.

LONG, Richard (b. 1945)
218 *A line in Ireland* 1974. Courtesy of the artist.

LOUIS, Morris (1912–62)
78 *Untitled* 1959. Magna acrylic on canvas 264.2 × 193 (104 × 76). *Photo Kasmin Gallery, London.*

80 OMICRON 1961. Synthetic polymer paint on canvas 262.3 × 412 (103¼ × 162¼). Waddington Gallery, London.

McCRACKEN, John (b. 1934)
214 *There's No Reason Not To* 1967. Wood, fibreglass 412.1 × 45.7 × 8.9 (120 × 18 × 3½). Nicholas Wilder Gallery, Los Angeles.

MACK, Heinz (b. 1931)
156 *Light dynamo* 1963. Kinetic sculpture 57.1 × 57.1 × 31.7 (22½ × 22½ × 12¼). The Tate Gallery, London.

MAGRITTE, René (1898–1967)
13 *Exhibition of painting* 1965. Oil on canvas 80 × 65.1 (31½ × 25⅝). Collection Alexander Iolas, New York, Paris, Milan, Madrid, Rome, Geneva.

MANZONI, Piero (1933–63)
104 *Line 20 metres long* 1959. Ink on paper. Collection Edward Lucie-Smith, London.

MANZU, Giacomo (b. 1908)
175 *Fruit and vegetables on a chair* 1960. Gilded bronze 100 (39⅜).

176 *The Death of Abel* 1964. Bronze 92.1 × 62.9 (36¼ × 24¾). St Peter's, Rome.

177 *The Death of Pope John* 1964. Bronze 92.1 × 62.9 (36¼ × 24⅜). St Peter's, Rome.

MARINI Marino (1901–80)
172 *Horse and rider* 1947. Bronze 162.6 (64). The Tate Gallery, London.

MARTIN, Kenneth (b. 1905)
202 *Rotary rings* 1967. Brass 54 (21¼) high, 17.8 (7) at broadest. Axiom Gallery, London.

MASSON, André (b. 1896)
9 *Landscape with precipices* 1948. Oil on canvas 205.7 × 254 (81 × 100). Galerie Louise Leiris, Paris.

MATHIEU, Georges (b. 1922)
58 *Battle of Bouvines* 1954. Oil on canvas 250.2 × 600.1 (98½ × 236¼). Collection the artist.

MATISSE, Henri (1869–1954)
30 *Zulma* 1950. Gouache cut-out 238 × 133 (93¾ × 52⅜). Statens Museum for Kunst, Copenhagen.

31 *The Snail* 1953. Gouache cut-out 726.4 × 983 (286 × 387). The Tate Gallery, London.

MATTA, Roberto (b. 1911)
10 *Being With* 1945–6. Oil on canvas 455 × 221.9 (179⅛ × 87⅜). Pierre Matisse Gallery, New York.

MEADOWS, Bernard (b. 1915)
169 *Standing armed figure* 1962. Bronze 162.6 (64). Gimpel Fils Gallery, London.

MICHAUX, Henri (b. 1899)
55 *Painting in india ink* 1960–7. 74.9 × 105.1 (29½ × 41⅜). Galerie Le Point Cardinal, Paris.

MIDDLEDITCH, Edward (b. 1923)
43 *Dead chicken in a stream* 1955. Oil on board 136.5 × 109.2 (53¾ × 43). The Tate Gallery, London.

MIKI, Tomio (b. 1938)
108 *Ears (detail)* 1968. Plated aluminium 17.1 × 15.9 × 7 (6¾ × 6¼ × 2¾). Minami Gallery, Tokyo.

MILLARES, Manolo (1926–72)
54 *No. 165* 1961. Plastic paint on canvas 81.3 × 100.3 (32 × 39½). Courtesy Marlborough Fine Art Ltd, London.

MIRÓ, Joan (1893–1983)
36 *Blue II* 1961. Oil on canvas 269.2 × 355.6 (106 × 140). Pierre Matisse Gallery, New York.

MOON, Jeremy (1934–73)
91 *Blue Rose* 1967. Oil on canvas 218.4 × 251.5 (86 × 99). The Tate Gallery, London.

MOORE, Henry (b. 1898)
165 *Internal and external forms* 1953–4. Elmwood 261.6 (103). Albright-Knox Art Gallery, Buffalo, N.Y.

166 *(Lambert) Locking-piece* 1963–4. Bronze 292.1 (115). Collection Banque Lambert, Brussels.

MORELLET, François (b. 1926)
159 *Sphère-trames* 1962. Aluminium 217.2 (85½) diameter. Indica Gallery, London.

MORLEY, Malcolm (b. 1931)
219 *St John's Yellow Pages* 1971. Oil on canvas 403.9 × 348 (159 × 137). Ludwig Collection, Wallraf-Richartz Museum, Cologne.

MORRIS, Robert (b. 1931)
211 *Untitled (circular light piece)* 1966. Plexiglass 61 × 243.9 (24 × 96) diameter. Dwan Gallery, New York.

MOTHERWELL, Robert (b. 1915)
18 *Elegy to the Spanish Republic no. LV* 1955–60. Oil on canvas 177.8 × 193.3 (70 × 76⅛). Contemporary Collection of the Cleveland Museum of Art.

NAKIAN, Reuben (b. 1897)
181 *The Goddess of the Golden Thighs* 1964–5. Bronze 386.1 (152). Courtesy of the Detroit Institute of Arts.

186 *Olympia* 1960–2. Bronze 182.9 × 182.9 (72 × 72). Whitney Museum of American Art, New York. Gift of the Friends of the Whitney Museum.

NEVELSON, Louise (b. 1900)
191 *Royal Tide V* 1960. Wood, painted gold (21 compartments) 205.1 × 259.1 (80¾ × 102). Private Collection.

NEWMAN, Barnett (1905–70)
74 *Tundra* 1950. Oil on canvas 182.9 × 226.1 (72 × 89). Collection Mr and Mrs Robert A. Rowan.

NOLAN, Sidney (b. 1917)
119 *Glenrowan* 1956–7. Ripolin on hardboard 91.4 × 121.9 (36 × 48). The Tate Gallery, London.

NOLAND, Kenneth (b. 1924)
79 *Cantabile* 1962. Plastic paint on canvas 168.9 × 163.2 (66½ × 64¼). Collection Walker Art Center, Minneapolis.

81 *Grave Light* 1965. Plastic paint on canvas 259.1 × 228.6 (102 × 90). Collection Mr and Mrs Robert A. Rowan.

OLDENBURG, Claes (b. 1929)
123 *Study for Giant Chocolate* 1966. Enamel and plaster 26.7 × 11.4 × 11.4 (10½ × 4½ × 4½). Robert Fraser Gallery, London.

136 *Store Days* 1965. Action. New York. Photo Robert McElroy.

OLITSKI, Jules (b. 1922)
86 *Feast* 1965. Magna acrylic on canvas 236.2 × 66 (93 × 26). Collection Catherine Zimmerman. Brookline, Mass.

OPPENHEIM, Dennis (b. 1938)
232 *Reading position* 1970. *Photo courtesy of the artist.*

PALADINO, Mimmo (b. 1948)
240 *It's always evening*, 1982. Mixed media on canvas (centre panel of tryptich) 219.7 × 480.1 (86½ × 189). Private collection. *Photo Prudence Cuming Associates.*

PAOLINO, Giulio (b. 1940)
230 *Apotheosis of Homer*, 1970–1. Tape recorded sound and 32 photographs. Studio Marconi, Milan.

PAOLOZZI, Eduardo (b. 1924)
189 *Japanese War God* 1958. Bronze 152.4 (60). Albright Knox Art Gallery, Buffalo, N.Y.

201 *Etsso* 1967. Aluminium 139.7 × 121.9 × 78.7 (55 × 48 × 31). Hanover Gallery, London.

PENCK, A. R. (b. 1939)
244 *T3 (R)*, 1982. Acrylic on canvas 299.7 × 198.8 (118 × 78¼). Galerie Michael Werner, Cologne.

PASCHKE, Ed (b. 1939)
237 *Minnie*, 1974. Oil on canvas 128.9 × 96.5 (50¾ × 38). Courtesy The Art Institute of Chicago.

PHILLIPS, Peter (b. 1939)
110 *For men only starring MM and BB* 1961. Oil on canvas 274.3 × 152.4 (108 × 60). The Calouste Gulbenkian Foundation, London.

PICASSO, Pablo (1881–1973)
28 *Massacre in Korea* 1951. Oil 109.9 × 169.5 (43¼ × 66¾). Collection the artist.

178 *Head of a woman* 1951. Bronze 54.6 (21½). The Solomon R. Guggenheim Museum. The Joseph H. Hirshhorn Collection.

6 *The Woman of Algiers* 1955. Oil on canvas 114 × 146 (44⅞ × 57½). Collection Mr and Mrs Victor W. Ganz.

PIGNON, Edouard (b. 1905)
46 *The Miner* 1949. Oil on canvas 92.1 × 73 (36¼ × 28¾). The Tate Gallery, London.

PISTOLETTO, Michelangelo (b. 1933)
106 *Seated figure* 1962. Collage on polished steel 125.1 × 125.1 (49¼ × 49¼). Kaiser-Wilhelm-Museum, Krefeld.

POLLOCK, Jackson (1912–56)
14 *Number 2* 1949. Oil, Duco and aluminium paint on canvas 97.8 × 481.3 (38½ × 189½). Munson-Williams-Proctor Institute, Utica, N.Y.

15 Jackson Pollock at work. *Photo Hans Namuth, New York.*

POMODORO, Arnaldo (b. 1926)
180 *Sphere no. 1* 1963. Bronze 120 (47¼) diameter. Collection The Museum of Modern Art, New York.

POONS, Larry (b. 1937)
84 *Night Journey* 1968. Acrylic on canvas 274.3 × 315 (108 × 124). Collection Carter Burden, New York.

RAUSCHENBERG, Robert (b. 1925)
96 *Bed* 1955. Combine painting 188 × 7.6 (74 × 3). Collection Mr and Mrs Leo Castelli.

97 *Barge* 1962. Oil on canvas 203.2 × 988.1 (80 × 389). Leo Castelli Gallery, New York.

RAYSSE, Martial (b. 1936)
107 *Tableau simple et doux* 1965. Assemblage with neon light 194.9 × 130.2 (76¾ × 51¼). Collection André Mourgues, Paris.

REINHARDT, Ad (1913–67)
75 *Red painting* 1952. Oil on canvas 365.8 × 193 (144 × 76). The Metropolitan Museum of Art, New York. Arthur H. Hearn Fund, 1968.

RICHIER, Germaine (1904–59)
164 *The Hurricane* 1948–9. Bronze 153.7 × 194 (60½ × 76⅜). Musée National d'Art Moderne, Paris.

RICKEY, George (b. 1907)
149 *Six squares, one rectangle* 1967. Stainless steel 81.3 × 40.6 × 33 (32 × 16 × 13). Staempfli Gallery, New York.

RILEY, Bridget (b. 1931)
142 *Crest* 1964. Emulsion on board 166.4 × 166.4 (65½ × 65 ½). Rowan Gallery, London.

RIOPELLE, Jean-Paul (b. 1924)
52 *Encounter* 1956. Oil on canvas 99.7 × 81.3 (39¼ × 32). Wallraf-Richartz Museum, Cologne.

RIVERS, Larry (b. 1923)
130 *Parts of the face* 1961. Oil on canvas 74.9 × 74.9 (29½ × 29½). The Tate Gallery, London.

ROSENQUIST, James (b. 1933)
131 *Silver skies* 1962. Oil on canvas 198.1 × 41.9 (78 × 16½). Collection Mr and Mrs Robert C. Scull.

ROSZAK, Theodore (b. 1907)
185 *Invocation I* 1947. Steel 75.6 (29¾). The Solomon R. Guggenheim Museum, New York. The Joseph H. Hirshhorn Collection.

ROTHENBERG, Susan (b. 1945)
246 *Beggar*, 1982. Oil on canvas 100.3 × 128.3 (39½ × 50½). Willard Gallery, New York. *Photo Roy M. Elkind.*

ROTHKO, Mark (1903–70)
20 *Orange Yellow Orange* 1969. Oil on paper mounted on linen 123.2 × 102.9 (48½ × 40½). Collection of the Marlborough-Gerson Gallery, New York.

SCHNABEL, Julian (b. 1951)
239 *Humanity asleep*, 1982. Painted ceramic relief on wood 275 × 365.8 (108¼ × 144). The Tate Gallery, London.

SCHÖFFER, Nicolas (b. 1912)
158 *Chronos 8* 1968. 300.2 (118⅛). Collection the artist.

SCHWARZKOGLER, Rudolf (1941–69)
138 *Action* May 1965. Vienna.

SCOTT, Tim (b. 1937)
205 *Trireme* 1968. Steel tube, acrylic sheet, painted 457.2 × 396.2 × 167.6 (180 × 156 × 66). Waddington Gallery, London. *Photo John Goldblatt.*

SEGAL, George (b. 1924)
222 *Girl on a red wicker couch* 1973. Mixed media. *Photo Sidney Janis Gallery, New York.*

SMITH, David (1906–65)
195 *Hudson River landscape* 1951. Steel 228.6 (900) long. Collection Whitney Museum of American Art, New York.

196 *Voltri VII* 1962. Steel 304.8 (120) wide. Collection of the Marlborough-Gerson Gallery, New York.

197 *Cubi XVIII* 1964. Stainless steel 294 (115¾). Courtesy Marlborough-Gerson Gallery, New York.

SMITH, Richard (b. 1931)
117 *Soft Pack* 1963. Oil on canvas 213.4 × 175.3 (84 × 69). Joseph H. Hirshhorn Collection, New York.

118 *Tailspan* 1965. Acrylic on wood 119.9 × 212.7 × 90.2 (47¼ × 83¾ × 35½). The Tate Gallery, London.

SMITH, Tony (1912–80)
207 *Playground* 1962. Wood mock-up to be made in steel 162.6 × 162.6 (64 × 64). Fischbach Gallery, New York.

SMITHSON, Robert (1938–73)
217 *Spiral Jetty* 1970. Great Salt Lake, Utah.

SOTO, Jesús Rafael (b. 1923)
147 *Petite Double Face* 1967. Wood and metal 60 × 38.1 (23⅝ × 15). Collection Mr and Mrs Serge Sacknoff, Washington. *Photo courtesy Marlborough-Gerson Gallery, New York.*

SOULAGES, Pierre (b. 1919)
57 *Painting* 1956. Oil on canvas 150.5 × 194.9 (59¼ × 76¾). Collection The

Museum of Modern Art, New York. Gift of Mr and Mrs Samuel M. Kootz.

STAËL, Nicolas de (1914–55)
67 *Agrigente* 1954. Oil on canvas 65.3 × 81 (25⅝ × 31⅞). Private Collection, Paris.

STANKIEWICZ, Richard (1922–83)
193 *Kabuki Dancer* 1956. Steel and cast iron 203.8 (80¼). Collection Whitney Museum of American Art, New York. Gift of the Friends of the Whitney Museum.

STELLA, Frank (b. 1936)
82 *New Madrid* 1961. Liquitex on canvas 193 × 193 (76 × 76). Kasmin Gallery, London.

83 *Untitled* 1968. Acrylic on cotton duck 243.8 × 487.7 (96 × 192). Collection Lord Dufferin. *Photo Kasmin Gallery, London.*

STILL, Clyfford (1904–80)
27 *1957-D no. 1* 1957. Oil on canvas 287 × 403.9 (113 × 159). Albright-Knox Art Gallery, Buffalo, N.Y. Gift of Seymour H. Knox.

SUTHERLAND, Graham (1903–80)
32 *Somerset Maugham* 1949. Oil on canvas 137.2 × 63.5 (54 × 25). The Tate Gallery, London.

SUVERO, Mark di (b. 1933)
190 *New York Dawn (for Lorca)* 1965. Wood, steel, iron 2,377 × 2,255 × 1,524 (936 × 888 × 600). Collection Whitney Museum of American Art, New York. Gift of the Howard and Jean Lipman Foundation Inc.

TAKIS (Takis Vassilakis, b. 1925)
153 *Signal* 1966. Collection John de Menil, Houston, Tex.

154 *Electro magnetic* 1960–7. Kinetic sculpture with electromagnet. Formerly Galerie Iris Clert, Paris. *Photo John Palmer.*

TANGUY, Yves (1900–55)
12 *The Rapidity of Sleep* 1945. Oil on canvas 127 × 101.6 (50 × 40). Courtesy of The Art Institute of Chicago. The Joseph Winterbotham Collection.

TAPIÉS, Antonio (b. 1928)
53 *Black with two lozenges* 1963. Oil on canvas 411.5 × 330.2 (162 × 130). Private Collection, Buenos Aires.

THEK, Paul (b. 1933)
100 *Death of a hippie* 1967. Pink painted hardboard, wax body 259.1 × 320 × 320 (102 × 126 × 126). Stable Gallery, New York.

TINGUELY, Jean (b. 1925)
151 *Metamachine 4* 1958–9. Painted metal construction 182.9 (72). Private Collection. *Photo Courtesy of the Staempfli Gallery, New York.*

152 *Homage to New York*, 1960. Jean Tinguely with the piano and the meta-matic machine. *Photo David Gahr.*

TOBEY, Mark (1890–1976)
22 *Edge of August* 1953. Casein on composition board 121.9 × 71.1 (48 × 28). Collection The Museum of Modern Art, New York.

TOMASELLO, Luigi (b. 1915)
146 *Atmosphère ébromo-plastique no. 180* 1967. Wood cubes, white paint and fluorescent green and orange 200 × 200 (78¾ × 78¾). Collection the artist.

TUCKER, William (b. 1935)
206 *Memphis* 1965–6. Plaster 76.2 × 142.2 × 165.1 (30 × 56 × 65). The Tate Gallery, London.

TWORKOV, Jack (1900–82)
76 *North American* 1966. Oil on canvas 203.2 × 162.6 (80 × 64). Collection the artist.

VASARELY, Victor (b. 1908)
140 *Arny* 1967–8. Oil on canvas 249.9 × 249.9 (98⅜ × 98⅜). Galerie Denise René, Paris.

141 *Metagalaxy* 1959. Oil on canvas (62⅝ × 57⅞). Galerie Denise René, Paris.

WALKER, John (b. 1939)
89 *Touch-Yellow* 1967. Acrylic and chalk on canvas 266.7 × 518.2 (105 × 204). Collection the artist.

WARHOL, Andy (b. 1930)
1 *Brillo boxes* 1964. Silkscreen on wood 33 × 40.6 × 29.2 (13 × 16 × 11½). Leo Castelli Gallery, New York.

132 *Race riot* 1964. Acrylic and silkscreen enamel on canvas 76.2 × 83.8 (30 × 33). Leo Castelli Gallery.

133 *Green Coca-Cola bottles* 1962. Oil on canvas 209.6 × 144.8 (82¼ × 57). Collection Whitney Museum of American Art, New York. Gift of the Friends of the Whitney Museum.

WESSELMANN, Tom (b. 1931)
128 *Still-life no. 34* 1963. Oil on canvas 121.9 (48) tondo. Collection Mr and Mrs Jack Glen, Kansas City.

129 *Great American Nude no. 44* 1963. Assemblage painting 265.7 × 243.8 × 25.4 (81 × 96 × 10). Collection Mr and Mrs Robert C. Scull.

WOLS (Wolfgang Schulze, 1913–51)
50 *The Blue Pomegranate* 1946. Oil on canvas 46 × 33 (18⅛ × 13). Collection Michel Couturier, Paris.

YOUNGERMAN, Jack (b. 1926)
73 *Totem black* 1967. Oil on canvas 312.4 × 205.7 (123 × 81). Betty Parsons Gallery, New York.

Index